SYNDICATE
Wife

SYNDICATE Wife
THE STORY OF ANN DRAHMANN COPPOLA

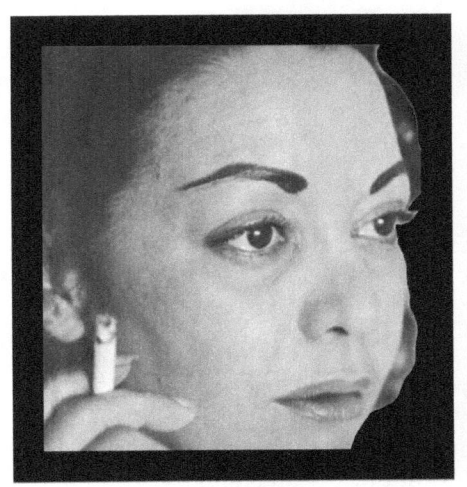

Hank Messick

COMMONWEALTH BOOK COMPANY
St. Martin, Ohio

To the memory of Robert F. Kennedy,
whose fight against organized crime
made this book possible.

© 1968 by Hank Messick
© 2021 by Commonwealth Book Company

All rights reserved. No part of this book may be reproduced in any form or by any means without the prior written consent of the publisher, excepting brief quotes used in reviews. Printed in the United States of America.

ISBN: 978-1-948986-33-5

Commonwealth Book Company
St. Martin, Ohio

Preface

Organized crime is a cancer on our society. It takes billions of dollars a year from the public for narcotics and gambling and extortion.

Its sickness starts with the protected corner bookmaker and goes through the corrupt public officials, and businessmen "on the take."

For many years the U.S. Government has been combatting this blight and has called on local governments to do the same. The Federal program uses the combined resources and facilities of twenty-six Federal agencies under the over-all direction of the Justice Department.

The Internal Revenue Service plays a major role in this vital program. In the last seven years our investigators have been responsible for the conviction of more than 2,100 criminals who violated Federal tax laws.

In recounting the conviction of "Trigger Mike" Coppola, Mr. Messick reveals the painstaking investigative work required to secure the conviction of a major underworld figure. Agents Richard Jaffe and Joseph Wanderscheid, who worked on this case, are typical of the dedicated men engaged in this program.

We in the Revenue Service have learned that the battle against crime can be won only if it has the full support of the American public. Books such as Mr. Messick's play a major role in laying the groundwork for that support.

SHELDON S. COHEN
Commissioner of Internal Revenue

HANK MESSICK (1922-1999) was born in Happy Valley, NC, and educated at the University of North Carolina and the University of Iowa. He began his investigative journalism career in western North Carolina and in 1956 began working at the *Louisville Courier-Journal*, Kentucky's largest newspaper. For the next several years Hank investigated and reported on the Newport, Kentucky, vice industry. He later worked for the *Miami Herald* and the *Boston Traveler*, also investigating organized crime and corruption in those communities. After 1967 he wrote full time, authoring 19 books, mostly about organized crime and its influences in American life.

Hank Messick with wife Faye celebrating their 14th wedding anniversary at the Beverly Hills Country Club, Southgate, KY, June 9, 1961.

Foreword

Much of the research for this book was accomplished under Ford Foundation grants. In that connection I would thank Mr. Mark Ethridge, Sr., former publisher of the Louisville *Courier-Journal* and until recently a member of the board of the Ford Foundation.

In the sometimes less than forthright world of journalism, Mr. Ethridge was an inspiration.

If there is a "lesson" in this history, it is that Organized Crime can be beaten in specific situations but only by extraordinary effort on the part of individuals and united action by communities.

Ann Drahmann Coppola was at once a product and a victim of today's amoral society. Courage she had from birth. Ultimately she achieved a degree of understanding and with it compassion. Ironically, one of her final notes was scribbled on the back of a "sick" greeting card which carried this printed message:

> WISDOM COMES WITH AGE
> too damn late to do any good

While we may hope mankind will learn wisdom before it becomes too late to use it, there is little reason for optimism. Individuals, therefore, who do achieve a measure of understanding must make their own lonely choice even as did a former syndicate wife.

HANK MESSICK

Fort Lauderdale, Florida

"As God is my judge, I shall tell only the truth."
ANN DRAHMANN

"Death shall be a blessing to me." ANN DRAHMANN

Prologue

THE WOMAN WHOSE DARK BEAUTY CAPTIVATED AN OVERlord of organized crime sat at a desk in the bedroom of a fashionable hotel. From behind a shuttered window came the street sounds of Rome. The woman ignored them. She poured Scotch from an almost empty bottle and drank it neat. For hours she had been writing and drinking. Now only one message remained. She picked up the ball-point pen and resumed writing.

The ex-wife of Trigger Mike Coppola was preparing to die.

She wrote hurriedly, unsure as to how much time remained. The last letter was addressed to Harold Moss, Internal Revenue Service attaché at the American Embassy in Paris. Moss had handled the international aspects of "Operation Babysit." The letter began:

"I am writing this letter to you because I know you are a person who always knows exactly what to do and, what is more important, you are completely dedicated to your Government . . .

"You know I have never lied to you or anyone else working for our Government, so please believe me when I tell you no one murdered me. I am going to commit suicide by drinking Scotch and I will take nemutals (a great many), enough I hope to kill me. You will also notice my door shall be locked from inside making it impossible for anyone to have murdered me.

"Please have this letter made public as I want so very much for people to know what I have felt and feel since becoming Ann Drahmann once again . . .

"I would like the two girls I met in the Eve of Roma's beauty salon and the couple I met in the bar at the Excelsior Hotel to know how very much I appreciated the fact that they did not treat me as though I had the Plague. I can't mention their names as Mike Coppola could make it very rough for them if he knew they spoke to me. But, anyhow, thank you from the bottom of my heart for speaking to me.

"Please tell my family not to grieve for me. I couldn't rest in peace if I thought I made them unhappy. Please, my darling sisters and brothers, don't grieve. I want to be with Mama and Charley. As you all know, all my life I could never face reality . . .

"Mr. Robert Kennedy, please do not lose the courage of your convictions. Don't allow gambling in Newport or Covington, Kentucky. It isn't the gambling that is so bad, but the dope peddling, prostitution, fencing and hideout for every wanted criminal that is so horrible. Frank 'Screw' Andrews is Mike Coppola's main and most important man in Newport. Screw handles all the dirty work for Mike and Tony Salerno.

"Mr. Kennedy, why are the city officials of Newport allowed to take money from gangsters to permit such horrible things to take place in Newport? I suggest, do not only wipe out the gangsters but please wipe out the city officials. In my wildest dreams I can't imagine how Washington can allow people working for cities, states and Washington to play both ends to the middle by accepting money to uphold the law and then accepting money from gangsters to break the law. Please, Mr. Robert Kennedy, stop this. Don't give up.

"My daughter, Joan, what can I tell you? I love you so very much. Please be happy and good, darling. You, my baby, have been such a joy to me. I kind of grew up with you so forgive me for any blunders. Please, Joan, go back to the States. Our country is a wonderful country. I hate and despise Europe. What the hell do they have to show for their thousands of years? A damn bunch of ruins.

"Mr. Moss, please believe me. I am taking my pills this minute. No fanfare, no publicity, no autopsy. Tell my family—I think it is against my religion—I want to be cremated and my ashes strewn over Mike Coppola's home.

"I am so tired and depressed it is impossible for me to go on trying to live. Wouldn't it be a joke if it should be a heck of a lot worse wherever it is one goes after death?

"Thank you, Mr. Moss, for your past kindness and may God bless you and your family. I have never lied to you and please see that justice is done. Also, please do everything to make Coppola pay his lien. After all, a million dollars is a drop in the bucket to him. Don't let all my work in the past two years go to the devil.

"Mike Coppola, someday, somehow, a person or God or the Law shall catch up with you, you yellow-bellied bastard. You are the lowest and biggest coward I have had the misfortune to meet.

Ann Drahmann

"Please excuse English but I have been drinking and I am so tired."

The letter to Moss was found tucked into the frame of a wall mirror. Ann was dead on the bed, the pen still clutched in her hand. On the wall above the bed was written:

"I have always suffered. I am going to kill myself. Forget me."

But in those hours before death she made certain she would not be forgotten.

> "I learned at an early age it
> was most admirable not to
> be a stool pigeon." ANN DRAHMANN

One

ANNA AUGUSTINE, AS FOND OF PRANKS AS ANY OF HER classmates, was tempted when one of the girls suggested they play hookey from school that afternoon. The Western Hills Viaduct was to be dedicated. It was a big event for Cincinnati in the mid-thirties. Important officials would make speeches. There would be bands. It would be exciting. A lot of older boys would be there.

The thought of her mother checked the impulse. A widow with seven children, her mother was patient and kind but she had firm ideas about rules and the value of education. She might never learn of the escapade but it would still be a breach of trust.

Only Marion went back to school with Anna when the noon recess ended. The other three girls went off gaily to see the ceremony. Sister Arcadia immediately noticed their absence. Months before she had placed the five friends in the front row where she could keep an eye on them. They weren't bad girls, just high-spirited, but a tight rein was needed. Now with three seats vacant she came to Anna. Where were the missing girls?

The dark-haired Anna could be stubborn on occasion and this was such an occasion. It was one thing to play hookey but it was something else to snitch on friends. Anna refused to talk.

Sister Arcadia also had a stubborn streak. Anna's refusal was defiance, and the nun prided herself on keeping her girls submissive. When Anna continued to refuse, she was ordered to stand in front of the class. The teacher picked up the long, springy stick she kept in reserve as the ultimate weapon. Anna eyed it apprehensively, her brown eyes almost black with fear. But she shook her head. She would not talk. The teacher lost her temper. Eighth-grade girls were almost women. It was high time they learned to respect authority. The beating began.

Anna tried to hold back the tears. Her older brother had impressed upon her the virtue of courage. She had listened enthralled when he would return from visits across the Ohio River in Newport. His tales of such people as Bob Zwick, "the Fox of Gangland," and Zwick's girl, Dago Rose, were exciting. Zwick had only recently been convicted after a long and bloody career as a hijacker and hired gun. The newspapers had written much about his "stoical indifference." And Anna had been thrilled to learn that the jurors who convicted him had used the light tan purse of Dago Rose as a ballot box when they decided whether "the Fox" would live or die.

The nun used the stick with vigor, her anger increasing as Anna refused to break. And when the girl could stand the pain no longer, she ran from the classroom. The tears came now, unrestrained. She was still sobbing when she reached home and the arms of her mother. The last reserve gave way and she blurted out the full story.

Agnes Augustine was a native of Italy. Religion was very important to her and had become more so since the death of her husband, Antonio. Again and again she had impressed upon her children that a nun or priest could do no wrong. But as her daughter sobbed out the story, Agnes was ready to make an exception. The whipping could be justified. After all, Anna had disobeyed a direct order. But Sister Arcadia had no right to give such an order. After all, the Catholic Church had survived in the early days of Roman persecution only because Christians had refused to inform on each other.

To Anna's astonishment, her mother took her by the arm and led her back to school. For a little time Anna felt betrayed, but the feeling was forgotten as Agnes Augustine confronted Sister Arcadia and gave her a bitter tongue-lashing. Speaking sometimes in Italian, sometimes in English, the mother blistered the nun for attempting to turn her daughter into a stool pigeon. The teacher was dumbfounded. Mrs. Augustine had always seemed so meek, so willing to bow to the wisdom of the Church. And perhaps, after all, she did have a point. Certainly she thought she had one.

Peace was restored, but Anna was never to forget her mother's actions. To be a stool pigeon was the unforgivable crime. No matter the provocation, no matter the justification, it was better to endure than to squeal.

The girl who as a syndicate wife was to break this unwritten commandment was born July 2, 1921, in Cincinnati. It was a time of beginnings. The amoral society in which she was to move was taking form and shape.

Of the many factors that made the Ohio River city a center of corruption in 1921, not the least was the long and sometimes bloody history of religious strife. German Catholics bore the brunt of the violence but the Italians who came later fell heir to the problem.

The first Catholics came down the Ohio from Pennsylvania. Many were refugees from the Whiskey Rebellion. They brought with them certain "liberal" attitudes toward liquor and gambling. Conflict developed quickly between these newcomers and those people of Scotch-Irish descent who followed Daniel Boone through the Cumberland Gap and pushed northward through Kentucky.

Hostility developed into the weird Know-Nothing movement, which reached its peak in the United States shortly after religious persecutions in Germany brought a new flood of immigrants. Again the Ohio River was a convenient route from the east and thousands of "Godless Germans," as the Know-Nothings called them, stopped at Cincinnati or settled on the south bank along both sides of the Licking River in what was to become Newport and Covington, Kentucky. The *achtafurtzigers*—forty-eighters—soon clashed with the "Red-blooded White Americans" and riots were common on both sides of the Ohio. The same forces made Louisville, one hundred miles to the south and west, a battleground. "Bloody Monday" in Louisville was the equal of the racial riots that more than one hundred years later were to make some American cities into disaster areas.

Prejudice created in those early days was to last more than a century and help fashion a moral stalemate in the area. With the population almost equally divided between Protestant and Catholic, the old distrust prevented unity of action for community good. Northern Kentucky, shut off from the Bluegrass by a barrier of hills and bad roads, grew closer to Cincinnati for economic as well as ethnic reasons. Italians, arriving in the early years of the twentieth century, found the area across the river a happy hunting ground, a no-man's land of law enforcement. It became known as "Little Mexico"—a place to hide, rest, and plan new forays.

In 1921, the area was ripe for the opportunities for quick wealth that Prohibition was to bring. Cincinnati citizens were still talking about the World Series of two years before. Something had smelled badly at the time but the details had remained hidden until a few months before Anna's birth. A trial in Chicago made it clear the Series had been fixed by Arnold "the Brain" Rothstein, a New York gambler whose crown as king of the layoff bettors was ultimately to be worn by a friend of Anna Augustine.

From headquarters in the Sinton Hotel, agents of Rothstein bribed the ballplayers and almost killed organized baseball.

Of more current interest were the activities of George Remus, locally known as the "King of the Bootleggers." From his marble palace on Price Hill, Remus ruled a fantastic liquor empire. Recognizing early the potential of Prohibition, Remus sold his lawbooks in Chicago and moved to the center of the distilling industry of Kentucky, Indiana, and Ohio. Under existing law, bonded whiskey could be diverted for commercial products such as hair tonic and medicine. Remus bought up entire warehouses of liquor, established or purchased drug companies to "buy" the whiskey, secured the necessary "permit for withdrawal," and placed hundreds of thousands of gallons of bonded booze on the bootleg market.

From his field office in "Death Valley" outside Cincinnati near the Indiana line, convoys of trucks rumbled daily and sped untouched through the streets of neighboring cities. Other cargoes were shipped in boxcar lots. During one three-month period Remus deposited $2,700,000 in Cincinnati banks. Federal agents estimated he owned one-seventh of all the bonded whiskey in the United States. His net worth was believed to be in excess of $70,000,000.

In later years, Remus admitted that to win the necessary freedom of operation he spent $20,000,000 for protection. He literally taught law-enforcement officials on both sides of the Ohio, and on every level of government including the federal, to hold out their hands. Worse, he convinced the citizens of the area that such a gesture was part of the American Way of Life.

Anna was only three months old when Remus' empire collapsed. Unbribed federal agents from other cities raided Death Valley. As Remus explained it:

"Men have tried to corner the wheat market only to learn there is too much wheat in the world. I tried to corner the graft market but there isn't enough money in the world to buy up all the public officials who demand their share of graft."

In other words—Remus had created a demand he was unable to supply. The demand remained to trouble the generation that came of age with Anna. Remus dispensed more than whiskey. The chloral hydrate served forty years later to George Ratterman, reform candidate for sheriff of Campbell County, was vintage Remus. And Anna, as the ex-wife of a syndicate gangster, was to plead with almost her last breath for an end to the corruption that Remus had loosed.

Anna was almost a year old when Remus went to prison. With him went twelve associates, members of the so-called "Remus Ring." Several of these men—Buck Brady, Peter Schmidt—were to return to build gambling empires in the decade following Prohibition. Anna would know them all in years to come.

The second phase of the bootlegging business, the manufacture of home-brew, followed the Remus period. At one time an estimated three thousand "speakeasys" served Cincinnati. Much of the rotgut came from across the river, where on some days smoke from "alky cookers" obscured the sun over the Licking River valley. Newport became a wild town as such men as Howard Vice discovered.

Vice was so tough his talents were employed as a bodyguard for Jackie Kennedy, beer baron of Toledo. Kennedy was engaged in a death struggle with Peter Licavoli. Vice quit and returned to Newport when Kennedy refused to heed his warning that "Miss Tiger Woman," as the newspapers called her, would betray him. Shortly after his return, she led Kennedy into a death trap on the streets of Toledo.

A woman was also Vice's undoing. His mistress, "a dead ringer for Jean Harlow," provoked a feud between Vice and Charles "the Wop" Lafata. A fight developed. In the confusion someone else shot Lafata and Vice was blamed. Charged with murder, he walked out of Newport's jail and stayed free for two years. Recognized in Nashville, he was returned and ultimately sentenced to life-imprisonment. Investigation later revealed that Vice was framed because leaders of the underworld considered him too independent. More than that, they wanted some real estate he owned and they took it.

The frame was later developed into such a fine art in Newport, it became unnecessary to murder people, but several bloody years were to pass before its potential was fully recognized.

Another independent sort who was to cause syndicate gangsters much trouble was Peter Schmidt. Schmidt, who went to prison with Remus, was a man of vision despite the soul of a miser. He began his adult life driving a one-horse cart for hire. From there it had been but a short step to driving liquor-laden trucks for Remus under the supervision of Buck Brady, superintendent of transportation. When released from prison he invested his bootleg profits in a building on Monmouth Street in downtown Newport.

Newport had two main traffic arteries, both connecting with the bridge to Cincinnati. Each morning thousands of honest citizens drove north along Monmouth to the offices and factories across the river. Each evening they came south over York Street en route to their homes. Major casinos, which depended largely on traffic from Cincinnati, developed along both streets.

Schmidt named his new building the Glenn Hotel, after his son. It was to have a long and notorious history. Bob Zwick lived there and was often seen in the lobby, where he held a submachine gun by a shoulder strap while chatting with fellow hoods who had fled to "Little Mexico" to escape the heat in surrounding states. David Jerus, known locally as "Jew Bates," found a home there after taking part in the St. Valentine's Day Massacre in Chicago. Decades later, a reform candidate for sheriff was arrested there after having been drugged in a Cincinnati hotel.

But Pete's plans called for more than a dirty three-story hotel and he was progressing toward his grander goal when abruptly there came an interruption. The one-thousand-gallon-a-day still he was operating on Kentucky Drive outside Newport was raided by federal agents sent in from Washington. Pete wounded one of the raiders and was sentenced to five years in prison. When he was released the bootleg era was about over and the gambling era began. Far to the north the Cleveland Syndicate had switched from booze to gambling. The newly organized National Syndicate had allotted the area south of Lake Erie to the Cleveland crowd and already they were moving into Cincinnati. Everywhere pressure was being applied to local gamblers who were given the choice of joining the syndicate or getting out of business. Some ex-lieutenants of Remus, such as Sam Schraeder and Red Masterson, did ally themselves with the syndicate. Others, such as Buck Brady and Schmidt, fought a losing battle for years.

The small gambling operation Schmidt conducted at the Glen Hotel was not too important, but it couldn't be overlooked. Nor had Pete's tightfisted nature endeared him to local hoods. It became a popular routine to display contempt for Schmidt. Dave Whitfield, who won title to Vice's property after his conviction and was now a partner of Masterson, was one man who delighted in "dingdonging" Schmidt. Ready to assist was Larry McDonough, who had seen early the possibilities in slot machines. Together they made a habit of urinating in unison in the lobby of the Glenn Hotel.

Schmidt swallowed the insults, saved his money, and bided his time. His vision was as grand in its way as the one Remus almost made a reality. Ten years later, Bugsy Siegel dreamed the same dream and fabulous Las Vegas sprouted on the sands of Nevada.

When at last he was ready, Schmidt moved quietly. He bought a hill in what was to become Southgate, some two miles south of Newport on the road to Frankfort, Kentucky. For years there had been a nightclub of sorts there, the Old Kaintuck Castle. Schmidt converted it into the Beverly Hills Club, the first casino worthy of the name in Campbell County. To bring in revenue while waiting for Cincinnati to "discover" the new joint, Pete operated a still nearby. Liquor might now be legal but some people in Newport had become accustomed to home-brew and didn't like—or couldn't afford—"fancy store-bought stuff."

An early visitor to the Beverly Hills was Moe Dalitz, one of the four charter members of the Cleveland Syndicate. Years later, little Anna Augustine was to entertain him when he came calling on Trigger Mike Coppola in Miami Beach. But in those early days Dalitz called himself "Davis," perhaps to protect his parents, who operated a respectable laundry at Ann Arbor, Michigan. With his partners, Sam Tucker, Morris Kleinman, and Louis Rothkopf, he ran liquor across Lake Erie in armor-plated boats during the smuggling phase of Prohibition. During the fourth phase, which continued until 1937, his syndicate, in conjunction with Meyer Lansky in New York, operated the largest illegal distilleries ever found.

When the syndicate turned to gambling as the industry of the future, it won control of plush casinos in and around Cleveland. It had expanded to the Arrowhead Club outside Cincinnati on the Ohio bank and was in the process of taking over what was later to be known as the River Downs racetrack outside the Queen City. For some months it had been eyeing Kentucky and indeed had made one foray which ended in disaster. Using a local attorney as a front, the syndicate built a dog track near Newport and operated it for thirteen days. State police closed the illegal track on orders of Governor A. B. "Happy" Chandler, then a young and still idealistic politician.

It was while in the area in connection with the dog track that Dalitz visited the Beverly Hills. He was immediately impressed with the possibilities and ordered into motion the necessary machinery to get possession. But Pete was stubborn and declined to accept the syndicate as a partner. The technique perfected by the syndicate of using local men as fronts for their ventures didn't appeal to Schmidt. Not even the almost unlimited bankroll the syndicate could supply was sufficient bait. He had his dream. There was no room for compromise.

The syndicate was forced to take sterner measures. On February 3, 1936, the Beverly Hills burned to the ground. A five-year-old girl, niece of the caretaker who lived in the building, died two days later of burns.

Officially the fire was something of a mystery. Schmidt was quoted as saying he merely operated a dairy out there on the hill. No roulette wheels—just cows. Police unofficially spread the word for "liberal" citizens that Pete's still had blown up, causing the fire. But here are a few facts they neglected to mention:

Red Masterson was seen buying a can of gasoline on the night of the fire. He told the man who spotted him to read the paper next day to find why he needed gasoline.

Edwin Garrison, who had once worked for "Legs" Diamond and Dutch Schultz in New York, actually set the blaze and was burned on the leg when the flame whooshed back to the can he was holding.

Garrison was taken to the home of Dave Whitfield, that friend of Masterson, for emergency treatment.

After the child died a scapegoat was needed. An anonymous call sent police to Whitfield's home where evidence was found. Whitfield was imprisoned after a quick trial. The syndicate rewarded him when he was released by giving him Vice's property and a job. Once again the virtue of keeping silent was demonstrated to the community.

Masterson also was rewarded. In years to come he was given a small piece of syndicate-controlled casinos and the title "Enforcer." In effect he became the unofficial police chief of Newport.

In 1960, during one of Anna's frequent visits to her old home, Masterson was made a Kentucky Colonel by Governor Bert T. Combs. A long list of good deeds was attributed to a man who had been twice tried for murder and acquitted on grounds of self-defense, who had served prison terms for robbery and narcotics violations, who had been shot during the Brady Rebellion of 1946—but of them all the most remarkable was the statement:

"He helps in the fire-fighting field."

Garrison was not so lucky. He escaped death with Dutch Schultz when he missed a train from Cincinnati to New York, but he twice made the FBI's "Most Wanted" list and served many years in prison for assorted crimes.

Schmidt, meantime, was ready to try again. In April 1937, he opened the new Beverly Hills. It was now so elaborate he expanded the name to the Beverly Hills Country Club. Governors of several states attended the grand opening. A reporter covering the event wrote:

"Peter was toasted opening night by the official life of four states. His rise has been meteoric. There's none, 300 miles around, that stands shoulder high to him now. His Beverly Hills dominates its world."

The elaborate new casino only made the Cleveland Syndicate more eager. Immediately a new campaign of harassment began. Less than two months after the grand opening, the club's bankroll was stolen by six men armed with submachine guns. The "dingdonging" continued. Pete was forced to import hired gunmen. Pressure was applied to stop this and Schmidt was reduced to hiring Negroes as guards. In the underworld of Newport-Cincinnati, the use of Negroes was indeed a last resort. First-generation Americans, needing someone to whom they could feel morally superior, felt the Negro was beneath contempt. The anti-Negro sentiment was to be demonstrated again and again over the years in such corrupt cities as

Biloxi, Mississippi; Hot Springs, Arkansas; Phenix City, Alabama; Gretna, Louisiana; and Cicero, Illinois. The worst of the racial riots in 1967 came not in the South but in Northern cities having large numbers of first- and second-generation Americans.

Despite his precautions, the pressure on Schmidt continued. Sam Tucker, a charter member of the syndicate and for a decade its branch manager in Newport, once talked to the author about it. Sitting in his plush home in Miami Beach, Tucker recalled that Pete finally gave up the struggle. People just kept bothering him, Tucker explained, and he became unable to hire muscle for protection. Conditions became so bad at last that Schmidt tried to bribe other underworld groups by permitting them to come in and operate. One gang from Toledo actually ran the club for three months, Tucker said, but they couldn't make a go of it either. People bothered them too.

Finally Pete surrendered and turned the Beverly Hills over to the Cleveland Syndicate, which took charge even before a final settlement was worked out. Pete was so weary he didn't even demand cash. Actually, said Tucker, the Cleveland boys got the joint for free. A small down payment was taken out of the profits they had already made while running the club. Future payments came from future profits. For, magically, all troubles ceased and the casino became the mint Schmidt always knew it could become.

Newport attorney Charles E. Lester handled the details and on November 18, 1940, the Beverly Hills became the legal property of the Cleveland Syndicate. Pleased with Lester's legal abilities, the syndicate put him on retainer—a mistake it was later to regret. And with its foot in the door, the syndicate began to expand. The Lookout House across the Licking River on a hill overlooking Covington became the next major target. And control was obtained in time for Anna—who now called herself Ann—to find a job when she needed one badly.

Ann had become a beautiful girl. Her dark brown eyes were her most attractive feature, set as they were in an oval face with black, arching eyebrows that matched her hair. She was five feet four inches tall and weighed a compact but well-rounded 115 pounds. Her complexion was medium and later after exposure to the Florida sun was to become stylishly dark. Men turned to watch as she walked by and the girl-woman was hungry for their flattery.

An unhappy experience contributed to her maturity by cutting short her girlhood. A young sailor fell madly in love with her and literally swept her off her feet. Almost before she knew it, the sixteen-year-old girl was married and pregnant. A daughter, dark-haired and brown-eyed, was born on July 19, 1938. The husband was discarded and almost forgotten. Ann, who had stopped playing with dolls only a few months before, found her daughter a delight. Named Joan, the baby soon replaced Ann's mother as the center of her world.

Yet delightful as she was, the baby posed problems. Ann had to find work. An older brother had some ideas. He worked at the Flamingo Club in Newport, which officially was owned by the Levinson boys: Ed, "Sleepout Louis," and Mike. That was enough for the underworld of Newport, where the use of "fronts" was an accepted practice. Years were to pass before the relationship of the Levinson boys to Trigger Mike Coppola became known.

The Flamingo had little to offer a girl in search of an honest job but her brother had connections. Sleepout was a friend of Jimmy Brink, who ran the Lookout House. In fact, Brink, Levinson, and Ed Curd had been indicted in 1936 by a Kenton County grand jury inspired by an attack of virtue. They had beaten the gambling rap, as usual, with little trouble. Indeed, some of the leading businessmen of the area had come to their aid. Nor was there any real trouble two years later when an injunction against gambling was issued for the Lookout House. No effort was made by local law-enforcement officials to halt gambling, which became bigger than ever when the syndicate cut itself in.

A huge, rambling frame building, the Lookout House offered various cozy bars, a good restaurant, and a casino from which one could see across the Ohio to the towers of Cincinnati. Brink, who had built it up, began as a bootlegger in the days of Remus. Like Schmidt, he switched to gambling. Unlike Schmidt, he had no desire to fight a costly and hopeless battle with the syndicate. So in 1941, when syndicate planners decided a two-county operation in Kentucky would be useful, Brink was willing to talk terms.

Sam Tucker, whom Brink called "the gentleman of the boys," handled the negotiations for the syndicate. A complicated deal resulted. Brink was permitted to retain ten per cent of the Lookout House and was given ten per cent of the Beverly Hills as well. He received $125,000 in cash and was permitted to remain as general manager of the club. Syndicate experts were sent in to help—Alvin Giesey as accountant and Sam "Gameboy" Miller as casino troubleshooter. Miller's varied assignments for the syndicate ranged from Miami Beach to Tucson.

A two-county operation permitted the syndicate a degree of insurance. If, for any reason, the "heat" went on in Kenton County, the suckers from Cincinnati's convention halls could be diverted to the Beverly Hills. Or vice versa. Then, too, there was a unique folk custom of the area which the syndicate—ever sensitive to local mores—felt obliged to honor. During grand jury sessions three times a year, it was believed that respect for law and order should be demonstrated by closing major gambling activities. Luckily the sessions usually lasted less than a week and the intervals were so well spaced it was possible to use them for vacations and remodeling. But by having a two-county operation and making sure the respective grand juries had a staggered schedule, it was possible to keep a casino going in one county while the other was respectfully dark.

With the conquest of the Beverly Hills and the Lookout House, the syndicate began the process of consolidation. Various handbooks and minor casinos in downtown Newport and Covington were taken over or put out of business. Of these, the largest was the Yorkshire Club in Newport, across York Street from Sleepout's place. Since the style of the Beverly Hills, to say nothing of its hours of operation, didn't permit a handbook there, the syndicate concentrated that phase of the gambling business in the Yorkshire. Twenty years later, the boys at the Yorkshire were reporting for tax purposes gross wages of more than $200,000 a month. What the real total was only the syndicate knew, but educated guesses placed the handle as high as $2,000,000 monthly.

Red "the Enforcer" Masterson was given the job of bringing peace and stability to the area. The syndicate knew only too well that random killings, holdups, and muggings, to say nothing of overgreedy bust-out operators, were bad for business. Such a town attracted punks, but the syndicate had no desire to operate "Little Mexico." It was the convention business of Cincinnati and the high-rollers from Louisville and Atlanta it wanted to attract. And Masterson, on the whole, was effective. He roamed the town from his headquarters in the Merchants Club on Fourth Street. A word from "the Enforcer" was usually enough to quiet even the most reckless hood. If deeds as well as words were needed to convince, Masterson was ready to oblige.

All was going smoothly. Sam Tucker moved from Cleveland and took up residence near the Beverly Hills. He brought along his "kid brother," Garson, to handle the restaurant at the Beverly. The fact that a charter member of the syndicate would personally take charge was proof enough of the importance of the Kentucky operation.

Nevertheless, some problems remained. Schmidt, angry but patient, reopened his Glenn Hotel on Monmouth Street despite his promise to the syndicate to quit the gambling business. His old dream was still alive. And he had an ally in Attorney Lester, who was still on retainer for the syndicate. The retainer wasn't large enough to match Lester's greed so he got together with Schmidt—whom he had helped oust from the Beverly Hills—and planned a coup.

The political climate was right. Governor Keen Johnson was nearing the end of his term in September 1943. Scheduled to go out of office with him were Attorney General Hubert Meredith and his assistant, Jesse K. Lewis. Governor Johnson had been on friendly terms with the politicians who nominally controlled Newport. He appointed to office two key local officials—Commonwealth's Attorney William J. Wise and Circuit Judge Ray L. Murphy—who were destined to serve for twenty years without hampering the syndicate. Tucker and his aides had no inkling of what was brewing.

Lester was on friendly terms with Attorney General Meredith and Lewis. Plans were made quietly. The storm broke on September 20, 1943, when Lester and Lewis filed a civil suit in Circuit Court asking for an injunction against gambler and official alike. Ninety-two men and women were named as joint defendants. Officials were charged with accepting bribes to permit wide-open gambling.

Special Judge John L. Vest was later to declare:

"It staggers the human mind to comprehend at a single effort, the extent of depravity and utter disregard of the existence of all law, semblance of law, that are set forth in the petition."

The timing was excellent. The suit was filed as the Circuit Court office was closing for the day. Judge Murphy was out of town. There seemed to be no quick way action could be taken on the suit so gambling casinos opened as usual that night. But Lester and Lewis drove to a nearby county and there found a judge who signed a temporary restraining order which enjoined officials to stop non-enforcement of the law and authorized the seizure of gambling equipment. Armed with the order, "L & L," as they were called, returned to Newport after midnight and presented the order at police headquarters. All available men, including Acting Chief George Gugel, were rounded up and formed into raiding parties.

Apparently Gugel and his men were too astonished to pass a warning. The confused raiders found the first five clubs on their list operating as usual: the Beverly Hills, the Merchants, the Yorkshire, the York Tavern, and the Glenn Rendezvous.

The latter was the casino-nightclub in the Glenn Hotel. Lester was reluctant to hit it—after all, it was Schmidt's place—but Lewis saw no point in making an exception. Not too surprising, however, was the fact that little was found there, whereas it was necessary to hire moving vans to haul away gambling equipment from syndicate clubs.

Lewis estimated that $100,000 worth of equipment was seized. Some of it was burned but most of it—including a number of slot machines seized at the Beverly Hills—soon was back in action at the clubs.

The syndicate counterattacked. Tucker filed a petition in court which revealed the part Lester had played in the conquest of the Beverly and disclosed he was still on the payroll. Meredith and Lewis were forced to choose between dropping Lester as a special assistant or dropping the Beverly Hills group as defendants. They decided to retain Lester.

Shortly after the raids, the good citizens of Newport had a chance to express their sentiments. Five defendants won nomination to public office in the city primary election.

The Campbell County grand jury, forced to take note of developments, indicted a number of gamblers. Included were Sam Tucker and the mysterious Moe Davis, better known in syndicate circles as Dalitz. But, as usual, nothing came of the indictments as prosecuted by Commonwealth's Attorney Wise, and very little resulted from the suit filed by Lester and Lewis. Unexpectedly, a Republican governor, Simeon Willis, was elected in November. The new attorney general immediately dropped Lester and Lewis as aides. The suit survived awhile with the final act coming in 1944 when injunctions against gambling at all leading casinos in Campbell County were issued. No one paid any more attention to the injunctions than had been paid earlier in Kenton County when the Lookout House was enjoined.

The syndicate emerged from the crisis stronger than before and in a good position to cash in on the post-war prosperity everyone expected to develop in the wake of wartime restrictions.

Over at the Lookout House, Gameboy Miller had long finished his job of reorganizing the casino along professional lines and had moved on to new assignments. One of the men who replaced him was a veteran gambler named Charley Drahmann.

Long an associate of Jimmy Brink, Drahmann had an eye for women as well as dice. And very quickly he spotted the dark beauty of Ann. As a waitress in the Lookout House's restaurant, her beauty was wasted. After all, the restaurant operated at a loss as an annex of the casino. Drahmann decided Ann should be with the action. He installed her as a combination hostess and hatcheck girl in the "Little Club." The action was there, all right. It was the casino.

A few months later Drahmann decided Ann was wasted in the Little Club, too. He asked her to marry him.

"I'm a curious person." ANN DRAHMANN

Two

ANN COPPOLA OFTEN LOOKED BACK ON HER LIFE AS MRS. Charley Drahmann with nostalgia. In retrospect, her years as the wife of a syndicate casino manager seemed more tranquil than her career as the wife of a syndicate boss.

Drahmann was much older than Ann. She was only six when he married his first wife. That marriage lasted seventeen years and ended in divorce only after Drahmann met Ann at the Lookout House.

As an associate of Jimmy Brink, Charley never became a big man in the rackets. He was steady, reliable, and devoted to his boss—content to rise with Brink and, ultimately, to die with him.

Only once did Drahmann invest in a venture of his own. The 1937 Ohio River flood devastated that low-lying area of Newport known—for more than one reason—as "the Bottoms." It had been a slum area since the 1884 flood, replete with handbooks, brothels, and cheap cafés. Robert Cottingham owned such a café in the area —the 333 Club. The 1937 flood ruined him. In desperation he turned to Drahmann, who agreed to supply $500 for a half interest in a small handbook at the rear of the club. The operation continued for years, netting Drahmann between $100 and $200 monthly. After World War II, even this small profit dwindled as other handbooks were set up nearby. Cottingham died, and the operation was ultimately given to a faithful employee.

Casino business boomed after the syndicate took over the Lookout House. Brink, now a big shot on the local scene, followed Kentucky tradition and became known as a "sportsman," buying and operating the Lookout Stud Farm. Many syndicate executives were in the racing business, owning horses as well as tracks, so Brink had a ready-made clientele. He sold horses to such men as Pete Licavoli, then handling syndicate affairs in Arizona. Possibly Gameboy Miller arranged the deal. He had accompanied Licavoli to Tucson.

As Brink devoted less and less time to the casino, the responsibilities of Drahmann increased. He served as Brink's personal representative. George Todd worked in the same capacity for the syndicate. The two men hired and fired personnel, counted the cash each day, and, at intervals, divided the profits between the various interests. Originally each was on salary at $15 a day plus a small percentage of the profits. Later, as business increased, they were jumped to $25 a day and became junior partners of record.

The Drahmanns followed the example of the Brinks and bought a home across from Lookout Stud on the road to Louisville. Originally it had belonged to Bill McCoy, the man who claimed to have founded "Rum Row" off New York and—because of the high quality of his booze—gave to the language the expression, "the real McCoy." Ann, enjoying financial independence as well as prestige, became famous for her parties. They didn't compare, of course, to the huge "social events" sponsored by the Brinks at their mansion on the farm, but Ann could assure herself that she made up in quality what was lacking in quantity.

It was an interesting life, Ann decided. Her husband might be a gambler, engaged in violating state law daily, but that fact was of no importance in the "liberal" climate of the area. Top officials attended her parties, displaying the respect anyone close to big money and the powerful men of the syndicate automatically received. Top gangsters from Cleveland, New York, and Detroit dropped in occasionally when business brought them to Newport-Covington. There were also big-name stars from the entertainment world—a world so closely allied to organized crime as to seem but a separate division. Both the Beverly Hills and the Lookout House featured the best talent of Hollywood and New York as attractions to draw the suckers to the gambling tables, and many of them found their way to the Drahmann home.

Another advantage of being a gambler's wife lay in the syndicate's habit of closing its plushest joints during the winter season on Miami Beach. The assumption was that anyone with money to burn went south for the winter. From January to April such places as the Beverly Hills and the Lookout House shut down. It was customary to redecorate during the off-season, but always there was time for a lengthy vacation in Miami Beach or a trip to New York. Ann grew to love south Florida and dreamed of the day Charley would be able to buy a home there like so many of his superiors had done. Charley made no promises. He knew the gap between casino manager and syndicate boss. Besides, he was content. Ann was beautiful, popular, and passionate. Joan, Ann's child, seemed like his own daughter. His work was interesting and not too demanding. What more could a man want?

Often they talked as they sat over the meal that served as lunch for Ann and breakfast for Charley. Ann had a quick mind and a sharp if superficial interest in people and things. Charley, who sometimes felt he had two daughters instead of one, enjoyed drawing on his background knowledge. But more was involved. One never knew what might happen in a business so dependent on the whim of law officers and politicians. It was wise to brief Ann occasionally. Someday the knowledge might be useful to her.

A subject of continuing interest was the Eastern Syndicate. Ann understood about the Cleveland crowd—the dominant influence in the area and, indeed, the entire region. But why did they tolerate such competitors as Sleepout Louis at the Flamingo and Buck Brady at the Primrose? Where did that old grouch Pete Schmidt fit into the picture? And what about Frank "Screw" Andrews?

Charley would smile tolerantly and answer. He didn't know all the answers and admitted it, but he was in a position to make good guesses.

Sleepout and his brothers were products of Chicago, but the source of their power was in New York. They had come to Newport in the thirties and muscled in on Art Dennert at the Flamingo. The Cleveland Syndicate let them alone for a very good reason—among their friends the Levinsons numbered such men as Frank Costello and Trigger Mike Coppola.

The "business," explained Charley, was complicated. He didn't understand all he knew. Not even Jimmy Brink knew the full story and Jimmy moved with the big guys. But, as nearly as he could figure it, there was this national organization. Within it were separate groups—the Eastern Syndicate based in New York, the Cleveland crowd, and the Chicago boys. The names were misleading, he added, because each group had men from several cities. Then there were other organizations in such places as Kansas City or East St. Louis, to say nothing of Boston. Anyway, each had its own sphere of influence, but sometimes there was a bit of overlapping. In the old days this might have led to warfare between rival groups, but under the direction of the National Syndicate cooperation and joint ventures were the order of the day.

Newport-Covington was Cleveland territory, yet the Eastern Syndicate was permitted to operate on a limited basis. Miami Beach and Broward County, Florida, was just the other way around. There Meyer Lansky of New York ruled but the Cleveland boys had pieces of several clubs and owned a lot of real estate. In fact, one of the biggest casinos run by Lansky in Florida was one partly owned by Tucker and Company. Apparently the top men in the rackets felt a little competition was good; they could also close ranks quickly if anyone got too greedy or a threat to the common safety developed. Take that Rip Farley affair recently.

Ann poured another cup of coffee for Charley. She had been wanting to ask about Farley, but it was better to let Charley tell it in his own good time. There had been a lot of rumors. She wondered if her brother was involved.

The story as Drahmann told it was basically simple. Rip Farley, a mountain boy from Clay County, Kentucky, was as reckless as he was ignorant. His brother, Taylor, had operated brothels awhile until finding a steady job with Sleepout. Apparently Rip thought that gave him some protection. In any case, on February 18, 1946, he walked into the Yorkshire Club and stuck a pistol in the back of a dealer. The idiot didn't even bother to wear a mask. The dealer handed over $2,500—all he happened to have on the table—and Rip walked calmly out.

This, Charley explained, was defiance of the syndicate, the one challenge that had to be answered in kind. No man could be allowed to live to boast he had robbed a syndicate casino. It might give other people ideas.

The fact that Rip's brother worked at the Flamingo complicated things a bit. Taylor had learned a little sophistication under the guidance of Ed and Sleepout though he was still a hot-tempered hillbilly at heart. No point in starting a blood feud. Joint action was indicated.

Four days were necessary to get things organized. At 2:15 A.M. on Washington's Birthday, plans were ready, and Rip obliged by emerging from hiding. He was spotted on the street outside the Flamingo. With him was Taylor. A large, dark sedan which had been waiting down the unlighted street started its motor and crawled forward to pause at the curb in front of the club. The rear window was open. A voice called, "Taylor."

Three men were in that car—one representing the Eastern Syndicate, one representing the Cleveland Syndicate, and a hired killer known as Danny Meyers. His real name, by the way, was Aaron Meyervitz, and he had arrived in town only the day before.

Taylor Farley recognized the driver. After all, he saw him almost every day. He raised his hand in greeting as Rip turned to look.

The blast of a shotgun sounded on the silent street. Rip Farley, the man who had stuck up a syndicate casino, was cut almost in two. Even as he fell, a pistol barked from the front window. Taylor staggered, shot in the chest. He fell beside his brother. The black car roared away up York Street.

Great confusion followed, said Charley with a wry smile. City officials held conferences, issued orders, gave every evidence of sincerity. No one was really worried, of course. Then new complications developed.

Taylor, tough old hillbilly that he was, refused to die. Police placed guards at his hospital door to block any effort, they said, to silence him. No one thought there was a chance Taylor would finger the man he recognized to the police. Nor was he likely to take action against him. The guy had simply been attending to business. But Danny Meyers was another matter. He had pulled the trigger of the shotgun and killed Rip. According to the code of the hills, Danny had to pay. His identity had become an open secret.

Again there were conferences on the top level and decisions made. Just getting rid of Taylor wouldn't have been enough, Drahmann explained. Taylor had many friends who would have been obligated to carry on the feud. There was only one way out.

Two days later Danny Meyers was found dead in a snow-filled park in Pittsburgh. He was sitting at the wheel of a car stolen from a Cincinnati used car lot. At his feet were the butts of fifteen cigarettes, indicating he had sat there for a long time presumably talking to someone in the seat beside him.

At the end of the long conversation, a third man—so police

reasoned—put a pistol to the back of Danny's head and pulled the trigger. Rip Farley was avenged—the danger of a blood feud averted.

Ann didn't ask the names of the two men who had accompanied Meyers on his last ride. Presumably they were the same as the two who had ridden with him to gun down Rip. Such questions were better left unasked. But she knew enough to make some good guesses.

The shooting of Danny didn't end the turmoil on the political level, Charley admitted. Public indignation which could condone every crime but murder demanded at least a token investigation. A special "Court of Inquiry" was set up. As a result the liquor license of the Flamingo Club was revoked. A real blow at crime that proved to be.

Even Ann could laugh. She recognized a joke when she heard one. The club had reopened a few days later and, according to her brother, the bar did a bigger business without a license than it had done with one. In fact, Sleepout was happy. State Beverage Control agents now had no legal right to inspect the premises, and he could reduce the amount of "ice" that went regularly to state agencies.

Despite her resolution not to ask certain questions, Ann blurted out a good one. Did Nig Devine have anything to do with the Farley affair? She had heard talk—and Niggy was such a nice guy.

Charley told her to forget it.

Devine, whose real name was Blatt, was a mysterious, shadowy character on the Newport scene. He seemed supplied with unlimited funds and his business interests were varied. He had connections with Screw Andrews, who was beginning to become big in numbers. Rumor had it, and correctly, that Nig was also a power in a catering company which supplied syndicate restaurants with food. Most mysterious of all was his relationship to the Lassoff brothers, Bob and Ben, known locally as Big Porky and Little Porky.

A Newport cop who sometimes served as a one-man vice squad and had ambitions to become chief drank too much one night at a party and gave Ann "confidential" information.

It seems that the cop, for reasons he didn't explain, found it necessary to raid the "Bobben Realty Company" located in the Finance Building on the southwest corner of Fourth and York Streets. Bobben Realty was the Lassoff's layoff betting operation.

On the night following the raid, the officer continued, "I was getting ready to go up to Cleveland on an excursion. I like to drive at night and get where I'm going early in the morning. Anyway, as I was getting dressed, I got a call at home from Nig Devine. He asked me to meet him at the Terrace Plaza in Cincinnati.

"I went over there and asked him what he wanted. He wanted to know why I had knocked over his place, and I said, 'What place are you talking about?' He had a beautiful blond girl there and he invited me to climb on the broad and enjoy myself, but I refused and told him to get down to business and what place was he talking about.

"He says, 'the Bobben.' And I said, 'Well, that's Porky Lassoff,' and he said, 'Yes, but I'm Porky's partner.' So I told him, 'Well, I didn't know he was your partner, but even if I'd known it I'd still have knocked him off.' And he says, 'I know that, but why?' And I says, 'Well, I told the man to close up and he wouldn't. Once I give a guy an order, Nig, he's going to do what I tell him or he is going down.'

"And Nig says, 'Well, the son-of-a-bitch. Wait till I see him. Thanks. That's good enough for me.' And I went on to Cleveland and that was it."

Charley listened to the tale, smiled, and remarked: "Your friend had better watch himself. He's getting delusions of grandeur. The same thing happened to Buck Brady."

Brady had been superintendent of transportation for George Remus and had used his savings to buy a joint known as the Primrose Club outside Newport. It had grown slowly over the years until it began to compete in a modest way with the Beverly Hills. Brady, at sixty-eight, was a tough old bird and permitted no nonsense but the handwriting had been on the wall for months.

Enforcer Masterson began the campaign by passing the word that Brady had to go. If Buck didn't take the hint and come to terms with the syndicate, action would follow. And with the lesson of Rip Farley still fresh, few people doubted what that action would be like.

Brady was too experienced a campaigner to sit on the defensive. On August 5, 1946, he was waiting when Masterson left his Merchants Club in his new Cadillac. A block from the club another car pulled alongside Masterson and a voice called:

"Hi, Red."

Masterson raised his hand in automatic greeting. A shotgun blast ripped across the few feet separating the cars. So close was the range there wasn't time for the charge to spread. A large part of it hit the steel upright dividing the main window from the vent. Masterson fell from his still moving car, which crashed into others parked along the street. Several men leaped from the shooter's car, which also crashed. The role of the innocent bystander—be it man or car—was always tough in Newport.

The Enforcer was taken to a hospital in nearby Dayton, Kentucky. Despite the shootings over the years, Newport never had a hospital of its own. Police began a search of the area near the scene of the "incident." Brady was found hiding nearby in an outdoor privy. He had with him a revolver and a rifle.

The old bootlegger explained he just happened to be in the vicinity when he heard the shot. "I always run when I hear shooting," he added. Newport police charged him with breach of the peace. At his trial the deposed king of the bootleggers, George Remus, testified as to Brady's good character. "He is the salt of the earth," said Remus. True to the code, Masterson refused to finger Brady as the gunman and the charge was dismissed.

An ominous quiet settled over the city as Red recovered from his wounds. Few doubted that the Enforcer's reputation would require he strike back at Brady. If death was the penalty for robbing a casino, nothing less would suffice for attempting to murder a syndicate lieutenant.

Drahmann chuckled at the thought. There was only one thing wrong with that reasoning, he told Ann. Masterson was not the big shot everyone assumed. Top syndicate officials realized another killing would create heat, force reluctant officials to act against the casinos. Measured against the possible loss of revenue, the hurt to Masterson's reputation was unimportant.

Syndicate bosses drafted an ultimatum to Brady: "Get out or die." Buck, who had already been spending much time in Florida, was reasonable. He could retire there now, content in the knowledge that it had taken the big men—not a punk like Masterson—to make him quit. He turned the Primrose Club over to the syndicate and departed for Orlando and the orange grove he had bought there. Years later, Sam Tucker spoke admiringly of Buck, calling him "a tough old buzzard."

The Primrose was renamed the Latin Quarter. Dave Whitfield, who had helped burn the old Beverly Hills, got out of jail about then and was made manager. The syndicate had tried for years to spring Dave—going so far as to offer $7,000 and a prize bull to a state official for his help in arranging a parole. The official did his best as a series of letters between a syndicate representative and the official shows.

The appointment of Whitfield was something of a sentimental gesture—he had been a close friend of Brady.

Masterson, meanwhile, recovered from his wounds but never regained his old prestige. However, he kept trying.

Affairs in Newport were not always settled by force or the threat of force. Over the coffee cups, Drahmann briefed Ann on Pete Schmidt's latest bid for power.

Following the abortive Lester-Lewis coup of 1943, Schmidt played it cool. His Glenn Rendezvous developed into one of the most notorious bust-out joints in town. A far cry from Pete's dream, it nonetheless made enough money to finance a venture into politics. Pete didn't run himself. Instead, he turned a strolling musician, Robert Siddell, into a public figure and in 1948 almost elected him mayor.

The winner, James E. Deckert, decided he'd better curb Schmidt's power. Immediately after taking office he ordered the Glenn Rendezvous raided. Schmidt was arrested. Instantly, friendly officers struck back, hitting the Elks Club and seizing twelve slot machines. Great uproar followed as city officials lined up with one side or the other. Charles E. Lester, acting on behalf of Schmidt, made a formal charge that the raid on the Glenn Rendezvous was but an effort by Mayor Deckert to shake down Pete. A hearing followed, but by then the syndicate had moved to restore order and the charge was dismissed.

Fearing he was about to be backed into a corner again and forced to give up the Glenn as earlier he had given away the Beverly Hills, Schmidt pulled a fast one. Moving swiftly, he sold the hotel to the Eastern Syndicate as represented by the Levinson boys, Arthur Dennert, and Nig Devine. It was an astute move, permitting Schmidt to lick his wounds and wait for the next opportunity.

The Cleveland Syndicate waited also. A few months later Dennert was "accidentally" killed in an auto crash in Cincinnati. The

Cleveland boys claimed his share of the Flamingo Club and installed as their personal representative a friend of Charley named Kenny Bright. The Eastern group, accepting the power play in the same spirit the Cleveland crowd had accepted the purchase of the Glenn, made no complaints. Already Ed Levinson had departed for Miami Beach, where he operated handbook concessions in a leading hotel. Later he would move on to Las Vegas. The country was big enough —there were plenty of opportunities for trained men and enough loot to share.

With everything shaking down so nicely it was downright unfriendly for Senator Estes Kefauver to intrude. Of course the Kenton County Protestant Association was partly to blame for attracting Kefauver's attention. While the syndicate had been concentrating on affairs in Campbell County, the preachers in Kenton went on the warpath and hired that old veteran, Jesse K. Lewis, to assist.

The immediate target of the reformers was Commonwealth's Attorney Ulie Howard. Lewis filed charges in Federal Court seeking to have Howard disbarred on the grounds he had failed to do his duty by not suppressing gambling. After hearing the evidence, Judge Mac Swinford ruled:

"It is utterly impossible to listen to this great mass of testimony of widespread, flagrant, open and notorious violations of the gambling laws in this judicial district over a long number of years and conclude that he [Howard] made more than a token effort to discharge his duty and enforce them. Such an attitude on his part proves him to be properly accused of protecting law violators . . ."

Judge Swinford's words were harsh, yet, as Drahmann pointed out at the time, they added up to very little. Howard was disbarred in Federal Court, but he retained his title and authority. If Kefauver hadn't followed up on the publicity, the whole affair would have blown over. Instead, there suddenly was Crisis.

By the time hearings on Newport-Covington were scheduled, the boys had their defense ready. Jimmy Brink told the Kefauver Committee that the Cleveland Syndicate pulled out of the Lookout House on June 20, 1951. He had talked to syndicate leaders in Florida, he said, and explained to them that "they were in the way."

Similar stories were told about Newport—the syndicate had pulled out and invested its money in the Desert Inn in Las Vegas. If Kefauver wanted to chase the syndicate, let him go to Vegas. Newport-Covington was now controlled by "local" men.

Not too surprisingly, Kefauver and his aides were not convinced. They did take the hint, however, and probed the Desert Inn, but they returned again to northern Kentucky. The "heat" got really hot.

Kenton County ministers, encouraged by the high-level help they were receiving, remained active despite a smear campaign designed to show their efforts were all part of a communist plot to undermine local government. Local "liberals" accepted the smear, but in Frankfort politicians decided they could ignore the situation no longer. Unlike the Beverly Hills, the Lookout House was in a sixth-class city and state police could move in without an invitation from local authorities. A decision was made to move in.

On March 5, 1952, State Police Sergeant David Espie and Trooper C. R. Lockhart left Frankfort for Cincinnati. Dressed as civilians, they registered at a Cincinnati hotel and caught a cab for the Lookout House. It was a procedure thousands of visitors had followed over the years and no trouble was encountered until they reached the hatcheck girl. Ann's successor in that job informed Lockhart he couldn't be admitted unless he wore a necktie. After all, the Lookout House was a classy joint and Mr. Drahmann insisted on decorum. It was also a well-equipped joint—the girl produced several neckties and Lockhart rented one for the occasion. A porter assisted him in putting it on. The officers then went into the bar, which "was in the shape of a horseshoe with a stage at the open end. The stage was occupied by a male entertainer who played an organ and sang. Behind the bar were two liquor islands . . ."

Espie noticed that on the other side of the bar was "a small lighted alcove and a set of closed double doors on the left just inside the alcove. After watching both men and women go and come through these doors," Espie continued, "we left our stools at the bar and entered the alcove. I still had about a half of a glass of whiskey and soda in a glass I carried in with me.

"I tried to open the door by turning the door knob but it would not open. Thinking the doors were locked, I rapped. One of the doors was opened immediately by a man dressed in a civilian suit and he looked to be over fifty years of age. He told us to come in and that the doors were not locked. We entered the gambling room. I was still carrying my drink.

"Immediately in front of us was a chuck-a-luck table or birdcage game with an operator standing behind the table. Beside this table was a roulette table with an operator stationed behind it. Beside the roulette table was a blackjack table with a dealer. To our right along the opposite wall were two crap tables, both being operated by four operators each. To our extreme right was a balcony which was occupied by three elderly men. Two large safes were in the rear of the balcony . . .

"We noticed several things during the time we were in the gambling room:

"1. All operators of games wore white shirts with ties of various descriptions. Some operators had their initials monogrammed on their shirt pocket.

"2. All operators worked rapidly and skillfully which seemed to mark them as professionals.

"3. At fifteen to thirty minute intervals each operator would be replaced by another operator.

"4. A man dressed in civilian clothes was noticed bringing a tray of drinks into the room several times during the evening. These drinks were paid for and consumed by patrons in the gambling room. Another man was noticed to stop by each gambling table from time to time. He would take small brown boxes containing surplus cash from the tables and run them to the balcony where they were handed to one of the men sitting there. The men in the balcony would empty the boxes and count the cash. After the money was counted, the box was handed back to the money collector, who would return it to the proper table.

"5. The crap tables drew most of the gambling trade.

"6. About 2:30 A.M. we noticed several operators bring additional equipment into the gambling room and set up additional gaming tables."

The troopers decided they would need some sleep and returned to the Sheraton-Gibson Hotel. Next morning they contacted Lieutenant Jimmy Hughes and made plans for a raid that night. Espie was given a key assignment—somehow, from someone, he had to obtain a search warrant without tipping off the club.

Local reformers offered advice and arranged a meeting with a magistrate. When they arrived that evening, the magistrate was suffering from a bad case of the jitters. He told Espie he "didn't know how to draw up an affidavit or a search warrant and did not have any printed forms for this purpose. He also stated he was on the spot. He said he was not physically afraid of anyone but that he had a wife and kids."

Nowhere in the Newport-Covington area is there any record of a wife or children being deliberately injured by gangsters, but it was the first plea made by persons reluctant to do their duty.

Espie asked if the magistrate would cooperate if they could persuade an attorney, Andy Clark, to assist. "Halfheartedly," the man agreed. Clark was located and promised to help. Fortunately, enough time had been alloted so the delay wasn't fatal to the raiders. With Clark's help, the proper papers were at last drawn and signed, the waiting raiding party which had just come up from Frankfort was advised, and all watches were synchronized. Leaving a guard with the magistrate to prevent a tip-off—and to give him an excuse later—Espie and Lockhart went once more by cab to the Lookout House. Again they rented a necktie and entered the casino where they began playing chuck-a-luck with their backs to the door.

"We noticed," Espie wrote in his official report, "the dealer's hands hesitate in mid-air and then begin to fall toward the money tray on the table. Then his hands went suddenly straight up in the air and he backed away from the table, his eyes glued on the main entrance. We turned to see Trooper Barton standing just inside the door with a shotgun in his hand. Already well into the room were several state police officers dressed both in uniform and civilian clothes and led by Lieutenant Hughes.

"Hughes stated, 'This is a raid.'"

Lieutenant Hughes, who was later to be second in command of the state police under Colonel Espie, said the raiding party arrived in a bus. When it pulled into the parking lot, an attendant shouted, "You can't park that thing in here," and then made a dash for a warning buzzer mounted on a pole. One of the officers grabbed him in time. Bypassing the dining room, the troopers crashed into the casino, where Espie and Lockhart were waiting.

Among the eighteen persons arrested that night was Kenny Bright, the syndicate representative at the Flamingo Club, who had been taking a busman's holiday. Some $20,000 worth of gambling equipment was seized and—even more unusual—burned. News stories about the raid noted there had been an injunction against gambling at the club since 1938.

The Lookout House as a gambling casino did not reopen. Drahmann assured Ann at the time, however, that the closing was only temporary. Some political adjustments on the state level would be needed but eventually the heat would cool. Meanwhile, would she like to move to Miami Beach for a while? The boys were planning some big things down there.

Sam Tucker, branch manager of the Newport-Covington operation, moved to Miami Beach back when the syndicate was trying to convince the Kefauver Committee it had pulled out of the area. He left his brother, Garson, to run the Beverly, assisted by such "local men" as Sam Schraeder and John Croft. A lot of other area people were in Miami Beach to say nothing of the big shots from New York, Cleveland, Detroit, and Boston. Ann would feel at home there.

Ann was willing enough to go, but destiny took a hand. Eventually she would move south but not as Mrs. Charley Drahmann. On August 6, 1952—five months after the Lookout House closed—Drahmann and his boss, Jimmy Brink, were returning home from a preliminary business trip to Miami Beach. Flying conditions were perfect and Brink was a skilled pilot. Yet, for no apparent reason, Brink's private plane dove into the ground near Atlanta.

Rescuers managed to recover $16,200 in $100 bills that spilled out of the burning plane. Dog track records from Miami were also saved. Apparently the syndicate was preparing a new assignment for Brink and Drahmann, but Brink and Drahmann were killed instantly.

Years later, Sam Tucker told the author: "I often flew with Brink. I could've been in that plane just as easily as Drahmann."

History would have been much different if he had been riding in Charley's seat.

*"I have never been afraid
of burglars."* ANN DRAHMANN

Three

MONDAYS WERE ALWAYS TIRING. THE ANNDRA SHOP STAYED open until 8:30 P.M. that one night each week. At day's end, Ann Drahmann decided to relax. There was no need to go home. Joan, a big girl now at fifteen, was spending the night with Nancy Neiman in Fort Mitchell. The big house on Dixie Highway would be lovely.

Luckily a friend happened by and invited her to dinner. They left the Carew Tower, tallest building in Cincinnati, where the dress shop was located, and went nearby to the Frontier Room of the Netherland Plaza Hotel. The meal was leisurely. Always an extrovert, Ann was glad to have a companion. It was well after 11 P.M. when she drove across to the Ohio to Kentucky and headed home. The road took her by the Lookout House, huge and dark at the top of the hill. Twenty months had passed since it closed. Despite a lot of talk, no real effort had been made to reopen it. The do-gooders were still in the saddle in Kenton County.

Ann sighed. It wouldn't mean much for her on practical grounds if the club did reopen. George Todd, the syndicate's representative in the daily operation of the casino, had visited her a few days after Charley's funeral and given her $4,467.50 in cash. It represented Charley's ten per cent interest in what was left of the casino's bankroll. The sum seemed rather small to Ann but she was still too stunned by Charley's death to argue. Now, looking back, she could smile in irony. Less than $5,000 was Charley's share, yet everyone seemed to think she had safety-deposit boxes overflowing with $100 bills. Even Screw Andrews, who should know the truth, was always hinting and probing. Screw was big in numbers these days but he was becoming something of a problem. Always hanging around as if, somehow, he had a claim on her. Once in an effort to discourage his attentions she had told him she didn't need a man, that she had all the money she wanted. It was a lie on both counts, and maybe Screw knew it.

Arriving at 2725 Dixie Highway, just across the street from the Lookout Stud Farm, Ann parked the car and entered through the back door. Carefully she locked the door. The front door was always locked; she seldom even used it. Tossing off a quick slug of J & B Scotch, which Charley had taught her to like—he said it was more sophisticated than the bourbon most Kentuckians drank out of loyalty to local industry—Ann prepared for bed. As usual she left a night light burning. Since childhood she had been unable to sleep in the dark. Even Charley could not tease her out of the habit.

An hour later she awoke. Someone was shaking her shoulder. Slowly she opened her eyes. Two men stood beside the bed. One was pointing a gun at her. Above his mask he had heavy, dark eyebrows which seemed to grow together over the bridge of his nose.

"Listen, broad," said the gunman. "We know you've got a lot of money in this house. We want it. Where's your plant?"

Ann had never lacked physical courage, especially where men were concerned. And she was always curious.

"What's a plant?" she demanded.

The gunman laughed in half-conscious admiration. "The place you hide your money," he replied.

Ann was conscious of his eyes. The nightgown she wore was almost transparent. Charley had picked it out. Despite her fear she felt a tingle of excitement. It had been a long time since a man had been in her bedroom. Too bad there there two of them. She might try something if he . . .

The thought died as the other man picked up her platinum watch from the nightstand and put it in his pocket. Charley had given her that watch. It was set with forty diamonds. He had paid $1,500 for it at Meyer's Jewelry in Cincinnati.

Angry now, Ann got out of bed and put on a robe. The men watched her carefully. Well, there wasn't much choice, she decided. She picked up the keys to the secretary in the hall. They followed her, still watching as she unlocked the secretary and the metal box it contained. The man with the gun grabbed the box and quickly counted the cash. There were eighteen $100 bills in it. He pawed through the rest of the papers in the box impatiently.

"This is chicken feed," he growled. "Where's the real plant?"

"That's all there is," said Ann quietly. "I work for a living."

The men didn't believe her. "We know you've got a lot of money stashed here somewhere," said one of them. "You can't keep it in the bank on account of income taxes so it's gotta be here. You'd better tell us where it is."

Again Ann denied there was any more cash. The men searched carefully. Finding nothing, they held a whispered conference. Ann caught the words:

"The broad didn't give us no trouble about the eighteen. Let's blow."

"First we gotta tie her up," said the second man.

Black Eyebrows snatched a sheet from the bed and tore it into strips. Seating Ann, they tied her to a chair and gagged her. Then, suddenly, the big house was silent once again.

It took Ann more than an hour to chew through the gag and rock the chair to the window. She began screaming. The house was set well back from the highway and there was little traffic at that time of night. Luckily, Charles Brufach, the gardener who slept in a little cottage at the rear, heard her screams and investigated. Police were called.

Ann explained to the officers that she had taken the $1,800 out of the bank only a few days before. She needed the money, she said, to pay her country club dues, Joan's tuition at boarding school, and other bills. The cops were skeptical. They too had heard the gossip of vast sums left behind by a syndicate casino boss. In their eyes Charley had been a big shot. The fact that the real bosses from Cleveland and Las Vegas took the cake and left only the crumbs would have been news to them.

Those first few months after Charley's death had been an education for Ann. Pride had forced her to keep alive the fiction that Charley had left her well fixed. The truth was far from that. Insurance policies had provided only $5,338. When added to the money Todd gave her, Charley's entire estate came to less than $10,000. Of course she had the house but it was burdened with a huge mortgage and she had been unable to sell it. And when and if she did, the equity would be only about $4,000.

The one bright spot was the suit she had filed against the Brink estate for damages resulting from Charley's death. It seemed simple to Ann—the plane was owned by Brink and he was the pilot. No natural causes had contributed to the crash. It had to be pilot's error and for that Brink's widow should pay. Unlike Ann, she had been left with plenty.

In the crisis, Ann's mother and sisters had come to her aid. Somehow they raised the money and bought the dress shop in Cincinnati. Ann was paid $100 a week to manage the shop. Most people assumed she owned it and had purchased it with funds left by Drahmann. The sight of the young and pretty widow driving to work each day in her 1950 Cadillac—she had managed to keep the car—excited the imagination of many.

Sometimes Ann let her own imagination wander. She was only thirty-one when Charley died and she still had her face and figure. Joan, growing up slim and beautiful, was sometimes mistaken as a younger sister. Life still had promise. There was time enough to marry again, and God knows, she needed a man. But next time . . .

As part of her act, and to fill the void left by Charley, she gave many parties. They weren't lavish or formal, but they were nice. Over the years she had learned the arts of the hostess and the trick of putting people at their ease. The parties attracted a strange assortment of people. Some claimed to be old friends of Charley. Others were important gangsters. And her fame spread. Of course, some of her guests were married men on the make, hoping to take advantage of a widow. But that was all right too. Charley had been married when she met him. Marriage, in and of itself, was no great problem if the right guy came alone.

One of the men who dropped in frequently was Gil Beckley. Ann didn't know too much about him other than that he was a gambler and apparently a big one. Gil didn't talk business at parties but he did enjoy telling of his experiences with MacArthur in Japan. Somehow Beckley and a pal promoted for themselves a Geisha house and had it all to themselves for two weeks. To hear Gil tell it, they had a lot of fun. Those Japanese girls must be nuts, Ann decided.

Curious as always and more than a little intrigued, Ann asked some discreet questions. Gil had come to Newport from Indianapolis, she learned, and had taken Nig Devine's place in the Bobben Realty Company. Nig moved south to Miami Beach for a while, where he was associated with Petey Arnold of Chicago and Joe "the Blimp" Sonken in Mother Kelley's Nightclub. Now he was in Vegas and reportedly a partner with Ed Levinson in the Fremont Hotel and Casino.

Bobben Realty, as everyone knew, had long been the layoff-betting center for much of the country. Under Gil's direction it had become bigger than ever, but the Kefauver blight made it too hot to operate and Gil moved the whole deal to Canada. He was still going strong up there, and he intended to return to Newport as soon as things settled down as inevitably they would. Meanwhile, he came often to visit and invariably dropped by to see Ann when he was in town.

Something was on his mind, Ann decided. Something beside the two things men were usually thinking about when they came calling on her. She puzzled about it. Somehow it annoyed her to find Gil staring at her across the room, coolly, speculatively, as if she was one of the Beverly Hills cows that Sammy Schraeder was always bragging about. Sammy was a big wheel at the Beverly now. She could remember when he was just another punk. Funny how he should be so proud of his cattle. Jimmy Brink used to brag about his thoroughbreds in the same irritating way.

Sleepout Louis Levinson was another frequent visitor. Now that Eddie was such a big shot in Vegas, Sleepout was the big man at the Flamingo in Newport. Ann smiled. Somehow the nickname "Sleepout" when applied to the fat, lazy Louis was funny. Years ago Charley had explained the origin of the name. The boys at the Flamingo sometimes got involved in marathon poker games that continued until they became more a test of physical endurance than skill. Louis developed the habit of "sleeping out" a hand or two every so often. He never left the table—just leaned back and snoozed. Brief as they were, the naps kept him refreshed and playing until everyone else finally tossed in their cards.

Sleepout was all right, Ann decided. Her brother liked working for him. Sleepout's wife, Mildred, was a pain in the behind. The Levinsons had a fine home on a hill in the best neighborhood of Campbell County, the suburb of Fort Thomas. Most of the bigger gamblers lived there—it was like Shaker Heights in Cleveland or

Grosse Point in Detroit. Just a high class residential community with nary a handbook in town. Matter of fact, there wasn't even a liquor license and the town's honest police chief, Louis Cook, made sure no one operated without one.

Cook, a rarity in northern Kentucky, had been chief before she was born. His son, Henry, was the United States Attorney for the Eastern District of Kentucky. Some of the boys had grumbled when he got the job—he was so square it hurt. Once as acting county judge, he closed the entire county down for two weeks. No one doubted he would do it again if given a chance. Luckily, the "feds" had never found a handle in Newport and Henry had been unable to do anything.

But back to Mildred—she liked to brag. Always talking about the fine home just up the street from Lester's place, or Louis's standing in the community and in the syndicate. What's more, she was so critical. Every time she came calling it was like standing an inspection. Where Sleepout was friendly, Mildred acted as if she hoped she would find something wrong. Almost she seemed jealous. But of what? Ann couldn't figure it out.

Screw Andrews was another matter entirely. Ann never doubted what he wanted. Few women did where Screw was concerned. Big, arrogant, with a thin black moustache and cold eyes, Screw gave the impression of controlled power. Maybe his arrogance came from pushing Negro numbers writers around. One thing was certain—he was greedy and ambitious. Always he was hinting that with a little extra capital he could get a lock on the numbers racket in the Greater Cincinnati area. Already he had eliminated some of the competitors by the simple expedient of killing them. With his connections at City Hall he could get away with murder by calling it self-defense. Yet his insistence that she had money, or would have it soon, was tiresome. He was laying the groundwork for something—while, at the same time, always hoping for a quick ride in bed. Once it occurred to her that he might not really mean it, that, instead, he was testing her virtue, but she dismissed the thought with a laugh. Screw's animal appetites were only too well known. No one had to wonder how he got his nickname.

Ann shrugged. A lot of things were going on. Maybe Charley might have understood them but they baffled her. The talk at her parties always turned to politics, and that was always confusing. The ally of yesterday was the enemy of today. That old buzzard Pete Schmidt, who had been down so many times she had lost count, was riding high again. Pulling the strings as usual was that pallid old ghost, Charley Lester. He, too, seemed indestructible. Once she had asked Drahmann why the syndicate tolerated the troublemaker. Charley had sighed.

"I don't really know," he said, "except maybe they figure that someday he'll be useful."

"Useful for what?" persisted Ann.

"To take the rap, maybe," replied Drahmann. "The guy's smart, all right, but maybe he's got too much hate in him. He doesn't like anybody."

Be that as it may, Lester was still active and still causing trouble in the weird political arena that was Newport. In retrospect, much that puzzled Ann can be explained. The Cleveland Syndicate, its well-developed intelligence system functioning perfectly, had been forewarned of the Kefauver heat. Deciding that consolidation was in order, it permitted Kenton County and the Lookout House to go almost by default; it prepared for the storm in Campbell.

With its major casinos—the Beverly Hills and the Latin Quarter—outside Newport's city limits, the syndicate sought to direct the coming heat on the town. Newport was sure to attract attention anyway. The scores of brothels, bust-out joints, and handbooks could hardly be overlooked. Even so, Newport could be closed completely without seriously hurting the syndicate. Indeed, the lack of action inside the city would hurt the independents and send more suckers to the suburbs. Of course, Newport had to be kept under control. Too much heat might lead to a citizen's revolt which could close down the entire area.

Exactly that happened in Kenton County, but the syndicate's plans worked so well the revolt was stopped on the west bank of the Licking River and never spread to Campbell.

The first step was to blunt the Kefauver attack. Red Masterson was assigned the job. By discreet financial contributions and covert encouragement on the political level, a group of sincere but naive businessmen were inspired to form the Newport Civic Association and to field candidates. They campaigned on a platform of moderation—"Clean up, not Close up." It was easy to convince the reformers that whatever their ultimate goal, this was the way to begin. The syndicate's political stooges were told to cooperate and the "liberal" voter was sold the idea that if brothels and bust-out joints weren't regulated they would give the area a bad reputation and scare away the rich sucker upon which the economy allegedly depended.

The campaign was so successful that when the Kefauver Committee turned to Newport it found a reform group holding public office. No one questioned the sincerity of the NCA though there were doubts as to its effectiveness. Yet, on the whole, committee investigators decided, it was better to encourage the reformers than to blast them.

Inevitably, the NCA clashed with the Schmidt-Lester faction, which, for reasons of local advantage, was sometimes supported by Levinson and Andrews. Other allies included the madams, bookies, and owners of slum property, who opposed a clean-up as strongly as they would have fought a close-up. To their way of thinking there was very little difference.

Schmidt, his old dream still alive despite the loss of the Beverly Hills and the Glenn, had prepared for opportunity by constructing on Fifth Street between York and Monmouth the $700,000 "Glenn Schmidt Playtorium." A sprawling, one-story building, it contained a beautiful bar, an excellent restaurant, a large bowling alley, and, of course, a swank casino. In the basement was a large assembly hall where, for years to come, anti-reform rallies were held.

So large and new, the Playtorium could not be missed by the eager beavers of the NCA. A raid was ordered by City Commissioner Charles Eha after a little private snooping. In quick revenge, a faction of the police department long controlled by Lester, struck back at the syndicate-run Merchants Club.

Detective Jack Thiem led the raid on the Merchants, headquarters of Red Masterson, and marched a long line of gamblers down Fourth Street to the police station. Thiem had become something of a one-man vice squad of the style made famous during the period by Pat Purdue of Miami Beach. He got his start after the Rip Farley murder when a so-called "hoodlum squad" was set up. Since then he had gone regularly into gambling joints, collaring punks who might recklessly try to follow Rip's example. Ordinarily, he never bothered the gamblers. Years later he told the author why:

"The police didn't recognize gambling as a wrong. Including myself. Now the gambling was there. I knew it was there. Every policeman knew it was there. Every public official knew it was there. Every citizen knew it was there. The doors were wide open. You could stand on the street and look straight into gambling joints. For years you could do it. Nobody was kidding anybody. I'm not saying I wasn't guilty of letting gambling go, but I was not against gambling because I was raised in the atmosphere of gambling. Besides, I was not a vice squad man. I was head of the hoodlum squad."

Thiem claimed that eventually he changed his mind about gambling "when I felt the creeping influence of the gambler at City Hall," but he didn't take immediate action. As he explained:

"There are things you have to get from the inside when you find yourself in such a muddle as Newport. You have to start figuring— how do I learn the angles enough to do something about it and not get my head chopped off while I'm trying? So you take a step down the road into crime and the further you step into it the more you learn but the more off-color you become—from white to gray to the point, when you've learned enough to do the job, you're black enough to be framed. I got to know the underworld very well."

As far as the NCA was concerned, the chunky Thiem had this to say:

"The NCA in the beginning was made up of very sincere people who really wanted to do something about the situation, but they didn't have the least idea as to who were the culprits. Due to the fact that I had worked so diligently to learn how to cope with the situation, I was probably twenty years ahead of my time. The rest of the citizens weren't ready for my type of action. I went to the fellow leading the NCA and offered to lead the battle for them. They insulted me and told me I was a crook. So I backed away, and after all the years I had spent in getting ready to lead such a fight I wound up as the opponent of people who wanted the same thing I did. It ended up being a battle between the NCA and myself instead of me and the NCA against the underworld."

And the syndicate couldn't have been happier.

Toward the end of 1951, with the life of the Kefauver Committee expiring, the syndicate passed the word—the NCA had served its purpose and was no longer needed. In the upcoming election the reformers were to be defeated.

Such a situation was made to order for Schmidt, advised by the wily Lester. Since 1943, he had been trying to get his protegé, Robert Siddell, elected mayor. Now with the NCA candidates largely discredited—the good citizens were disillusioned and the crooks were angry—and Jack Thiem busy fighting NCA leaders, Siddell had his chance. He won easily, defeating the NCA and the candidate supported by the syndicate.

At last Schmidt had the political power he had sought so long. The syndicate was still supreme in the county outside Newport but inside the city Schmidt was boss. And he had his old dream. As Thiem told it:

"The minute Siddell was elected, Pete Schmidt called from his Playtorium, called down to headquarters and asked me to stop by. He told me he was going to put a second floor on the Playtorium and put offices up there. He was going to use those offices to take over ALL the rackets—the race wire service to the bookies, the numbers, the whole shooting match.

"He said that I was going to be his 'Enforcer.' I told him I was like hell. The only thing I was going to enforce was him—and right now."

This was part of the switch that puzzled Ann. From ally of Schmidt in fighting the NCA, Thiem suddenly became his enemy. Some thought the syndicate was responsible. Thiem maintained he was but fighting crime in his own fashion.

And, it developed, Schmidt was a little premature in assuming he had complete control. The syndicate, perhaps thinking Schmidt might go too far, pulled some strings. Oscar Hesch was appointed city manager and he promptly ordered a bingo game at the Playtorium raided. Police judge and future mayor Alfred Maybury promptly dismissed the charges against Schmidt and declared from the bench:

"Oscar Hesch is owned body and soul by the Cleveland Syndicate."

As if to disprove the charge, Hesch moved next against the Glenn Hotel. It was about the only joint left in town giving the Playtorium competition. Even the Flamingo had curtailed action while waiting for the storm to pass.

Jack Thiem, fighting an increasingly lonely battle, struck back at the Playtorium. The second of two raids he conducted was a spectacular affair. Financed by someone—years later Thiem declined to say whom—he employed a group of private detectives in Louisville. En route to Newport they were deputized on the charter bus. Halting in front of the Playtorium, the "deputies" crashed into the place waving axes and guns.

Unhappily for the success of the raid, one of the private eyes had tipped Schmidt, who was waiting with his old friend Police Chief George Gugel. The raiders arrested Schmidt. Gugel arrested the raiders. Caught in the melee was *Courier-Journal* photographer George Bailey, who made the mistake of snapping a picture of Gugel and Schmidt. The chief ordered him taken into custody and Bailey was happy when he arrived at the police station—he had feared he was to be given a "Newport nightgown," as a blanket of concrete was known locally. But the arrest of Bailey was an error too. The *Courier-Journal* raised hell and ultimately Gugel was indicted in Federal Court for violating the photographer's civil rights. He paid a $1,000 fine and went back to work.

But the raid was the last straw as far as Lester-Schmidt were concerned. Thiem had to go. The simple thing to do was to frame him. And they did.

The detective fought back. Turning down an offer presented by Screw Andrews to leave town in return for having the assortment of charges dropped, Thiem demanded a hearing. With Lester guiding the proceedings, the outcome was inevitable. Little effort was made to conceal the farcical nature of the proceedings. Lester's management of a hearing in which he had no official status became so obvious that Thiem's attorney moaned:

"This is prosecution by proxy."

Even that statement went into the record without being denied.

A broken man at the end, Thiem left town and headed for Las Vegas, where that old Newport personality, Ed Levinson, gave him a job as security officer in the Sands Hotel casino.

While all this was going on, Screw Andrews was quietly extending his control of the numbers racket. Sometimes, however, his actions became a bit loud—as loud as pistol shots.

Born Frank Andriola in Cincinnati in 1911, Screw's first scrape with the law came as a juvenile when a gun with which he and some friends were playing went off accidentally and killed a bystander. In the next few years he was arrested more than forty times. Eventually he became active in the numbers racket in Cincinnati, but after an arrest in 1945 and a stretch in prison he shifted his headquarters to Newport where the law was more flexible.

Numbers, in those early days, was a competitive business and Negroes had a big share of the action. Two of Screw's competitors were "White Smitty," a pale-skinned Negro, and Melvin Clark. Of more immediate concern was Steve Payne, who ran a Negro nightclub in Newport known as the Sportsman's Club.

Shortly after Screw moved across the Ohio, Payne's body was found in a ditch along Kyles Lane in Kenton County. He had been shot several times in the head. Mentioned as a suspect was Screw Andrews, but, as usual, the probe soon hit a dead end and was forgotten.

Court records show, however, that on May 3, 1948, a little more than a month after the murder, the Sportsman's Club was sold to Nig Devine, that friend of Ann Drahmann and a big shot in the Eastern Syndicate.

A few months later the club passed from Devine to Charles O. Derrick, a local magistrate. Thirteen months after that it officially became the property of Screw Andrews.

The numbers racket was no longer just a local operation.

Shortly before the final transfer of the club to Screw, Newport police led by City Solicitor Morris Weintraub drove by the club to raid the numbers headquarters of White Smitty. It was one of the most successful raids in Newport history—up to that time. Sixteen men were arrested and $19,668 was seized. White Smitty's operation was destroyed. Everyone assumed the fact that the enterprising Mr. Weintraub just happened to be Screw's attorney was only a coincidence. After all, Weintraub's reputation as a prosecutor had been established long before. He was the man who prosecuted Jack Thiem.

Andrews was now free to give his attention to his last remaining competitor, Melvin Clark. He decided to be subtle.

When the Sportsman's Club became his property, he also acquired two of the late Steve Payne's brothers as aides. Presumably their presence made the transition from black to white control more acceptable to the Negroes who patronized the joints and provided the great bulk of numbers action. One of the brothers, Bull Payne, was given the job of managing the Alibi Club, which Screw had also obtained.

Early on January 13, 1952, a shoot-out occurred in the Alibi Club. According to police reports, Clark gunned down Bull after an argument over a bar bill. The story had it that Clark came into the joint with a white woman and was told "that down here we don't mix." White women weren't wanted in Negro clubs even if the clubs were owned by a white man. Clark left, so the story continued, without paying the bill. Payne was sore. When next the two men met, Payne allegedly pulled a gun and Clark killed him.

That was the official line and Clark helped it along by pleading self-defense. But secret testimony made available to the author discloses that a girl friend of Clark gave another version:

"He [Clark] told me that the guy he killed didn't have any good reason to shoot at him. He felt that Bull Payne had been put up to kill him by Screw."

Be that as it may, Andrews moved heaven and earth to convict Clark of the killing. His efforts became so obvious that even Judge Ray Murphy was quoted as saying:

"One report has it that a Negro nightclub owner has been instrumental in efforts to have Clark convicted so that he could take over Clark's numbers racket interests."

The truth sometimes comes from unlikely places.

But convicting anyone for anything was a chore in Newport, which is one reason the frame became so popular. It was more easily managed. Then, too, some of the boys felt Screw had gone too far if rumor was right that he had attempted murder by proxy.

The murder charge was dropped and Clark was convicted on the lesser count of carrying a concealed weapon. Instead of going to jail, he was put on probation. One of the conditions was that he stay out of Kentucky during the probation period. This was all to the good as far as Screw was concerned, but someone slipped up and made the probation period far too short. Screw had barely finished absorbing Clark's writers when Clark returned to Newport and opened the Coconut Grove. Soon he was back in the numbers business and posing a growing threat.

The matter became moot when Andrews killed Clark on July 18, 1955. The shooting occurred outside the Alibi Club. Detective Pat Ciafardini, an old friend of Lester and Andrews, said Screw surrendered to him personally. The body of Clark was found in an alley. Ciafardini said the dead man was holding a revolver with five empty cartridges. It was self-defense said Andrews, and Pat agreed.

Weintraub was too busy campaigning for Happy Chandler, the no longer young or idealistic politician, and was destined to be named Speaker of the House when Happy was elected to his second term as governor. But available to defend Andrews was another Chandler man, Andrew Jolly.

The simple case of self-defense became complicated when reporters found an eyewitness. A University of Cincinnati coed, she was Clark's girl friend. Miss Evelyn Farmer talked to reporters. She had accompanied Clark to the rear of the Alibi Club and waited there in the car as Clark went in to discuss buying some slot machines for the Coconut Grove. Suddenly she heard a shot. A "dead silence" followed, and then came several more shots . . .

Clark appeared in the wide gap of the fence. "He was crawling toward me," Miss Farmer said. "He was trying to tell me something but there wasn't any sound. There was nothing in his hand. Then all at once his hand went up and he rolled over on his back."

That this story conflicted with Ciafardini's account was obvious to all, but Miss Farmer had more to tell. She ran across Central Avenue to the Congo Club, another Negro night spot. Someone there called the police. She sat down at a table.

"I was sitting there," she continued, "with my head in my hands. I heard three more shots. Everybody started for the door. I saw this guy coming down the alley, around the corner of the parking lot. He crossed Central Avenue. He was about ten feet away from me. By that time I had gone to the door. He faced me. He said: 'I'm looking for the bitch that was with him.'

"I looked down and saw he had a gun in his hand. It was hanging at his side. It was Screw. I just stood there. He looked around. Everybody looked the other way when he looked at them. He continued up the alley past the Congo. Everybody told me: 'Get out.'"

Miss Farmer got out—all the way to Toledo where the FBI and the reporters found her. She came back to testify. Belatedly, Clark's body was dug up and an autopsy performed. It uncovered several bullets in the body. Several other strange circumstances came to light, but, despite everything, Jolly won an acquittal for his client on the grounds of self-defense.

Shortly, thereafter, Ann Drahmann was taken to New York by Screw, Gil Beckley, and Sleepout Louis. Avowed purpose of the trip was to see the heavyweight championship bout between Rocky Marciano and Archie Moore. Real purpose was to introduce Ann to a man who for some time had been looking for a suitable wife.

The man was Trigger Mike Coppola, boss of the numbers racket in East Harlem and an overlord of the Eastern Syndicate.

Years later, Ann was to write: "Screw Andrews is Mike Coppola's main and most important man in Newport." By then she knew the facts.

Meanwhile, she had discovered why her parties had been so popular and why Gil Beckley stared at her so often in that peculiar way.

"You would think the King was walking in when Mike walks into Harlem." ANN DRAHMANN

Four

THE MAN WHO WAS TO BECOME FEARED AS TRIGGER MIKE Coppola was born July 29, 1900, near Salerno, Italy. Guiseppe and Angelina Coppola, his parents, sailed five months later for the United States. Port of entry was New York City and it was there in 1918 his father became a naturalized citizen under the name Joseph.

Michael, one of nine children, was considered lucky to finish the seventh grade. By age 14 he was labeled an "incorrigible delinquent" and was sent to truant's school. Thereafter he was charged at regular intervals—grand larceny, pickpocketing, felonious assault, disorderly conduct, and homicide. In those early years he went to jail five times—the last a thirty-month stretch in Sing Sing Prison for grand larceny.

Paroled in 1925, he could consider his apprenticeship behind him. There was still time to cash in on the profits of Prohibition. The Reinfeld Syndicate was bringing Canadian booze by the shipload out of the St. Lawrence River and around and down the coast to "rum rows" off Boston and New York. Arnold Rothstein, the man who fixed the 1919 World Series, is generally credited with organizing the business but he dropped out to concentrate on gambling and narcotics. Men who were to become famous took over: Frank Costello, Bill Dwyer, Irving "Waxey Gordon" Wexler, Joe (Doto) Adonis, Meyer and Jake Lansky, Abner "Longie" Zwillman, Charles "Lucky" Luciano, Louis "Lepke" Buchalter, Dutch Schultz, and many more.

At first, competition was fierce, and bloody, but by 1929 a degree of cooperation was achieved. Out of this experience ultimately grew the Eastern Syndicate.

Coppola proved his ruthlessness under such bosses as "Mad Dog" Coll and "Legs" Diamond, and gained the nickname "Trigger Mike" in the process. The nickname proved to be very useful to a man not physically impressive. Only five feet, five inches tall, he needed a reputation to win the respect he thought his due.

In a little known chapter of the period, the New York gangsters cooperated closely with the emerging Cleveland Syndicate, which ruled Lake Erie from Detroit to Buffalo. Occasionally, despite the efficient organizations supplying liquor, a shortage would develop in one region of the country. The Clevelanders would make up the deficit from their supply. Or, in turn, New York would send liquor west if a temporary shortage developed in Ohio. Later, during the final phase of Prohibition, the two syndicates worked closely in operating the largest illegal distilleries ever found in the United States. The Molaska Corporation listed Meyer Lansky's father-in-law as an officer along with fronts for Moe Dalitz, Sam Tucker, and the rest.

Trigger Mike, as a rising star in the east, had every opportunity to meet the men who later were to control Newport and invest millions in Miami Beach, Las Vegas, and Havana.

Coppola hid his activities behind a number of occupations. In 1929 he listed his employment as clerk. In 1930 he said he was a barber. Caught with the goods in 1933, he admitted he was a bookmaker, but by 1936 he claimed once more to be a clerk. By 1942 he had promoted himself to "restaurant owner," and in 1944 on Miami Beach he was a "betting commissioner."

When the National Syndicate was formed in 1934, Coppola ranked high with the top men in New York and was able to cut himself into the numbers racket in East Harlem. The opportunity came when Ciro Terranova, known as the "Artichoke King," became unpopular with his men because of a certain unwillingness to share the loot. His power stemmed largely from the fact that he was a nephew of Lupo the Wolf, an early "Black Hand" boss in East Harlem.

The Black Hand is sometimes confused with the Mafia and those writers who in the fashion of the day seek to trace all organized crime back to a Sicilian secret society have made much use of it. During the early years of the big Italian immigration, the Black Hand flourished as cynical Italian-Americans capitalized on the newly arrived sons of Italy's ignorance and fears. In New York, Boston, and New Orleans, and as far west as Cincinnati and Louisville, a few crooks exploited their former countrymen. However, as the new citizens learned their way around and became aware of their freedom, the organization withered and died. So it was that in East Harlem, the rank and file shoved aside Lupo's nephew and accepted Coppola in his place.

The shift gave Trigger Mike control of only about one-fourth of the number profits in East Harlem, but it put him in position to claim the numbers empire of Dutch Schultz when that racketeer fell out of favor with the bosses of the Eastern Syndicate.

The "Dutchman" had been hiding from the Internal Revenue Service—over the years the one enemy of organized crime that was most effective—when the National Syndicate was organized. His holdings were considered fair game and both Coppola and the Cleveland Syndicate took quick advantage. Schultz "beat the rap" and returned to business but any inclination he had to resent his losses became a moot point when syndicate gunmen burned him down at Newark, New Jersey. Just before he was murdered, Schultz had returned from Cincinnati, where the Cleveland Syndicate was in the process of taking over the Coney Island Race Track, which they renamed River Downs. One of his aides, Edwin Garrison, missed the train that night in Cincinnati and so lived to burn the old Beverly Hills Club out from under Pete Schmidt.

Coppola, happy that Schultz could not challenge his takeover, moved to consolidate his position in East Harlem. Originally, the area was Jewish. Then came the Italians and then the Negro. In more recent years it has become necessary to speak of "Spanish Harlem," as thousands of job-seekers from Puerto Rico have settled in the area. Nevertheless, it has always been a slum area, a "Hell's Kitchen," where "melting pots" simmered but never quite succeeded in reducing various ethnic and national characteristics to any single standard. One thing the inhabitants have always had in common, however, is poverty, and, as an outgrowth of that, a fascination for the numbers racket. As elsewhere, numbers are the stuff of dreams. Bets can range from a dime to a dollar, and the lucky winner collects at 600 to 1. Of course, there are only enough winners to keep the dream alive. Schultz pioneered in ways to "fix" the number so that the winner was always the one receiving the least play by the suckers. Coppola carried on the tradition and it is safe to assume that wherever numbers is big business ways are found to control the payoff—from Miami to Boston. In Newport, Screw Andrews was no exception.

An associate in the Harlem enterprise was Joey Rao, who had survived a feud with Mad Dog Coll in 1931. Coll, by then an outlaw among outlaws, went gunning for Rao with a submachine gun. He missed his target but killed one child and wounded four others in the street-side assault. Other gunmen soon eliminated the "Mad Dog."

As late as 1947, New York police were reporting that Rao and Trigger Mike shared "in the profits derived from the allocation of choice spots for curb stands when the Holy Feast celebration was taking place in Harlem."

An officer explained to the author that East Harlem is largely Catholic. Late each summer a week-long celebration similar to "a county fair" is held. Streets are crowded with hot dog stands, gambling wheels, and amusement devices. Professional gamblers from all over New York compete for choice locations. Coppola and Rao had the final word on such matters and took their cut. How much of the profits went to the Church was, as in the case of many bingo games, anyone's guess.

Coppola, meanwhile took himself a wife. His growing power and prestige seemed to require it. Moreover, he had fallen in love and when sentiment and power didn't conflict, he had no difficulty in making up his mind. The girl was Doris Lehman, a tall and young dancer with dark hair and eyes. They were married in 1943 and their first child, Michael David Coppola, was born the following year.

There exists today a photograph of young Michael David Coppola at about age three. He is standing on the streets of East Harlem. Joey Rao holds one hand and Trigger Mike the other. Rao, wearing glasses, a hat, and a sports shirt, looks like a middle-aged merchant. The shorter Trigger Mike is dressed in jacket and slacks. A huge ring shows on the little finger of his left hand. The boy, wearing a coat and sport pants, stares almost wistfully at the camera. He has his mother's beauty and it is emphasized by the grim bulk of the swarthy men beside him. Somehow he looks lonely.

Tragedy was about to strike the Coppola family but, except for the child, it was not undeserved. The affair started with the murder of Joseph Scottoriggio.

Just before dawn on Election Day, 1946, Scottoriggio left his apartment at 400 East 105th Street. As Republican district captain, he had an important and perhaps vital role to play in the election that day. Congressman Vito Marcantonio was seeking reelection against Republican Frederick V. P. Bryan. A victory by Bryan would upset the delicate political balance that permitted Coppola to operate so freely. Pressure had been applied to swing Republican votes to Marcantonio, and Rao and Coppola were the chief instruments applying the pressure. Scottoriggio was only 37 years old, but he controlled 600 votes in the district and in a close election they could be decisive.

Unknown to Scottoriggio, he had been much discussed at a meeting the night before at Trigger Mike's apartment. One of those in attendance at 347 East 116th Street was another Republican district leader. Also present in addition to Coppola and Rao were Doris Coppola and her father, David Lehman. The political situation was reviewed. The district leader disclosed that Scottoriggio planned to support Bryan against Marcantonio.

Coppola decided the matter was important enough to require the presence of the congressman. After he arrived the discussion continued. Then Coppola decided that Scottoriggio should be put out of action for one day—Election Day.

So it was that a few hours later as Scottoriggio left home that morning, his watching wife saw him pause at a streetlight. Four men appeared out of the gloom and assaulted him. They knocked him to the sidewalk where they pounded and kicked the helpless man repeatedly. At least a score of early-morning commuters witnessed the episode, but no one moved to interfere. In East Harlem one minded his own business.

Police arrived after the assailants faded into the blackness. The injured man was taken to the hospital where first reports indicated he was not fatally hurt. With Scottoriggio out of action, Marcantonio won the Democratic and American Labor Party nominations but failed to achieve the complete sweep he wanted when he lost the Republican nomination to Bryan. It was the beginning of the end for the man who had started in politics as the protégé of Fiorello H. LaGuardia. He was reelected to Congress but two years later the

Democrats followed the Republican lead and dropped him. Once again, however, the American Labor Party kept him in office. He backed Henry A. Wallace's unsuccessful bid for the presidency and was defeated for the mayoralty of New York. And in 1950, all forces united to defeat his bid for a new term in Congress.

The end for Scottoriggio came much quicker. Six days after the election he died of his injuries. A long probe into the political murder began. Quickly Coppola came under suspicion. Police decided to tap his phone only to discover the wily Trigger Mike didn't have one in his name. He paid a woman down the street for permission to run wires from her house to his apartment. When her number was called, a bootleg phone rang in Coppola's living room. Years later, police officers were to tap Mike's phone in Miami Beach. They listened in immediately and were in time to hear Mike warning all his friends that his phone was tapped.

Baffled, the New York detectives sought another angle. Coppola and Rao were arrested as material witnesses and held in lieu of $250,000 bond each. Immediately they sought a reduction and New York Supreme Court Justice Aaron J. Levy obliged by cutting the figure to one-tenth. The men easily posted the $25,000 and went free. A few years later Justice Levy died, leaving in his hotel suite a suitcase containing $600,000 in securities. Crime and politics go hand in hand, as the Scottoriggio case repeatedly illustrated.

Marcantonio was questioned and, as expected, denied everything. Officers were left with two possible witnesses—Mrs. Coppola and her father. They had vanished.

Reasoning that Coppola would entrust his wife only to someone he trusted implicitly, police began checking possibilities. Eventually the leading suspect became Frank "Butsy" Morelli, considered the syndicate overlord of New England, with headquarters in Providence, Rhode Island. Ultimately, Morelli testified before a grand jury—a mistake that cost him his position in the underworld.

The story gradually came out. Immediately after Trigger Mike's arrest as a material witness, Doris had taken her son and father to a relative's home in Queens. From there they flew to Miami Beach and stayed awhile on Palm Island in Biscayne Bay. Al Capone had been first to discover the beauties of Palm Island, and in later years such characters as Ed Curd—a Kentucky associate of Sleepout Louis—made his home next door. From the sunny south, the fugitives flew north with the robins and stayed at Morelli's mansion in Providence.

Unable to stay hidden from the greatest hunt since the search for Louis Lepke, Mrs. Coppola and her father followed Lepke's example and surrendered. They appeared before the grand jury. On the basis of their testimony, the jury indicted both of them on perjury charges.

Trigger Mike was on the spot. If his wife purged herself of the charges by telling the truth, he would go to jail. If she didn't talk, then ten years in prison awaited her. Mike was in a quandary. It seemed that neither muscle nor money could get him off the griddle. Reports reaching police had him half crazy with worry. Aggravating the matter was the fact that Doris was pregnant.

Did sentiment now conflict with policy? No one was sure. As far as the investigators were concerned, the break was unexpected and tragic. On March 17, 1948, Doris Patricia Coppola was born. Next day, Mrs. Coppola—still under indictment—died in the hospital. Of complications from childbirth? That was the assumption, but no autopsy was performed and, contrary to his religion, Mike had the body cremated.

The case against Coppola died with Doris. Charges against her father were dropped.

A wave of sympathy swept the underworld, which considered that both Trigger Mike and Doris had lived up to the code of silence despite tremendous pressure. In contrast, Morelli had talked. Reportedly, Harold R. Danforth, ace investigator of the district attorney's office, forced him to squeal by threatening to reveal some personal secrets. Those secrets were never made public but Butsy was finished as a ganglord. His place as boss of New England was taken by Raymond Patriarca, who ruled serenely until indicted in 1967 by a federal grand jury in Boston.

Patriarca was skilled in the necessary arts a top gangster must have when he moved into Morelli's job. Ten years before he had been sentenced to serve from three to five years in prison for armed robbery. Eighty-four days later he walked out of prison with a pardon. The resulting uproar brought the impeachment of Massachusetts Governor's Councillor Daniel H. Coakley. Investigation revealed that Coakley personally drafted the pardon petition, which presented Patriarca as a virtuous young man anxious to be released so he could support his old mother in Providence. Raymond did go home to his mother upon release, but only for a change of clothing. Thereupon he departed for Miami Beach with a dazzling blonde. His interest in south Florida remained high, and years later he was associated with his friend Trigger Mike in some business investments there.

In 1948, however, Coppola was displaying his skill in turning misfortune into profit. Even death could be made lucrative. Funeral services were held for Doris at Ferncliff Mausoleum, 207 East 116th Street, and the underworld turned out to pay tribute to the departed and, perhaps more important, curry favor from the living King of Harlem. As they signed the guest register at Ferncliff they also listed the contribution they were willing to make to assuage Trigger Mike's grief. The sums ranged from $5 to $1,000, but the great majority were in the $20 to $100 class. Many of the names were famous or destined to become so—Dio, Gallo, Pellegrino, Carfano, Felice, DeMartino, Genovese, Erra, Salerno, Carbo, Catena, Oremento, Amato, and the like.

Butsy Morelli, apparently trying to brazen it out, signed his name boldly, listing his address as 315 Mt. Pleasant, Providence. Not everyone found it necessary to sign his full name. Albert Anastasia, so-called "Lord High Executioner of Murder, Inc.," simply wrote "Albert" in large letters. There was only one Albert of consequence in the syndicate, but he only contributed $50. In contrast, Vincent "Jimmy Blue Eyes" Alo gave a century note.

The contributions totaled $13,615. The undertaker's bill was $3,033.20. The mausoleum cost $9,000. Total cost of the funeral was $12,083.20, leaving Mike with a neat profit of $1,531.80. Shortly thereafter he bought a new Cadillac for $4,008.29, paying cash as usual, and employing a front to handle the transaction. It was a technique he continued to use in the future.

A period of transition now began for Coppola. He was restless in New York. Some people thought he felt guilty about something. In any case, the Scottoriggio affair had brought him too far into the limelight and his continued presence in the big city was certain to mean continued investigation. More and more his thoughts went to Miami Beach, where he had sat out much of World War II. In 1946, he had filed his income tax return there, listing his address as 5138 Cherokee Avenue. On his Selective Service questionnaire he had given his occupation as "Betting Commissioner of Sporting Events."

Business was such that a return to Florida was practical. In 1947 he had invested in the Manhattan Cigarette Company—an act which as much as anything proved his growing power in the rackets. For Manhattan Cigarettes had been a syndicate operation from the beginning. Michael Lascari, foster brother of Lucky Luciano, and Joseph "Doc" Stacher founded the firm in 1936. Later Longie Zwillman, the so-called "Al Capone of New Jersey," took Doc's place. Another partner was Jerry Catena, in later years considered to be Vito Genovese's successor in the Eastern Syndicate. Joe Adonis was another top mobster with a piece of the business. Joe Massei, the notorious ganglord from Detroit, provided $5,000 to Coppola to buy into Manhattan Cigarettes. Massei had worked with and for the Cleveland Syndicate in its rum-running days and moved to Miami Beach in the forties. He had an interest in the Miami Provision Company, which supplied food to syndicate-controlled hotels and restaurants, as well as to the homes of individual gangsters. A friend, and also former Cleveland Syndicate associate, was John Angersola, who, under the name "King," had prospered in the construction business in Miami. Angersola joined Massei in urging Mike to move. All he had to do was turn the cigarette business over to Ben DeMartino. The numbers racket could be left in the capable hands of Tony Salerno and Joey Rao. They would keep away rivals and make sure Mike got his cut of the action, which by then was grossing $250,000 a day. Or so police estimated.

Angersola had a plush home waiting for Coppola at 4431 Alton Road on Miami Beach. While real estate records show Mike didn't become the official owner until November 1950, Angersola later swore he turned the house over to his friend in 1948, immediately after the death of Doris. Mike gave him $1,000 in cash and, as Angersola put it:

"The house as far as I was concerned was his the day he came down here. I told him to come down here."

Total cost of the huge house was said later to be $30,000. It was a bargain in every sense of the word. Other, and smaller, homes in the same area have sold for $100,000 or more.

Coppola maintained his apartment in New York until July 1950, when he made his final break with his home town. Thereafter he would return at intervals for consultation with top syndicate hoods or to check the progress of the assorted rackets of East Harlem.

Ultimately, he was content to let couriers bring his share of the loot to Miami Beach.

With Coppola's background, he had little trouble in finding projects on Miami Beach suitable to his status. The sophisticated underworld along Florida's Gold Coast respected money and power. Coppola had both so he was welcome. Quickly he joined Jack Friedlander to operate a casino at the Club Collins. Friedlander was a partner in the S & G Syndicate, which controlled bookmaking on Miami Beach for years prior to Estes Kefauver's journey to Florida. Ben Cohen, the brains of the S & G and political boss of the city, became Coppola's personal attorney.

Miami Beach in addition to being a good place to live and work was a vacation spot for hoods. Mike was able to renew acquaintance with the Levinson boys of Newport, with Nig Devine, Gil Beckley, and Screw Andrews. Many visitors were looking for capital and Coppola, who had cash to spare, developed a shylock business—as the racket was locally known—which was to grow with the years. He also became a banker for the bigger bookies and accepted tremendous amounts of layoff business from bookies who were financially strapped for cash.

Working with gangsters of Jewish descent posed no problems for Mike. The Eastern Syndicate contained people of all ethnic backgrounds in the very top ranks. From Rothstein to Lepke to Lansky, the descendants of East European Jews had proved their value in situations requiring moxie as well as muscle. For all his growing pride, Coppola had no illusions that organized crime was the exclusive domain of Italian-Americans despite occasional newspaper stories about the Mafia. If he needed proof, Meyer Lansky lived just up U.S. 1 in Broward County. Years before Lansky had been co-boss with Bugsy Siegel of the Bugs and Meyer Mob, a forerunner of Murder, Inc. Today Lansky, while still retaining his power in New York, was casino boss of the Southeast and the Caribbean. He had operated in Havana prior to World War II and would have returned had not his friend, Dictator Batista, lost power temporarily. Meanwhile, he dominated the plush casinos a few miles north of Miami Beach in Broward County, and had a piece of Costello's Beverly Club outside New Orleans. No one in his right mind called Lansky a tool of the Mafia. Coppola, whose primary gambling interests remained the numbers racket, accepted Meyer as a co-equal in the National Syndicate.

When Lansky in 1952 reestablished Batista in Cuba and began a gambling boom there, Coppola followed the example of other syndicate hoods and invested in the Sans Souci there. It was peanuts compared to Lansky's Riviera and didn't even compare with the Cleveland Syndicate's holdings at the Nacional. But Coppola was happy and a few years later when his old friend Albert Anastasia challenged Lansky's authority in Havana, Mike made no move to help his fellow Italian-American.

The wealth that came rolling in, growing larger and larger, was not reflected in Coppola's income tax returns as revealed later by Ann. In 1946, he listed his income as $10,500, and claimed it all came from gambling. Next year, he said his luck went sour. Only $5,000 was reported. By 1948, he had his salary as an officer of Manhattan Cigarettes to supplement his gambling wins so he listed $14,012. In 1949 the total rose to $18,362, but in 1950 it was down to $14,489.

What his income actually totaled can only be estimated but in view of later developments it is safe to assume he reported only a minute fraction of the real amount. His accountant kept no work papers in connection with Coppola's tax returns.

With much of his money coming from New York it was logical that interest should remain high there in Coppola's activities. A 1952 probe by the New York State Crime Commission into waterfront racketeering disclosed that Anthony Strollo, also known as Tony Bender, was a power on the docks. Backing him, the commission said, were those old pals, Joey Rao and Trigger Mike.

The commission's findings led to the expulsion of the International Longshoreman's Association from the American Federation of Labor. The AFL organized a rival union to take control of the piers from the gangsters and an election was ordered by the National Labor Relations Board. The syndicate rallied its forces. Murder and beatings were common, but Coppola's boys had long before learned how to get out the vote. The ILA won and the threat to Trigger Mike's power ebbed with the tide. In 1967 a high official created a sensation when he commented that the ILA had gangster connections. Exactly why that was news, the official couldn't comprehend.

Another probe in 1953 dug up some ancient history. Coppola, it was discovered, had been active in years past with Lepke in garment industry racketeering. Lepke had long since been executed for murder but the racket remained and so did Coppola's interest.

Meanwhile Coppola became associated with several of Lansky's principal lieutenants in on-track bookmaking in Florida. Such men as Frank Ritter and Max Courtney handled the bets at the track while Coppola provided part of the bankroll. Several years later the lieutenants were to be in charge of casino gambling on Grand Bahama Island after Castro's victory in Cuba forced Lansky to relocate his Caribbean gambling empire.

In December 1955, the Thoroughbred Racing Association ejected Trigger Mike from Tropical Park outside Miami and then banned him from all member tracks. It was a blow to Mike's pride although the action received little publicity, but he didn't protest too strongly. After all, he had something else very much on his mind—a young widow whose dark hair and eyes reminded him of Doris.

For despite his many and varied interests, Trigger Mike found the big house on Alton Road a lonely place. His sister cared for the children and he had found a blond mistress who didn't remind him of Doris to take care of his physical needs and to serve as a companion on the town. The job was not too demanding—a person in a position to know later reported that Mike wanted a woman only on Sunday afternoons and, even then, was a "flop" in bed. Nevertheless, Mike felt his position in the rackets and in the community demanded he have a wife. Such a person wouldn't be easy to find—the qualifications were complicated.

Friends began a quiet search, prompted as much by selfish reasons as sentiment. The lucky sponsor could hope to win the friendship of both parties. Translated into practical realities that could mean prestige, operating capital, and muscle if needed.

In Newport, Screw Andrews and Sleepout Louis conferred and agreed Ann Drahmann would make a suitable candidate. She had dark beauty comparable to Doris's, and that was what Mike really wanted. Her family background was superior to Doris's—both parents being native-born Italians—and her years as a casino manager's wife had given her the sophistication needed in syndicate social circles. Andrews conducted some tests to make sure she was not an easy conquest. Virtue is not the highly valued commodity some Mafia experts have said, but in a wife a degree of restraint and respectability would be necessary. Mike certainly didn't want a tramp. Levinson assured himself that she was ambitious—eager for the big time.

When all doubts were satisfied, and the boys took their time, Gil Beckley was recruited. The Royal Mounted Police was making it hot for Beckley in Canada and he was preparing to move back to Newport and into the Glenn Hotel. He called on Ann several times and approved the choice. Beckley was necessary—highly traveled, polished, and so intelligent as to win Rothstein's old title as "the Brain." His approval was essential if Mike was to be convinced. Beckley also had some ideas about the introduction. As a layoff bettor, he was very interested in fights—in fact, he got himself into some hot water a few years later for his part in arranging the Patterson-Johannsen bout. Coming up was the long-delayed battle between Champion Rocky Marciano and aging Archie Moore. A lot of syndicate money was on the line. Odds were that Coppola would be in New York for the bout. Why not take Ann to see the fight and arrange discreetly for Coppola to meet her? The rest would have to be left to Cupid. If for any reason Mike wasn't interested after viewing the merchandise, Ann could be returned to her dress shop in Cincinnati none the wiser.

Sleepout and Screw thought it a splendid approach. Beckley contacted Fat Tony Salerno—who sometimes helped him in the fight racket—and got Tony's promise he would have Mike in town. All that remained was to persuade Ann to make the trip. It wasn't difficult. She wasn't particularly interested in boxing, but she was curious as to why the boys should so suddenly invite her. Besides, the trip might break the monotony, get her out of the rut.

It did.

"He pursued me like I don't think too many women have been pursued." ANN DRAHMANN

Five

THE MARCIANO-MOORE FIGHT DREW 61,574 CUSTOMERS INTO Yankee Stadium. They paid $948,118 to see age fall before youth. As the suckers read it, Moore put up a valiant battle before being knocked out in the ninth round. He even managed to deck the invincible champion in the early minutes.

Ann Drahmann watched with the rest but her mind was on a battle more ancient than boxing and, as she saw it, a lot more fun.

The merry group of fight fans had traveled from Cincinnati to New York by train. Included in addition to the Levinsons and Andrews were the Martin Millers. A man of many aliases was Miller. Known variously as Meyer Berman, Martin Berman, Abe Miller, Joe Miller, and Martin Miller, he had been involved for years in the syndicate gambling clubs of Newport and was a friend of Red Masterson, Big and Little Porky Lassoff, and the rest. His wife, Nikki, went along on the trip as did the wives of the other men. It was all very respectable.

After reaching New York on September 20, the party was steered to an Italian restaurant in East Harlem. Beckley and Salerno were co-hosts and the guests were given red-carpet treatment. A fat little man Ann assumed was the restaurant owner kept coming over to the table to ask "if everything is all right." Many of the dishes he personally served to Ann, assuring her he had also prepared them. Ann was impressed with the food and with the little man's obvious efforts to please. Near the end of the dinner she noticed him watching her from across the room. Much to the amusement of Screw Andrews, she left the table and walked over to the "owner."

"You're a wonderful host," she said. "If we're in New York again we'll come to see you."

The little fellow seemed a bit nonplussed by Ann's words. He mumbled something and bowed as if to cover his confusion, but his eyes followed Ann back to the table. Andrews poked Levinson in the ribs with his elbow. Sleepout responded with a smile.

No one bothered to tell Ann that the little man was Trigger Mike Coppola. At that stage of the game, the decision was still up to Mike. If he decided she was not what he wanted in a wife, she could continue to assume the swarthy-faced man with the little scars was just a restaurant owner trying to please out-of-town guests. But the conspirators had been watching Mike as closely as Mike had been observing Ann—they felt confident they had scored heavily.

Their confidence was justified. Coppola was in a near-trance. In the brunette beauty of the stranger, he saw, or thought he saw, the essence of his first love. Her mistake in assuming he was but a restaurant owner delighted him, as did her warm friendliness. Doris had been like that, a bit naïve but strong. Watching Ann, he could almost imagine that Doris had not died, and in letting himself dream for a second he felt a peace he had not known for years. Hard and tough was Mike Coppola, but the feelings of guilt that had possessed him since Doris died he had been unable to shake off. Now, perhaps, he could begin again.

And Trigger Mike was happy.

Next day before the fight Beckley told Ann part of the truth. He made no mention of Mike's place in the rackets. Let her find that out in her own time and way. No, say nothing about the numbers racket or the shylocking business. Tell her only that the "restaurant owner" was a very wealthy man who dabbled in the stock market and was very interested in finding a new wife. He had fallen in love with her at first glance.

Ann seemed to accept the story. If the boys wanted to play games, it was all right with her. Suddenly a lot of things made sense. In years to come she kept up the fiction until she almost believed she was deceived into marrying a gangster. But in her more honest moments she acknowledged she knew the score from the first. If Coppola wanted to assume she was a dumb broad, then fine. The huge mass of flowers delivered to her hotel room the morning after the dinner seemed to indicate he liked her in that role. Life with Charley had been nice. No question of that. Charley had loved her and love compensates for many things. But poor Charley—already she was thinking in those terms—had been unable to make his alimony payments to his first wife on time. When he died she had resolved that when she remarried—and she had no doubt she would remarry—it would be to a top man in the rackets. Trigger Mike was as near to the top as a girl could get. All she had to do was keep him hooked.

Quickly it was apparent that even this was no problem. Mike had been well briefed before meeting Ann; he knew her background and he had testimony from men who would not dare to lie. The dinner had been enough to sell him. He was hooked, indeed. Ann began to wonder how best to slow him down. After all, there had to be a period of courtship. He couldn't be allowed to think she was too eager. Later, it might make a difference. Besides, she wanted to know more about the guy before crawling into bed with him as his wife.

The time in New York became a pursuit. Mike was everywhere. Candy, flowers, jewels poured in. He was always around, respectable but ever pressing. It was a relief to return to Cincinnati, to get away from her shadow for a little while.

The return was something of a triumph. Even Mildred Levinson, usually so catty, treated her with respect. The men took it for granted that it was just a matter of time before she was Mrs. Trigger Mike. So, for that matter, did Ann.

It was quicker than even she suspected. Her respite from courtship was brief. A few days after resuming work a customer commented about the Mutt and Jeff types standing outside the shop. Ann glanced out incuriously. There stood Mike, short, stocky, and expensively dressed. Towering beside him was Fat Tony Salerno. They were arguing about something. As she watched, Mike impatiently thrust a huge box into Salerno's hands. A moment later Fat Tony was in the Anndra Shop, looking like a mountain in the feminine atmosphere. He presented the box with Mike's compliments. Would Ann dine that night with Mike? It was very important to Mike.

The box contained candy. Ann sampled a piece and smiled sweetly at the nervous gangster. Yes, she would be delighted to dine with Mr. Coppola. He could pick her up when the shop closed. And thank him for the candy. It was delicious.

That's the way it went for the remainder of the week. With Tony playing the role of John Alden, Trigger Mike pushed his courtship. Between dates he conducted business in Newport with Sleepout and Screw. On his hotel registration card he had listed his address as 633 York Street, Newport—the home of the Flamingo Club. But his business, however important it might seem to Andrews, took a back seat to the pursuit of Ann. Again she was relieved when, reluctantly, he told her he had to go home to Miami Beach.

Again it was a short recess. Coppola returned. Ann sensed the beginning of impatience on his part as if he was wearying just a little of his role. Still courtly in his fashion, he spent money as if he had an inexhaustible supply, but there was now an air of ownership about him. Any doubts about Ann's reaction, any fears she might reject him, had been discarded. As far as he was concerned it was merely a matter of setting the date and that he was eager to do.

She set the date—December 28, 1955. Mike presented her with a huge diamond ring and left for New York.

Peace was wonderful and there was much to do. Ann began hunting for someone to buy the Anndra Shop. Her mother and sisters were the legal owners but they had no use for it. There was also the house Charley had left. Compared to the mansion on Alton Road described by Mike, it wasn't much more than a shanty but it was still hard to sell. There was also a decision to be made about Joan. She was a senior in boarding school and didn't want to leave in the middle of the school year. Ann decided to buy her a car to compensate in part for the absence of a mother. Coppola said he would pay for it.

Social life took up a lot of time. The elite of underworld society combined to honor Trigger Mike's fiancée. One party followed another and Screw Andrews turned up at all of them. Was he keeping an eye on her for Mike, making sure she didn't do something to upset the wedding plans? It seems that way but Ann gave no hint as to her suspicions. The role of the dumb broad was still appropriate.

Life in the Newport-Covington area was about back to normal after the upheavals caused by Kefauver and the ambitions of Lester-Schmidt. The reformers had managed to elect a county judge, Fred Warren, but events had demonstrated the truth of Lincoln Steffens' observation that honesty in a public official is not enough to assure good government. Warren was honest, yet despite his sincere efforts he had been unable to do anything about syndicate rule in Campbell County.

Elected in 1953 as the candidate of the Campbell County Civic Association, an outgrowth of the now dead NCA, Warren had promptly fired the chief of county police. Just as promptly the ex-chief found a job with Sleepout while Warren beat the bushes for an honest replacement. After several failures he thought he had succeeded. His candidate was a personal friend and former army officer. Great precautions were taken to keep the appointment secret until the new chief could make an undercover study of conditions. Law required the chief's picture be on file at the courthouse. Warren sidestepped the requirement by photographing the man from the rear. All seemed to be going well when, after about three weeks, the chief came to Warren's home one night and asked to be relieved. Under questioning, he admitted he had been paid off.

Ann heard the inside story at the time. It was years before Warren learned the truth from Big Jim Harris, former marshal of the suburb of Wilder. Harris, who operated a big brothel, the Hy-Dee-Ho Club, while wearing a badge, said the man came to him for advice as soon as Warren offered him the chief's job. He wanted to know how he could make some quick money out of the opportunity. Marshal Harris told him.

During the three weeks as undercover man, the chief visited a different gambling joint each night. He drove a different car each night. Before starting out he would phone Harris and give him the license number and a description of the vehicle. Harris, in turn, would call the operator of the club and, also, the Cleveland Syndicate, and tip them the anonymous chief was paying a visit. If they didn't believe him they could check the parking lot.

The entire routine was designed, Harris explained, to convince the syndicate that Harris and Harris alone had the new chief in his pocket. Any deals would have to be made through him. When the point finally was accepted, syndicate lieutenants met above the Yorkshire Club and reluctantly agreed to pay the money the chief, through Harris, was demanding—$5,000 a month. Harris took his cut and gave the rest to the chief. He also tried to persuade him to continue in office, but the man had one idea from the beginning—make some quick dough and get out. He got out—and Warren, still not understanding how things were done, continued his search for an honest man.

The syndicate was no more amused than Warren by Harris' role in the deception. The boys at the Yorkshire had additional reasons to dislike the big marshal: those joints he operated in Wilder were taking money from the Latin Quarter. Harris had organized many of the Cincinnati cabdrivers. The beds in his brothel were wired for sound and any sucker who had second thoughts about his night in Wilder was permitted to hear a recording. All in all, the syndicate decided, it would be a good idea for Big Jim to take a long vacation,

In searching for ways and means it was discovered that two years earlier state police had raided the marshal's joint at the same time they hit the Lookout House. Belatedly, Commonwealth's Attorney Wise decided the grand jury should investigate and Harris was indicted on pandering charges. The witnesses were those arrested in the state police raid. Harris retained Charley Lester to defend him and, as he put it later, "I gave Charley $1,000 and he didn't even show up for court." The first jury was unable to reach a verdict. Wise—who could be relentless on occasion—tried again. Some of the witnesses later admitted they lied in court, yet Harris was convicted and sentenced to three years. He wasn't happy, though he could still be philosophical:

"It's a wonderful town for framing somebody," he observed.

With Harris out of the way and Pete Schmidt getting old, the syndicate could feel a new era of peace was at hand. True, Warren still had two years to serve, but his effectiveness was no threat and the end of the Civic Association was but a matter of time. This prediction proved correct—Andrew Jolly, who had so successfully defended Screw—succeeded Warren and promptly ordered his chief of county police to stay out of incorporated areas unless invited.

Schmidt, meanwhile, had made his final move. Fearing the day might come when gambling laws would be enforced, he protected his investment in the swank Playtorium by moving the casino into an adjoining building which he built next door—the Snax Bar. Rumor had it that an underground tunnel connected the two buildings, though to all intents it was a separate operation. The Snax Bar had a little area up front about the size of a large broom closet where one could buy coffee and sandwiches. An electronically controlled door led to the huge casino-handbook at the rear. Ex-mayor Siddell operated it for Schmidt and the joint took considerable business from the syndicate's downtown clubs. Business was booming and there was no hurry.

Thus it was that everyone was in a good frame of mind and ready to celebrate the triumph of the local girl who had made good—the next Mrs. Trigger Mike Coppola.

Of the three states most convenient to Cincinnati, Indiana offered the most liberal marriage laws. Lawrenceburg was the nearest town—just across the Ohio-Indiana line on the north bank of the river. It was something of a wild area as far as law enforcement went. Long after slot machines went into hiding in Newport, they could be easily found in the vicinity of Lawrenceburg and other Indiana river cities. The slots had originally been placed in the region by Frank Costello and could be found in candy stores and supermarkets. The FBI confiscated 3,457 slots valued at $957,000 in a raid in 1952. The raid came after Senator Kefauver sponsored a law which gave the feds jurisdiction. Those slots left in Indiana were survivors of a more wide-open day, but they helped create an atmosphere suitable to the marriage of one of Costello's top associates.

The wedding itself was very simple—just the bare necessities to make it legal. The festivities came that night at the Beverly Hills Club outside Newport.

Over the years the syndicate had vastly improved on Pete Schmidt's original dream. The club had been enlarged and remodeled several times since Pete surrendered it fifteen years before. It sat on top of a large hill overlooking the highway to Frankfort. The front side of the hill was landscaped and kept neatly mowed. From the highway the building looked like a brick and concrete fortress, and in many respects it was just that. A long driveway curved up the left side of the hill to the club. Legend, kept alive by syndicate propagandists, maintained that machine guns were mounted higher on the hill to cover the driveway. Since that day in 1947 when armed raiders literally captured and sacked the syndicate-controlled Mounds Club outside Cleveland, the boys had taken precautions. The raiders later paid for their daring with their lives; meanwhile no one wanted to risk another assault. The Beverly Hills was as impregnable as money could make it. If necessary it could withstand a seige. Its basement contained a separate power plant and water system. Deep-freeze units were stocked with enough food for weeks. An elaborate electronics network permitted observation of any section of the building.

Only the top people were invited to the wedding party. Trigger Mike, happy though he was, had no desire to entertain all the hoods in the Newport-Covington area. Not even the Beverly Hills could hold such a crowd. The elite got invitations while the punks went on about the business of robbing the suckers and thus earning the small salaries paid by the big shots. Somewhat to Ann's regret, Mildred Levinson didn't attend. Ann put it down to jealousy.

The wedding party dismounted from their Cadillacs and Imperials at the front door. Inside the lobby was a huge circular bar. Straight ahead was the theater-restaurant, built on descending levels to permit an uninterrupted view of the stage. At the right rear of the restaurant was a door which opened on a carpeted passage leading to the huge casino. One could also enter from the lobby but it was common practice to herd the customers into the dining area, feed them well and cheaply, entertain them with top Hollywood stars, give them a chance to play some bingo. The cards distributed to bingo players bore a stamped notice on the reverse side: "Property of the Desert Inn, Las Vegas, Nev."

After the show and the bingo, the star of the evening made a conspicuous jaunt through the restaurant and into the casino. Like sheep, most of the diners followed. Such stars as Jimmy Durante refused to serve as high-priced shills in this fashion. Others such as Gordon and Sheila MacRae would go into the casino and sit for a while without gambling. Such stars as Frank Sinatra did gamble, sometimes using their own money. Sinatra lost $30,000 in one evening at the Beverly when he stopped there for a final fling before buckling down to work on a movie in Indiana.

The Coppola wedding party had choice seats for the show and choice steaks. Ordinarily, for such a guest, everything would have been "comped"—as Morris Kleinman, one of the owners of the Beverly, put it. "Comped" meant "complimentary" or, as Sleepout Louis called it, "free gratis." However Trigger Mike was in an expansive mood that night—he dropped a $1,000 bill on the table. The tab came to $960. Whether Mike was paying, or just leaving a tip, Ann wasn't sure. The party which began at 7:30 P.M. broke up at 4:30 A.M.

There was no honeymoon as such. Mike had wasted enough time on the courtship. Urgent matters were waiting his attention in Miami Beach. Moreover, they weren't kids. Both had been married before. Why waste time with a lot of romantic nonsense?

Leaving Joan in school, the newlyweds flew south to Miami

Beach, where the big house on Alton Road was waiting. The house sat on a corner lot which was roughly 100 feet wide and 120 feet deep. One entered by a small hall. To the right of the hall was the living room and flanking it an enclosed porch or Florida room. To the left of the hall was the huge kitchen and dining room. Equipment in the kitchen alone had cost thousands, Ann decided. It resembled the restaurant in New York where Mike first displayed his cooking skills. He soon made it apparent that the kitchen was second only to his collection of ivory.

A small loggia was to the left of the kitchen and a maid's room at the rear. Behind that was the garage, which opened on to 44th Court.

At the end of the short hall in the center of the building was another enclosed porch and behind it a huge screened patio. One of Mike's first acts after marriage was to order a large swimming pool costing about $10,000 installed at the right rear of the patio. A concrete block wall sealed off the rear of the lot.

The second floor was spacious, containing four bedrooms and two baths. Ann thought so many bathrooms—there was one and a half downstairs—a bit superfluous, but Coppola assured her that in Florida a bath per bedroom was the norm.

A strange combination this Mike Coppola, Ann decided. Greedy, egotistical, and cruel, yet he loved beautiful things and could be very gentle. Indeed, in those first few days he treated her almost as if she were a piece of jade. Once, when half asleep, he called her Doris. Ann shivered. Mike's preoccupation with his late wife frightened her a little. Hell, Charley had been dead a lot less time than Doris and she never made such a mistake.

The household was arranged most efficiently. A housekeeper and a cook did most of the work inside and a yardman attended to the grass and shrubbery. Much of their groceries came from the Miami Provision Company in which Mike's old friend Joe Massei had an interest. Mike had some sort of arrangement with Joe to conceal the cost and it was not taken out of her budget. She received $160 a week, in cash, to pay other expenses.

Allowances to the children were generous—$8 to Michael David; $5 to the younger Doris Patricia, who was called "Deedee"; and $15 to Joan. As the children grew older the allowances were increased.

The "honeymoon period" of the marriage lasted three weeks.

One afternoon Mike went off to the track for a profitable interlude of booking and betting. Ejected a few weeks earlier from Tropical Park, Mike had not yet been banned from Hialeah where the horses were now running. Ann, left alone in the house, continued her task of rearranging her new domain.

In the tiny hall she noticed a large bookcase. On top of it sat a picture of Mike's former father-in-law, David Lehman. After Doris died the New York authorities dropped the perjury charge against Lehman on the grounds he was old and ill. Yet he had continued to live and to receive $200 monthly from Mike.

Ann stared at the picture, thinking of Mike's fixation about Doris. If ever she was to win a place as an individual in her own right, Mike's obsession would have to fade. Perhaps removing this picture would be a good start toward that goal. It didn't belong in the hall anyway.

She picked up the picture, stared at it incuriously, and turned away. Something, she couldn't be sure what, caught her eye—something odd about the bookcase. Mike was not a reader. Strange that he should have a bookcase in the first place. And this bookcase was more than it appeared to be. She began to examine it, taking her time. Excitement boiled within her as suspicion became certainty. There was something queer about the bookcase.

Almost an hour was required before she figured it out. On the wall above the bookcase was a picture of some flowers. When the picture was pushed aside, just so, and a drawer in the bookcase opened, a mechanism was triggered. The back of the bookcase slid upward, exposing a large compartment. In the compartment were stacks of money.

The new bride looked a long time before deciding that since she had gone so far it would be silly to stop. She counted the cash—$58,000 in $100 bills. There were also some bonds in the name of Mike's children.

Greatly excited, Ann replaced the money and closed the plant—years before she had asked some robbers in Kentucky what the word meant. A plant was all this could be. Yet why was it located here in the hall so near the front door? For convenience, she decided. Mike must have other plants as well. This one was kept handy when he needed a little cash to give to visitors who might have a sudden emergency.

Mike got in late from the track that day and Ann postponed her questions. After thinking about it all afternoon, she had concluded she should tell Mike about her find. Reasoning that once he recovered from the shock of realizing she was not Doris reincarnated, he would appreciate an intelligent wife, Ann decided to take the risks she knew frankness involved. Sooner or later he would learn the truth so why not now, at the beginning of marriage?

There wasn't time to talk when he returned. Martin and Nikki Miller, alias Berman, etc., were in town, as was Nig Devine and his wife, Ida. Ann had arranged for the three couples to go out for dinner.

The men got drunk during the evening and the women had trouble getting them to their homes and hotels. When Ann and Mike were at last alone in the master bedroom on Alton Road, she could conceal her new knowledge no longer. As she spread cream on her face, attempting to transform her new sunburn into a becoming tan, she mentioned her discovery.

"Why you flat-nosed, frog-eyed bastard," said Trigger Mike Coppola.

She sat stunned as Coppola ran across the room, cursing wildly all the way. He went to a cedar shoe rack. Ann watched as he fumbled with it, pushing something here and there. A section of the rack slid back. Mike produced a key. Despite her fear, Ann was beginning to feel curiosity. Another plant—perhaps the main one.

She had little time for wonder. Mike reached into the hidden compartment and grasped something. He turned, a pistol in his hand. Ann dived to the floor as he fired. The bullet hit the wall next to the bathroom door and Ann fled from the room.

Coppola didn't shoot again nor did he follow her downstairs where she spent the night in the unoccupied maid's room. Next morning, after hearing Mike moving in the kitchen, she slipped upstairs and began to pack her clothes. She had no intention of leaving, however. It was a bluff. Mike would never let her leave—of that she was sure. He would be the laughingstock of the underworld if his bride of three weeks walked out. Let him apologize, blame his rage on the heavy drinking bout with Nig Devine. She would accept the apology eventually. At least the bastard wouldn't call her Doris any more.

Ann was right, up to a point. Coppola didn't intend to let her leave. But he was in no mood to apologize. Just as she finished packing, he entered the room. Defiantly, she turned to face him. With one swift motion he knocked her down.

"If you leave me, bitch, I'll kill you," he grated.

Stubbornly Ann tried to get up. She was half erect when he hit her again.

"I'll kill you if you try to leave," he repeated. "No one walks out on Trigger Mike Coppola."

Flat on her back he left her. Ann licked her split lip and wearily climbed to her feet to begin unpacking. For better or worse she had made a choice. What, after all, was a beating? Charley had never beaten her but then Charley had never owned plants containing thousands of dollars. Speaking of plants—wonder how much the second one contained?

In her excitement, Ann forgot her bruises. She was to be disappointed however. A key was needed to open the hidden compartment and Mike had taken it with him. Well, good enough. She'd just have to wait her chance and have a duplicate made. There would be plenty of chances in the days ahead. Meanwhile, she'd better concentrate on learning how to live with the son of a bitch.

Her next lesson came a week later and it also followed a dinner party. Guests included two of the top men in the Cleveland Syndicate—Moe Dalitz and Louis Rothkopf. Dalitz had a new wife along, his third. The others he had divorced. Rothkopf was alone. His wife, Blanche, had killed herself the year before after a long and childless marriage. Ann couldn't know that Rothkopf was to follow his wife's example in less than a year.

For Ann it was the greatest triumph yet. The party at the Beverly Hills faded into nothing in comparison. These men had been the bosses of Charley Drahmann's boss. They were absolutely at the top of organized crime and had been there for a quarter century. And here she sat, the wife of a co-equal, while Coppola and Dalitz talked about the trip they had made to Arizona with Big Al Polizzi in 1936. Since then, using Peter Licavoli and a Newport man with a ring in his nose, Butts Lowe, the syndicate had developed the Tucson area. In the old days it had been just sand and lizards.

Perhaps the awe Ann felt at being on such intimate terms with men Drahmann had considered to be giants was apparent to Coppola. Certainly some of her feelings showed when she whispered the suggestion he should pick up the check. It was only about $300, but that wasn't the important thing for once.

Later that night in the privacy of the master bedroom, Mike made the point clear. He knocked Ann down again.

"Look," he said in his gutteral voice. "Get this straight once and for all. I don't want to tell you again. I'm Trigger Mike Coppola. When I go out with people I'm doing them a favor no matter how big they think they are. Mike Coppola don't take second place to nobody and don't you forget it."

Ann, flat on her back, looked up at the cocky figure scowling down at her. Well, she told herself, you've got what you wanted. And, perversely, despite the pain and humiliation, she felt a glow of pride.

"My daughter was a woman now and very beautiful." ANN DRAHMANN

Six

SOME TWO MONTHS AFTER HER MARRIAGE ANN DISCOVERED that she was pregnant. Wanting confirmation before she broke the news to her husband, she consulted a reputable doctor. After what seemed to be a prolonged examination, the doctor said that she was correct. But, he added gravely, he doubted if she would be able to carry the baby.

The examination, he explained, had revealed the presence of a tumor on the uterus. It wasn't malignant, not yet anyway, but it should be removed.

Stunned, Ann asked for time to think. The prospect of an operation didn't frighten her though the thought of Mike's possible reaction did. While he had made it plain he wasn't interested in more children, he was old-fashioned in an Old-World sense. Would he consider her "damaged goods" if she had the operation? Something less than the woman he had bargained so hard to win? It was very possible.

Ann couldn't decide what to do. If she tried to carry the baby and lost it, Mike would learn the truth. If she had the operation in secret, perhaps while he was away in New York, he might very easily find out and his rage would be all the greater. Secrets from Mike were hard to keep in Miami Beach where few people dared lie to him.

A solution of sorts came from an unexpected source—Mike himself. A few days after the visit to the doctor, Mike announced calmly at breakfast that he had arranged for her to have an abortion. When Ann stared in amazement, Mike grinned wolfishly.

"Your period is two weeks late," he said. "You're pregnant. Just leave everything to me."

Ann almost blurted out the truth. If Mike didn't want a child that badly there was no need for an abortion. A miscarriage was almost inevitable. Fear stopped her. She owed too much to Mike to risk his wrath. Among other things he had paid for her trousseau. He had given her furs and jewels. Could she risk losing this and the more to come by telling him about the tumor?

That afternoon with the children away, the abortion took place on the kitchen table. Called in to perform the abortion was a physician known to the underworld of Miami Beach as "Dr. D." He had long been Mike's personal physician. Ann had decided, however, that he was a poor example of the medical profession. About all you could say for him was he was always available.

The price, Mike informed her, was $1,000. For security's sake, he added, he would act as the doctor's assistant. And Ann, staring into her husband's swarthy face, realized he was anticipating the job. It was going to be great fun for Trigger Mike.

Mustering her strength, Ann walked into the polished kitchen. Mike placed a sheet over the table and she stretched out. "Like a lamb for the slaughter," she thought. In the back of her mind was the knowledge that if Mike enjoyed playing doctor so much it would be doubly dangerous to tell him about the tumor. Hell, he might decide to have Dr. D. cut it out then and there. She glimpsed his face as she drifted into unconsciousness—the bastard was actually smiling.

The abortion was a success—or so Mike declared. Ann, who felt sick and sore, wasn't too sure. Dr. D. was as awkward and inept as she had suspected. But then, if he had been a good doctor he might have discovered the tumor. Still, if he had found it, would he have said anything to Mike? She doubted it. He would have been just as reluctant as she to deprive Mike of his fun—to say nothing of the fee he would lose. No, her secret was safe with the syndicate doctor.

Her relief at having postponed the crisis—for the tumor was still there and growing—was tempered by the sickening thought the scene on the kitchen table might have to be repeated again and again. For now it seemed that Mike wanted intercourse only in hopes of making her pregnant. The act of love itself had little pleasure for him. And sure enough, within three months there was another session in the kitchen. Two others followed in the months to come.

Desperate, Ann decided she couldn't take any more. She had reached the limits of her endurance. The thought of the doctor's fumbling hands gave her nightmares. So, one day when she again realized Mike had achieved his purpose, she waited until she was alone in the house and called a reputable doctor. He promised to come quickly. Ann was ready when he arrived.

She was on the bed, moaning in pain when he came in. A sanitary napkin full of blood in the bathroom was mute evidence. Ann gasped between moans that large clots of blood had passed through her. The doctor, deciding she had suffered a miscarriage, took her to a hospital and, in Ann's words, "performed a clean-out but actually an abortion."

The blood in the sanitary napkin had come from her foot which she had cut with Mike's razor. Luckily the doctor didn't concern himself with her lower extremities. And as Ann rested in her private room at the hospital she knew a moment of triumph. She had cheated Dr. D. of $1,000 and deprived Dr. Coppola of an hour of sadism.

There were no more abortions and no more faked miscarriages after that. For some reason—and Ann could only assume the tumor was responsible—she never became pregnant again. Or maybe Mike was getting old. After a time he seemed to have lost interest. At any rate he quit trying. Ann was pleased. In the exciting world of Miami Beach it was possible to forget the danger within. As she put it later, "I could never face reality."

Miami Beach in 1956 was a thrilling place to live, especially if you were Mrs. Trigger Mike. Ann, curious as always, didn't understand all she heard or saw, but she couldn't help but know her husband was a very important person.

The Gold Coast of Florida was, Ann decided, very much like the Newport-Covington area of Kentucky in that the more things changed the more they remained the same. A lot of things had altered since those long ago days when she visited Florida with Charley. The S & G Syndicate, which in the forties controlled bookmaking, was no more—a victim of the Kefauver blight—even though some of its members were still active. Ben Cohen, the legal brains behind the S & G, was still a political power and the man to see if one had trouble with a parking ticket or a murder indictment.

Ann was able to evaluate Cohen's power by her own standard. Of the mixed crowd of gangsters, politicians, and businessmen who came regularly to consult with Mike, Cohen was the only one to be invited into the living room. All others talked to Mike in the Florida room, that glassed-in area designed to catch the ocean breezes and the sunlight. Ann wondered "who the privileged character was that deserved the living room," and she eavesdropped to find out. The conversation she overheard was mostly concerned with getting telephone service to bookie joints in which Mike had an interest. Cohen assured Mike not to worry—he would handle the details.

Four years later Ann got into a spot of trouble with Miami Beach police—they charged her with drunken driving, reckless driving, having no valid driver's license, and five counts of running red lights. She called Ben, who killed the whole thing for $160.

Also gone from the scene was Madam Sherry, a landmark in the Miami area for decades. Her brothels had been world famous, but in a world of call girls they were a bit too obvious. Madam Sherry had gone off to jail and the prostitution racket was in the hands of men who considered it a business rather than a cultural contribution.

The plush casinos Meyer Lansky had operated for the Eastern Syndicate were also too obvious in the new age and had long since closed their doors. The Colonial Inn, the Club Boheme, the Club Greenacres had their modern counterparts in Havana and were easily accessible. Vanishing with them had been such places as the Island Club in the Miami area, which Gameboy Miller had operated for the Cleveland Syndicate. Even the Frolics Club, to which Moe Dalitz's name was linked, had been torn down and replaced on its site overlooking Biscayne Bay by the blue and gold home of the Miami *Herald*.

With Lansky running Havana, however, Mrs. Trigger Mike Coppola could expect a warm reception. All she had to do was tell Mike that "the girls and I want to do a little gambling," and Mike would call Havana to make sure the best hotel suites and unlimited credit was waiting there for them. Ann enjoyed casinos—they were such good places to show off one's gown and jewels.

Despite the closing of the mainland casinos, however, there was plenty of local action. Much of it centered around the new and fabulous Fontainebleau Hotel on Collins Avenue. Mike used the place as his headquarters. She had to remember when calling him there to ask for Michael Kaplan. Cohen was also at the Fontainebleau a lot, maintaining a well-furnished cabana with a telephone that rang constantly. Occasionally Ann would pick up some gossip and store it away for future use. There had been much labor trouble during the hotel's construction. Barney Barnett, a Teamster union official, was employed by the hotel to "expedite" the labor problem. Barnett, she learned, placed stink bombs in the office of the Hotel Employees Union and stole their records. For good measure he ordered the lobby of the Fontainebleau stink-bombed, and then blamed the union.

It was all very curious, Ann decided. She didn't know that investigators had tapped Barnett's phone and heard the union official declare he made his living by "blood money." However, she did have a clue to Mike's influence at the hotel.

One day while making her weekly inspection of Mike's plants, she found a document concerning Glassman of the Fontainebleau. It stated that in event of his death, his heirs would have no claim on Coppola for recovery of a $20,000 loan to Coppola by Glassman. The document explained that no money was actually exchanged—it was merely a "personal accommodation" in case Mike was ever asked to justify his income.

Glassman soon sold out his "interest" in the Fontainebleau and dropped out of sight. Mike had another good friend who remained active at the hotel—Max Eder, alias Maxie Raymond.

Short and stocky like Mike, the owl-eyed Eder served one term in federal prison on a narcotics rap in 1929, though he managed to beat a variety of other charges over the years ranging from gambling to homicide. In the 1940s he became president of Eder Dresses, Inc., located in the New York garment district. Vice-president of the company was Frank "Cheech" Livorsi, a narcotics violator and an important figure in the Coppola-Rao gang that bossed East Harlem.

At the Fontainebleau Eder operated a linen shop in the basement but spent much of his time in the card room on the mezzanine where high-stake gin games lasted long into the night. Eder and Barnett were closely associated in the building trades and Coppola picked up $200 a week for permitting them to use his name on those occasions when a contractor seemed about to balk at their demands.

Shylocking, as the loan-shark racket was known, was big business for Trigger Mike. Day after day men came to Alton Road with hat in hand. On one occasion, after Mike had lost heavily in Las Vegas and was temporarily short of cash, he asked Ann if she would like to make a $10,000 loan at ten per cent interest. Cautiously, Ann inquired what security she would receive for the loan. Angrily, Mike replied that the 10 per cent was on a monthly basis. When you get that kind of interest, he added, you don't ask for security. Ann declined to become a shylock although the idea of getting $1,000 profit every month was tempting.

Ordinarily Mike had all the cash he needed to make loans. During the first year of marriage he made four trips to New York and came back loaded with $100 bills. Ann, who had developed the habit of counting his cash, found that as a general rule there was at least $200,000 on hand at all times and usually much more. Mike kept no bank account. When Ann received a check from the sale of her house in Kentucky, Mike sent it by runner to the Fontainebleau to be cashed.

Life, in spite of the beatings and the abortions, was still fun. A man of moods, Mike was not always surly. For months Ann clung to the hope that he really loved her as an individual, that the gifts of cash, jewels, furs, and cars he handed out so generously were merely an inarticulate man's way of expressing devotion. Eventually she was to write:

"He gave me this vast amount of material things to prove to people how big and successful he was and to feed his ego until he himself believed he was God Almighty."

In 1956, however, Ann could still feel gratitude on occasion and one such occasion came in March 1957. Ann's mother, a widow since 1926, was dying in Cincinnati. Mike flew there with Ann. Loyalty to kin was as important in his code as it was to Ann, who had always felt guilty for not living up to her mother's standards. When the end came, Ann could not bear to enter the room. It was Trigger Mike who sat beside the dying woman and Ann was comforted. Later, Mike was to use the little edge the episode gave him to hurt her cruelly.

With the funeral over, there was time to hear the latest area news. Everyone in Newport was talking about Hattie Jackson, a defiant madam who was about to get the "treatment."

Two years older than Ann, Hattie began her career as a prostitute at Hamilton, Ohio. Soon she drifted to Newport and found a job with Taylor Farley—brother of the late and unlamented Rip Farley. Taylor ran the 316 Club at the time. Part of Hattie's duties was to help him prepare payoff envelopes for police and public officials. Bagmen came up weekly to pick them up. Since the size of the payoff varied with each man, the chore of preparing the payments took time.

By mid-1949, things were getting too rough to suit Hattie. She moved on to other cities, determined not to return to Newport. In 1954, however, she did return—not to work, but to collect $3,400 Newport hoods had stolen from her in another city. Robert Siddell was mayor and he directed her to the real boss of the non-syndicate factions, Charles Lester. The pale Lester promised to recover her money. Instead he gave her a deed to a brothel in payment. With the deed went a partner, Raymond Bridwell.

Inflation caused the business to grow rapidly. The cops would demand a bigger payoff, which would necessitate hiring additional prostitutes, which, in turn, would cause the cops to come back for still more. It was, Hattie decided, a vicious circle. Adding to her worries was Bridwell's habit of slipping knockout drops into any customer's drink if he flashed a roll and otherwise behaving in a manner not suitable to a proper brothel. Madam Sherry in Miami would have understood Hatti's feelings. When Hattie objected, Bridwell threatened to frame her.

The dispute reached a climax on July 4. Bridwell locked Hattie in a room at the rear of the house. A friend cop came to her rescue and let her out. Hattie promptly changed all the locks on all the doors to keep Bridwell out. It was all very funny, according to Ann's friends.

Bridwell, a huge, illiterate man, one of three brothers in the business, filed suit against Hattie. Lester, as Hattie's attorney, filed a counter-suit which charged that Bridwell had put the liquor license of the club "in jeopardy by illegal sales of malt beverages and spiritous liquors, suffering and permitting unsavory characters to congregate in said barroom, pimping on behalf of prostitutes secreted by him on the premises, and by fingering customers for robbery and swindle."

On July 20, a stipulation of agreement was signed. It contained an admission by Bridwell that Hattie's charges were true. Judge Ray

L. Murphy, who had handled criminal and civil cases in the county since shortly after the syndicate takeover in 1940, dismissed Bridwell's suit.

That such admissions could be entered into a court record and solemnly noted by a judge was considered very amusing by the elite of the underworld. Mrs. Trigger Mike, wearing furs and diamonds, could share in the general chuckle. If nothing else, the episode helped prove how far she had climbed.

For Hattie Jackson it was another story. Shortly after her victory in civil court, she stood as a defendant before the same Judge Murphy charged with pandering. Cooperative Newport cops had helped Bridwell frame her as he had promised to do.

The first trial, as sometimes happened to the Jacksons and Big Jim Harrises of Newport, ended in a hung jury. Hattie created some excitement when she testified three city commissioners had been patrons of her brothel. The commissioners explained piously that they had but visited the joint to check on rumors of prostitution. Lester, as unpredictable as always, pulled out before the second trial and left Hattie to her fate. Before quitting, however, he persuaded her to sign the club over to another client.

As expected, Hattie was convicted the second time around and lodged in city jail to await sentencing. While she was waiting the grand jury came along on a tour of inspection. Such tours had become traditional, a way of giving the jurors something to do. They usually resulted in the admonition the jail needed painting. This trip Hattie took advantage of the opportunity to tell the jurors she would like to testify.

Commonwealth's Attorney William Wise—who had been in office almost as long as Judge Murphy—agreed to bring Hattie before the jury six days later. She was scheduled to be sentenced then, he explained, and thus one trip upstairs could serve both purposes. Meanwhile, Chief George Gugel came calling. He took a lid off the sewer in Hattie's cell and loosed an army of rats. Hattie took refuge on the top of a small table and sat there for five days and nights while the rats scampered below.

Just before she was to appear before the jury, Gugel ordered the rats killed and the sewer closed. And when Hattie was taken before the jury she had nothing to say. "I just don't feel like talking," the jury quoted her as remarking. No one bothered to find out why. With that detail over, she was then sentenced to five years in prison. Judge Murphy passed sentence.

Ann was back in Miami Beach when the last act of the drama was played. The possibility that she might someday regard Hattie as an ally never crossed her mind. Newport had not heard the last of Hattie Jackson however. And when next she returned to that river city no one laughed.

When school ended in Cincinnati, Joan joined the family on Alton Road. She had developed into a beautiful girl-woman, the same height and weight as Ann and the same dark hair and eyes. Even on Lincoln Road, that sophisticated shopping center on Miami Beach, eyes turned as she walked by. It was great fun shopping with Joan and feeling free to buy her the very best. Always she had seemed more like a sister than a daughter and it was somehow a renewal of youth to buy for her those things Ann as a girl had longed for in Cincinnati.

A high spot came on July 19. To celebrate Joan's eighteenth birthday, the entire family went to the La Ronde Room of the Fontainebleau. If there was a more expensive place to dine in south Florida, Ann didn't know where to find it. As always the waiters welcomed Mike as if he were a part owner and Joan was more than a little dazzled.

"I was so terribly pleased and proud of my wonderful daughter, I felt like shouting," Ann wrote later.

Mike also seemed proud. It was as if he were seeing Joan for the first time and realizing for the first time that she was beautiful. Ann became a little uneasy as she watched Mike's eyes. They reminded her, somehow, of those sessions on the kitchen table.

The feeling passed, lost in Ann's pride for Joan. Back home, Mike casually mentioned to Joan they would go next morning to Coral Gables and buy her a Thunderbird. The girl found it all too incredible and went off to bed in a daze. Mike watched her leave the room.

Left alone, the adults stared at each other. Ann got up, intending to thank Mike for his kindness to Joan. Without warning, Coppola seized her, twisted her around. Brutally he kicked "me in my rumpus." Ann fell to the floor, screaming with pain. "Every move I made was like the tortures of hell."

The kick, delivered by a pointed shoe, broke membranes near the anus. When Mike realized Ann was really hurt, he rushed to the telephone and called Dr. D. As usual, the doctor was available. Before he arrived, Mike warned Ann to say she had fallen on the cement floor of the patio. Apparently even Trigger Mike was briefly ashamed of himself.

The doctor gave Ann some shots which eased the pain and recommended the damaged area be sprayed with what Ann called a freezing process. For Mike, that promised to be almost as much fun as an abortion. Every day for three weeks, Ann stretched out on her stomach while the helpful doctor assisted by Mike "sprayed my rumpus." The doctor also gave her a cane to assist in moving about the house. When she needed it no longer Mike stored it away in his clothes closet.

Ann managed to conceal the episode from Joan. It was a calculated risk. Instinct told her that Joan should be fully informed about her new stepfather, but in the absence of immediate danger instinct could be ignored as the tumor was ignored. To admit the truth would be to admit failure as a woman and could only result in friction and continuing compromise. To tell would be to risk all she had worked so hard to gain, or so she told herself. It was easier to pretend that all was well. Mike helped in maintaining the fiction. He was always polite and considerate of Ann in the presence of Joan. What his motives were, Ann didn't dare ask.

On the other hand, the fear which made her cautious also drove her to new extremes. Whatever the future might hold, the more she knew of Mike and his business, the better it would be if a showdown came. It was obvious that even in his kindest moments he didn't consider her an equal. She was a woman and women by nature were inferior. He did recognize that she was not the shy, trusting person Doris apparently had been, and she scored that as a point in her favor. And the more she knew the better. She had no plans to use the information she obtained, but she felt it would someday be valuable.

The dumb broad act was one way of getting information and sometimes it would still work if she could catch Mike off guard. On the first Thanksgiving Day of their marriage, a large turkey and a pumpkin pie were delivered by messenger. The card was signed: "Radio."

Ann knew about Radio. He ran a joint off the 79th Street Causeway connecting Miami and North Miami Beach. Once Mike had mentioned there were more whores to be found along that causeway than any place south of Scollay's Square—except, maybe, in the area surrounding the Newport police station. But they weren't cheap—$100 a night was the usual minimum. The girls loitered in the classy bars and nightclubs that lined the causeway and if a drunk without a bankroll got too persistent the cops would remove him.

Why Radio should pay tribute to Mike with a turkey and pie was an interesting question. Was Mike the real owner of his joint? She had heard rumors he had hidden interests in several joints including a big one on Federal Highway north of Miami where Frankie Dio was a power.

Affecting innocence, Ann asked Mike for Radio's last name. Instantly he wanted to know why. Demurely, Ann explained that she had to write or call him to thank him for the turkey. Since she had never met the gentleman it wouldn't be nice to call him by his first name.

Coppola blew up. "You're out of your mind," he shouted. "That son-of-a-bitch ought to thank me for taking his damned turkey. If you say one word to him I'll break your neck."

Exactly what this proved Ann didn't know. Certainly, Mike felt no sense of obligation for the gifts. After eleven months of marriage she realized Mike considered such tokens as his due. He was courted by a strange assortment of people, from punks to respectable businessmen. The source of his power might be far away in East Harlem, but it was nonetheless real in Miami Beach. Surely not everyone who curried favor was worthy of contempt.

On the day before Christmas another turkey arrived from Radio. Mike carved it with a flourish on Christmas Day. "The bastard knows how to pick a good bird," he commented.

A better way to check on Mike was to open his registered mail that sometimes came when he was out of the house. Periodically, thick letters and thin packages arrived from Philadelphia. Ann took one such letter "and put it in a drawer where I could conveniently forget it until it became time to clean out the drawer and I could open it by mistake." She found ten $100 bills wrapped in a piece of newspaper.

Other information came when she persuaded Mike to let her buy some stock. Mike gave her $4,395 to buy 500 shares of Florida Canada, which later became the General Development Company.

The stock was purchased through H. B. Houser & Company of Toronto. Louis Chesler, portly friend of Mike and owner of a plush Miami Beach restaurant, was president of the fast-growing company. In a year Ann made a capital gain of $4,647. Mike didn't reveal the extent of his own investment though Ann learned it was large.

She also discovered he had money invested in south Florida laundries. When she laughed about it, Mike pointed out that her ex-husband's boss, Moe Dalitz, owned laundries in Cleveland and Detroit and had held them for years. They were sound investments, he insisted; he wasn't about to tell her the names of those he owned.

A hint of other business interests came one day on a visit to Cincinnati. Ann was telling her sister that homes in Florida were more expensive than those up north. Mike interrupted to deny it. He was in a position to know, he said, because he owned a construction company up north. Homes in Florida were a lot cheaper and that was a fact.

One day while searching Mike's wastebasket, Ann found pieces of a letter Mike had torn up and thrown away. She put it back together and found a plaintive note from David Lehman, Mike's former father-in-law. Lehman complained that the person in New York who had been assigned to pay him his pension of $200 a month had been forced to leave town in a hurry and he needed the money. Would Mike please make new arrangements?

Later she intercepted another letter from Lehman assuring Mike his money had arrived.

The Scottoriggio murder bothered Ann a great deal. Try as she might, she had been unable to fathom Mike's feelings for his first wife. He did not often speak of her but when he did his regret seemed tinged with a deeper emotion. At first Ann assumed it was but the stirring of conscience. Even Trigger Mike could feel guilty about putting his young wife into a position where to save him she had to perjure herself. Yet, as fits of black rage and beatings alternated with unexpected acts of generosity, she wondered if something more was not involved. Was there some dark secret about Doris with which even Trigger Mike Coppola found it hard to live?

Late in 1956, Mike returned from a week in New York. Ann waited until he left home next day to inspect the plants. The supply of cash had been renewed as usual; for once she didn't bother to count it. In the master bedroom Mike had also stored some papers. They concerned the Scottoriggio murder.

Ann never disclosed the nature of the papers, but, much later, she told a federal agent they provided the answer she had been seeking. She learned, she said, that Mike ordered Doris killed to prevent her from talking.

It was something to think about in the future.

> "He got a call from New
> York in regards to Costello." ANN DRAHMANN

Seven

ORDINARILY A TRIP TO NEW YORK WAS A GOOD TONIC FOR Mike. He usually returned with ego refreshed and a new supply of cash as visible evidence of his power. A visit in late March 1957, was an exception, however. Mike came home in a bad humor.

In his opinion the meeting had been unnecessary. Albert Anastasia, known to newspaper readers as the Lord High Executioner of Murder, Inc., was responsible for wasting everyone's time. Greedy old Albert had been at loose ends since the murder machine he put together had been decentralized, and he was getting restless. He wanted permission to cut in on Meyer Lansky's territory. As usual he had acted before asking and friction had already developed in Havana, where Lansky sat at the right hand of Batista.

Coppola backed Frank Costello in rejecting Albert's demands. Lansky was too big, had too much money and influence, to consider challenging. More, he had brains, executive brains. He had put gambling on an organized basis around the country and especially in Las Vegas. All the top men in the syndicate owed him a debt for that. Anastasia had tried to create a division in the ranks along ethnic lines. Lansky, he pointed out, was a Jew. All Italian-Sicilians should stick together in such a controversy, he insisted. Someone rather tartly remarked that Anastasia's old boss in Murder, Inc.—Louis Lepke—had also been a Jew. That drew smiles from everyone but Big Albert, who had raged and screamed.

Looking backward, Coppola decided Albert's outburst was the worst since Dutch Schultz raised hell because the boys wouldn't give him permission to knock off District Attorney Tom Dewey. The syndicate had no choice when Dutch wouldn't accept the decision but to knock off Dutch himself. Coppola had profited by Dutch's death—he got the numbers—and he hoped Albert wouldn't make it necessary to go so far. No question about it, Albert was on the downgrade. The cold cunning that had made his "hits" for Murder, Inc., almost scientific, had deserted him completely. Albert was still living in the past, unwilling to accept the fact that even crime has to change with the times.

In contrast to Albert's efforts to divide the syndicate by appealing to Mafia-type loyalties, Mike could remember how calmly Lansky took the decision to have his old friend and partner Bugsy Siegel killed. He had defended Bugsy, presenting in that cool, logical manner an analysis of the Bug's personality that explained his mistakes. But when the majority ruled that the good of the syndicate required action that would prevent future mistakes, Lansky accepted without protest. Even Lucky had been impressed.

Well, it was too bad about Albert. If he continued to make trouble something would have to be done.

"Did you have a nice time?" asked Ann, as she reached for Mike's hat and overcoat.

Coppola swung around. Was this bitch trying to be funny? She knew damned well he had gone to New York on syndicate business. Have a good time, hell! By God, he had to put up with Albert's stupidity but he didn't have to take any sarcasm from this woman.

As Ann took the coat from Mike's left arm, he spread two fingers wide and jabbed at her eyes. She ducked a fraction of an inch. The stubby finger missed the eyeball and crashed against the bone beneath. Pain and tears blinded her. Only dimly she was aware of Mike moving by her and into the home he loved so well.

The eyes swelled rapidly and turned very black. Ann wore dark glasses around the house, trying to conceal the condition of her face from the children. A reputable doctor was called—even Mike agreed this was a little out of Dr. D.'s field. Mike told the doctor his wife had tripped over a yard sprinkler, those stubby little devices that keep the grass green and almost high enough to conceal the source of the water. Ann, as usual, confirmed the tale.

By the first of May the worst of the discoloration was gone and Ann decided she would be able to travel. The Coppolas had planned a long trip, first to the Kentucky Derby in Louisville, then on to Cincinnati, and a flight from there to Las Vegas. While Mike gambled, Ann would take the Coppola children on to Los Angeles. Joan would break the trip in Cincinnati and visit friends and relatives.

Everyone had been looking forward to the trip. Sleepout Louis and Fat Allie Harris were going with them to Vegas and keep Mike company at the crap tables. It looked like a good vacation; suddenly it was threatened. Mike got a telephone call from New York. He listened intently, grunted at intervals, and hung up with a crash. As he entered the bedroom where Ann was finishing the last minute packing, his face was dark with anger.

"That crazy Albert," he said, in a guttural whisper. "He just tried to hit Frank."

Ann stared at him. She knew very little of the details though Mike had unbent enough to explain why he had been in such a bad humor upon his return from New York. Her eyes went to the packed suitcases. The troubles of Costello and Lansky had meaning only when translated into personal problems.

"Does this mean the trip is off?" she asked.

Mike shook his head. "I'll probably have to go back to New York soon," he said, "but not just yet. We'll take in the Derby and then see how things stand."

They stayed at their favorite hotel in Louisville, the square-shaped brick building on Broadway known as the Brown Hotel. The town was packed and local innkeepers made their usual killing. During Derby Week all prices escalated tremendously: food, drink, and accommodations. The Derby was the only attraction Louisville possessed to bring in thousands of visitors, so the local folks made the most of it. Even the wealthy sometimes had to share rooms, but not the Coppolas. As usual, Mike traveled in style.

The Derby had become a traditional social event for the underworld. Once it had been considered the property of high society and newspapers over the years had featured the big-name celebrities who attended. At least one reporter was assigned each Derby Day to observe and record the emotions of important people as their horses won or lost. But increasingly, the reporter had difficulty finding anyone to observe. The lords of the syndicate had replaced the fading royalty of Europe and as a rule they weren't eager to have their pictures taken.

A syndicate crap game somewhere in the suburbs had become as much a part of Derby tradition as the annual dinner of the Most Honorable Order of Kentucky Colonels, which usually took place at a leading hotel. Many of the syndicate's "moneymen" attended—those semi-respectable individuals who handled investments in such a way as to conceal the flow of "black money" from such places as Newport, Hot Springs, Biloxi, Gretna, Vegas, and Havana. Appropriately enough, the membership list of the order was a closely guarded secret. The Keeper of the Great Seal—who also kept the list—was the widow of a man who made a fortune in syndicate blackmarket liquor deals during World War II. To be a Kentucky Colonel was a mark of distinction in underworld circles and the hoods of Newport were always pulling political strings to be so designated. Businessmen who sometimes had to deal with the wealthy hoods coveted the honor too—it made mixing a little easier.

George Jessel was toastmaster at the 1957 annual dinner but the young "starlet" who accompanied him attracted more attention. She wore a long dress with a rudder at the bottom and a top that was open to the stares. To all who asked the inevitable question, she replied that her horse had something to do with King Arthur. However, she didn't remember his name. Those who acted on the tip and bet on Iron Liege were happy, but Round Table came in third.

No message from New York interrupted the festivities and Mike decided the expedition could continue as originally planned. Joan was dropped in Cincinnati and the reinforced party flew on to Las Vegas, where Ann was made welcome by her old friends Ed Levinson and Nig Devine. Mike began his routine of "standing them off" at the dice tables while Ann took the children on to Disneyland.

Four days later the call came and it was urgent. Regretfully, Mike dropped his dice and headed for a syndicate conference in New York. Ann was left with the chore of getting the children safely home.

Costello had been shot in the lobby of his apartment building on Central Park West. Earlier in the evening he had relaxed in restaurants with Miami Beach counterparts: L'Aiglon and Chandler's. A short, stocky man with a thin mouth, a large nose, and eyes that seemed perpetually narrowed, the so-called "Prime Minister" of the underworld had not been expecting trouble. He had come a long way since the days he pulled his slots out of New York under pressure from LaGuardia and relocated them in New Orleans and northern Kentucky.

The shooter was a large man and apparently an amateur. If, indeed, Anastasia was responsible, he had fallen far short of his old standards. Or perhaps the hired help was out of practice. In plain view of the crowd in the lobby, the gunman had shouted to get Costello's attention and fired one shot. Costello, startled by the shout, turned as the bullet creased the right side of his head. Only a novice would have tried a head shot in the first place.

Costello staggered to a chair and sat down. The gunman looked at him long and hard, apparently content. A professional of the old school such as Bugs Workman would have emptied his gun into the motionless target. This fat shooter simply turned and waddled out the door to a waiting car.

New York police, who might have been happier if a professional had been used, took Costello to Roosevelt Hospital. While the wound was being dressed, they went through the victim's coat. They found $800 and a brief memo which began:

"Gross casino wins as of 4-26-57—$651,284."

Investigation soon disclosed that the figures matched the first day's play of Las Vegas's newest sucker trap, the Tropicana. The casino had allegedly been constructed by Costello's old partner "Dandy Phil" Kastel, who began his career as an errand boy for Arnold Rothstein. Handwriting on the memo was identified as the work of two people—Michael J. Tanico, a cashier at the Tropicana, who previously had worked for Costello and Lansky at the Beverly Club in New Orleans, and Louis J. Lederer. The latter had an interest in Ed Levinson's Fremont Hotel in downtown Las Vegas. Under pressure from Nevada authorities, who found the heat too hot to handle, Lederer was forced to sell his piece of the Fremont. Sam Garfield, for many years an associate of the Cleveland Syndicate, provided the money for Levinson to buy out Lederer.

Thus the shooting in Central Park West set off ripples from Havana to Las Vegas. To the original problem of Anastasia's demands on Lansky was now added the difficulty of protecting hidden syndicate interests in Las Vegas. All this made Lansky more indispensable than ever.

Police picked up Vincent "the Chin" Gigante, a small-time gambler and ex-fighter, but he refused to talk. Ultimately he was acquitted of attempting to murder Costello. The Prime Minister, who all agreed must have been the shooter, refused to talk. Like Ann's his code frowned on stool pigeons. In any case, he knew the man who pulled the trigger was as much an instrument as the pistol itself. You can't get too angry at an instrument.

Exactly what was discussed at the meeting to which Coppola was so urgently summoned, Ann never learned. She knew without asking, however, that the syndicate would conduct its own trial and execute its own justice.

Ann returned home by way of Cincinnati to pick up Joan. The boys in Newport were not greatly concerned with the events in New York. Gambling was illegal in Kentucky and everyone knew it. If they didn't know it they had only to read the current issue of *Esquire* magazine. An article entitled "Sin City" was concerned with Newport. The author, Monroe Fry, had some fun with Newport officials, especially Mayor Maybury, who had succeeded Siddell. He had also dug deeply, mentioning such recent events as Big Jim Harris' troubles and the case of Hattie Jackson. He had even noted that corruption extended to some churches whose ministers didn't inquire too deeply into the identities of some of the generous contributors who helped pay their salaries.

According to the amused gossip some of the preachers had been upset by the article. A postman aptly named Christian Seifried had been given the go-ahead by his minister for a "Social Action Committee" composed of ministers and laymen of various churches. The group had decided to clean up Newport. Word had it they were going to city officials and demand action against prostitute and gambler alike.

Ann joined in the laughter. Compared to the problems that beset her husband, this threat was shadowy enough. When some pessimist pointed out that the troubles in Kenton County which closed the Lookout House began with just such a group of ministers, it was easy to reply that this time there was no Estes Kefauver available to fan the coals of discontent.

Mike remained tense and on edge throughout the summer. A big problem confronted the syndicate—what to do about Anastasia. Worse, from Mike's viewpoint, the heat was on in East Harlem. The cops were threatening his chief source of revenue. Ann knew better now how to handle him when he came in angry and tired from New

York. He wanted balm for his pride and he wanted it in large doses. It was an opportunity and she made the most of it.

The climax came when police raided one of the major counting houses in East Harlem. A counting house is where bets collected over a wide area are taken to be added up and the winners segregated so payoffs can be made promptly and runners and writers given their percentage of the action they have handled. Long before, the boys had learned to count the cash at another location—by separating the money and the records a degree of protection was assured. On the basis of records seized in the raid, police estimated this one counting house—and there were dozens—was doing a gross business of $35,000 a day.

Adding insult to injury, Coppola was spotted down the street and picked up for questioning. No one doubted his connections; proving them was another matter. He was soon released, but his pride smarted. A man of decision, Coppola decided instantly that New York was just too hot. He turned the business over to Fat Tony and headed south to stay. Tony soon followed and spent the winter on Miami Beach; eventually he went back to direct the racket. Mike's instructions were simple:

"Send my cut by courier."

In making the decision Mike was being realistic. He could trust Fat Tony and the organization he had perfected over the years. A man of Trigger Mike's status had no business attending to details even on a long-range basis. The rackets would go on without his personal supervision. They might even operate better if the top cops assumed he had retired. Meanwhile, he would get his cut and there was plenty to do in Florida and the Caribbean. On Alton Road his neighbors didn't know his reputation and there was surely nothing to fear from the Miami Beach cops or the Dade sheriff's office. As long as Ben Cohen retained his influence, there would be nothing to fear in the future. Ben had organized things well—a bagman called the Fruit Fly had been imported from New York to handle details and give Ben a certain amount of insulation. The Fruit Fly even had a cover—he operated some fruit stores on Collins Avenue.

The heat in New York increased with the death of Anastasia. After carefully considering the matter, the syndicate decided no other course was possible. Just as Bugsy Siegel signed his own death warrant a decade earlier when he defied the National Syndicate by helping a few rebels from Chicago in the Great Wire Service War, Big Albert had crossed beyond the pale with his attempt to muscle in on Lansky and knock off Frank. Mike, who took part in the deliberations, felt no regret at the death of his old friend. Albert deserved his fate.

On October 25, 1957, Anastasia was blasted as he sat in a barber's chair in the Park Sheraton. It was an efficient hit in the best tradition of the syndicate. Albert would have been proud of the manner in which it was handled. Murder, Inc., might be gone but the syndicate still had skilled killers on call and they handled the job well.

Two men wearing scarves over their noses and mouths, and dark glasses over their eyes, walked into the barbershop and stopped before Albert's chair. They had black gloves on their hands and black guns in their hands. The men fired for the body and then the head—no bungling here as in the shooting of Costello. Albert fell from the chair to the floor where one of the shooters administered the coup de grace by firing a bullet at close range into the base of Anastasia's skull. No chance of a slipup was intended.

Ironically, just twenty-nine years before, the mastermind of organized crime, Arnold Rothstein, was killed in the same hotel. That murder had also remained unsolved.

There is a pattern in organized crime, if people will look for it. Too often, however, a law-enforcement official sees only a fragment of the overall picture, and even a big agency may be concerned with only one phase of crime's varied activities. This is at once the weakness of law-enforcement and the strength of the syndicate. Until a coordinated attack is sustained against the syndicate, the organization will continue to operate and individuals will be replaced as needed.

Investigators found Anastasia's bodyguard. Very conveniently for the killers, he had been drinking coffee in a drugstore across the street while his boss was shot. The man's name was Anthony Coppola. What relation, if any, he was to Trigger Mike, no one bothered to note.

Back in Florida, things were stirring in a new field. Despite varied syndicate activity over the decades, the numbers racket had been neglected. The game as played in Florida was different from that in New York, Boston, or Newport—bets were taken on two-digit numbers instead of three. There were two principal areas of action instead of one—weekly bets on the Cuban National Lottery and twice daily drawings which were locally known as "bolita." The Cuban Lottery had been in existence since 1909 and had attracted a tremendous following among Negro and Cuban residents of the Gold Coast. Much of their faith was based on the fact that the drawings each Saturday in Havana were broadcast live by a Havana radio station. The doubters could tune in and actually hear the numbered balls roll down the chute and the winning number announced.

Local gamblers had long sensed, the tremendous opportunity if Batista could be persuaded to fix the winning number. Various individuals offered huge sums to the dictator, but he refused. The lottery was the one thing, and about the only one, with which he dared not tamper. To do so was to invite revolution.

Bolita was another matter. The winning number was selected in a ritual which had become traditional. Bets were sold by hundreds of writers who received fifteen per cent of the money they collected. Drawings were held at scattered locations to permit as many as possible of the players an opportunity to participate. Balls numbered from one to one hundred were placed in a sack and shaken in turn by the assembled players. The bag was then "tossed" to a "catcher," who grabbed the bag in one hand by clutching one of the balls inside. The ball was then tied off, the bag emptied, and the winning ball displayed. To the simpleminded players the procedure seemed foolproof, but the white operators had long before developed many ways of cheating. The methods ranged from palming the winning ball and substituting one with the desired number, to freezing the ball in advance and tossing it to a confederate planted among the players. He would fumble until he felt coldness through the cloth.

During the forties and early fifties, numbers were left to local gamblers. The syndicate was more concerned with casinos and horse parlors. But with such an expert as Trigger Mike on hand to advise as to the potential profits, the big boys took another look. A joint operation was agreed upon. Coppola, because of his reputation, would be kept in the background.

The Cleveland Syndicate, always eager to cooperate with New York, sent Fat Hymie Martin to the area. Long a lieutenant, Martin won his fame in a very messy Cleveland murder when he was still a young man. Convicted once, he was acquitted the second time around and had been rewarded with pieces of various syndicate casinos including those in Newport. Now he was tapped to organize the numbers racket in south Florida. The Eastern Syndicate sent down a man to help, and George Gordon—a friend of Ann from the Beverly Hills Club—was ordered to supervise the field men. Coppola was available for advice. Fat Hymie was an old friend and Coppola introduced him to his favorite "social clubs," where he renewed acquaintances with such old buddies as John Angersola and Joe Massei.

Martin began slowly, getting an okay first from Roy O'Nan, who at the time was chief bagman for the sheriff's office and coordinator of such individual bagmen as the Fruit Fly on Miami Beach and Red Rainwater for the Miami police department. Hymie offered his services, and syndicate funds, to the various independents of the numbers racket—such men as Fred Chapman and Jack Rainwater. Within two years most of them had joined his organization. When Allen B. Michell, an ex-Philadelphia cop, was elected sheriff of neighboring Broward County in 1960, Martin expanded northward. Soon he controlled eighty per cent of the racket from Palm Beach to Key West. Independents who refused to accept Hymie as banker were put out of business. Sometimes, when a "hot" number on which many had bet fell in Havana, it was necessary to delay the payoff a few days while additional money was rushed in from New York or Las Vegas, but payments were always made and everyone seemed reasonably happy.*

Even Mike Coppola settled down following Anastasia's death and his own retirement from New York. Somehow the little man seemed more relaxed, better able to enjoy the good life he could so easily afford. Even an occasional upheaval in Miami Beach politics didn't disturb him. Ben Cohen had everything under control.

Sheriff's deputies listening to Cohen's telephone conversations obtained ample evidence of the lawyer's abilities. They overheard discussion after discussion in which Cohen arranged to remove from office a police chief who had come under fire. His successor, handpicked by Ben, made a few public statements about reform. Few people took them seriously but one big gambler was worried enough to call for reassurance. Cohen told him the new chief was just fol-

* For the full story of the syndicate's role in numbers see *Syndicate in the Sun*.

lowing directions to calm the public. Nothing would change. A few moments later a reporter called from the Miami *News*. He began by apologizing and then explained he had heard rumors that Cohen had something to do with selecting the new chief. Before Cohen could deny it, the reporter hastily added:

"You know how it is. I don't believe in rumors and insinuations myself but my editors thought I ought to ask you about them."

Cohen made sympathetic noises and told the reporter not to worry—rumors never bothered him. Breathlessly, the reporter thanked him for his trouble—and hung up.

The deputies decided to tap Coppola's phone as well, but abandoned the idea when their informants reported that Mike knew all about the plan. People had tried to bug him before.

Almost before Ann knew it, Derby time was at hand once more. It was an uneventful trip. In Newport, Screw Andrews filled them in on the progress of the local reform drive. The Social Action Committee, as expected, had achieved nothing. Nevertheless, city and county officials had been unable to persuade them to forget the whole thing. The preachers were stubborn and it might be necessary to close a brothel or two to satisfy them.

Ann might have been happy during that period in 1958 had two things not worried her: the tumor she tried to ignore and Mike's growing interest in Joan, which she couldn't ignore. More and more he treated Joan like a princess, buying new cars, presenting expensive gifts, and maintaining in Joan's presence a kindly attitude toward Ann. Joan, who became more beautiful daily, was very popular. Mike made rather obvious attempts to discourage her interest in boys of her own age. Repeatedly he arranged dates for her with older men—such men as Frank "Lefty" Rosenthal. A convicted basketball-game fixer, Lefty was also active in supplying local handbooks with racing results and the "line" on upcoming sporting events. He was not the type of man Ann wanted Joan to be with, yet she could not take exception to him. He was Mike's friend and, if older, always acted the part of the perfect gentleman. Yet it seemed as if Mike were deliberately insulating Joan from her own generation, and Ann couldn't help but wonder why. Somehow her daughter was becoming cold and hard before her eyes—and guilt gnawed at Ann's heart.

One day she had to go to Cincinnati, where the suit she had filed long before against the Brink estate was at last coming to trial. She lost the case and, as she put it later, the fact that she had remarried and remarried Mike Coppola didn't impress the jury. The verdict came in early in the afternoon. There was no real need to return home immediately. Indeed, she had planned a visit with her sisters. The thought of Joan alone in Miami Beach with Mike caused her to change her plans.

"I had such an uneasy feeling," she explained later. "I knew I had to get home."

She asked Screw to pull some strings and get her on the next flight to Miami. Screw obliged and she took off at 11 P.M. Ann reached Alton Road in the early hours of the morning. She found her fears justified but not, perhaps, in the manner she had expected. Joan was very ill. Only Dr. D. was available at such an hour and for once he admitted his incompetence. Joan was rushed to a hospital where doctors diagnosed her trouble as virus of the stomach. Ann breathed easier—she had suspected appendicitis.

The crisis passed and life resumed its normal course. October arrived and Mike decided he needed a little excitement. A gambling fling in Las Vegas was agreed upon. Sleepout Louis and Mildred accompanied the Coppolas. They stayed at the Desert Inn, the pride of the Cleveland Syndicate's far-flung empire. Mike took $15,000 along but he ran out of cash very quickly. That posed no problem, of course. As Ann put it: "His credit was unlimited. I knew that because even I was able to get $11,000."

She lost the money loaned her by the eager pit bosses. The amount, however, paled into insignificance when compared to the losing streaks of Mike and Sleepout. Nevertheless, said Ann later, "He gave me a whale of a beating in Vegas, stating it was my fault we were even out there."

Coppola and Levinson became involved in a marathon crap game at the Riviera which lasted twenty-eight hours and tested even the endurance of the famed Sleepout. When it ended Mike had dropped $140,000 and Sleepout was more that $100,000 in the hole.

"It was the talk of Las Vegas," Ann remarked.

The beating followed the end of the game and it came in the Coppolas' suite at the Desert Inn. But Mike didn't have to pay for the room. As Sleepout put it:

"Neither of us paid anything. All we got was our telephone bills. A lot of people go there and get everything free gratis."

Asked why, Sleepout explained:

"Well, I don't have no rooms (at the Flamingo in Newport) but I do have bills. Like every day people come to the club. I sign maybe $70 worth of food bills for customers who come in and out. I know all the boys. When any of them come into our club, whatever he eats is free. If we had rooms I'd probably give them a room free too."

The syndicate takes care of its own.

Morris Kleinman, who lived near Coppola on Miami Beach, was once asked about the episode. He suffered a bad attack of memory and couldn't even remember when he first met Mike. He did confirm it was a custom at the Desert Inn to "comp" the rooms of certain guests, and he admitted that big gamblers were pre-rated as to the credit they might be given safely. When asked if he had talked to Coppola in the six months prior to the interview, the old bootlegger took the Fifth Amendment.

After working out his anger on Ann, Coppola got busy on the phone. He called Toronto and asked his broker to sell some General Development stock, but to do it gradually so the price wouldn't be hurt. There was no hurry, he emphasized. Mike then called Lou Chesler, the portly president of General Development and an old friend. He arranged to borrow $100,000 to take care of Sleepout's losses. The money was sent to Mike in Miami Beach and it was there a collector for the Riviera picked it up. The collector had no trouble finding the house—he had been there before.

"Whenever he was in town he came to our house every day," Ann explained.

Collectors sometimes serve as couriers, bringing cash to hidden owners while making the round of debtors.

But Mike's troubles weren't over. On October 13, Coppola and Levinson were trying their luck at the huge Stardust, across the Strip from the Desert Inn. Since the Cleveland Syndicate had leased the casino from John "Jake the Barber" Factor, the Stardust had become the second-largest money-maker in Nevada. Rumors about the heavy play at the Riviera had reached the FBI and the Clark County sheriff's office earlier and when Mike and Sleepout were spotted at the Stardust, two deputies were sent to pick them up. They were taken to headquarters and questioned. No charges could be made but the pair was advised to get out of town and stay out. Ed Levinson was reportedly furious "at this treatment of my brother." It seemed there were limits to what even Nevada authorities could stomach.

To make sure Mike didn't return, the Nevada Gaming Control Board placed his name in its "Black Book." Persons named therein are supposed to be banned from Vegas.

Sleepout was not included, thanks to the protests of his brother, but four years later when he sought a license as a partner of Ed, the authorities described him as "notorious" and refused. Exactly why Sleepout should be notorious while his brothers were acceptable is one of those minor mysteries of Nevada official thinking. Perhaps the nickname had something to do with it.

The list did cause Frank Sinatra some trouble later when as an owner of record he insisted on entertaining his good friend Mooney Giancana at his Nevada casino.

Coppola's basic mistake was in losing too heavily and thus calling attention to his background. Nevada officials could put up with a lot so long as it didn't attract attention.

More disgruntled than ever, Mike returned home. Ann was once more his punching bag. By now he had learned through experience that something more was necessary to hurt her sufficiently and relieve his hate. He found a new weapon, her love for her mother. Recalling that time in Cincinnati when Ann asked him to sit beside the dying woman because Ann's sense of guilt was too great, he snarled at her:

"Your mother fucked niggers. That's why you look like a nigger. You are a nigger."

It was the ultimate insult. "As long as I live," Ann said later, "those words will drive me out of my mind. I don't think anything I can do will wipe out the memory of that dirty swine's horrible remark."

Something worse was yet to come.

"It was loads and loads and loads of money." ANN DRAHMANN

Eight

THE COPPOLAS DINED ALONE ON DECEMBER 23, 1958. THE children had left for a party. Joan had a date and was taking her usual good time about dressing.

Mike had spent the afternoon at his favorite hangout, the Midtown Social Club, playing cards with Joe Massei. Ann had been busy finishing preparations for Christmas and checking the family Christmas list to make sure no one had been forgotten. It was a long list and most of the names were friends of Mike.

Several years later, after Joe Valachi spun tales about La Cosa Nostra to the McClellan Committee, the author compared the names listed by Valachi with those on Ann's Christmas list. Among the "soldiers" said by Valachi to owe allegiance to Trigger Mike, the following were on Ann's list five years earlier:

Philip Lombardo, Frank Livorsi, Teddy DeMartino, Tony Salerno, Dan Scarglatta, Ben DeMartino, Joseph Torrice, Anthony DeMartino, Joey Rao, Joe Stacci, and Al Rosato.

Also on Valachi's charts and Ann's lists were a lieutenant, Vincent "Jimmy Blue Eyes" Alo, and the man identified as the former "boss of all the bosses," Charles "Lucky" Luciano. The Coppolas listed his address as 464 Via Lasso, Naples, Italy.

The Coppolas also listed many people not mentioned by Valachi. Presumably he didn't consider them members of La Cosa Nostra. Some of the additional names included:

John Angersola, Joe Bommarito, John Croft, John Scalish, Ruby Kolod, Moe Dalitz, Louis Levinson, Ike Epstein, Al Polizzi, Max Raymond, Martin Berman, Tom Dragna, Gil Beckley, George Angersola, Louis Chesler, George Gordon, Lefty Clark, Meyer Lansky, Joe Rivers, Eddie McGrath, Jake Lansky, David Glass, Ralph Coppola, and many more.

Represented in this group are top bosses of the Cleveland, Eastern, and Chicago Syndicates. Together they made up much of the organization of the National Syndicate. It would be safe to assume that such a minor hood as Valachi never heard of many of them. He didn't move in their circles.

Had Ann needed additional assurance of Mike's standing in the rackets, the events at dinner provided it. Suddenly Mike slapped his open hand against his face. Cursing loudly in Italian, he pushed back his chair and rushed to the telephone.

"That stupid bastard," he exclaimed, as he dialed the number of the social club he had left an hour before.

Demanding to speak to the club manager, Coppola loosed a new torrent of profanity when the man answered. Finally he calmed down enough to issue orders. In a quiet voice more menacing than his curses, Mike commanded:

"Look in the deep-freeze unit and get the package I left there. The one that came in today. Send it over here right away."

Apparently the manager gave satisfactory assurance the package would be delivered. Mike returned to his meal, still cursing quietly. Ann didn't dare ask questions. Mike was obviously in no mood to answer them. But her mind raced. It was almost Christmas. Their third wedding anniversary was at hand too. Was this some special gift the unpredictable Coppola had ordered for her? Whatever it was it had to be valuable. She had never seen Mike so upset.

George the Wop, a flunky at the social club, arrived by taxi with the package before Mike finished eating. He must have set a new record getting there. Ann's curiosity was redoubled—it was such a large package. Perhaps another mink, she thought.

Without a word to her Mike put the package on a side table and completed his dinner. With the box in his possession, the emergency was past. Ann was too excited to eat her desert.

"What's in it?" she asked. "Please, Mike."

Obviously amused by her excitement, Coppola threw down his napkin and picked up the heavy package.

"Let's take it up to the bedroom," he suggested.

Ann quickly followed him and sat on the bed as Mike began fumbling with the cords. The box had been well sealed and he had trouble opening it. When at last he turned back the lid, Ann could scarcely believe her eyes. Money, tons of it. Loads and loads and loads of money.

Delighted with her reaction, Mike suggested she help him count it. Eagerly she agreed. As they worked, Mike condescended to explain.

"The courier came in from New York today and found me at the club. I was right in the middle of a big hand so I told him to stick it in the deep freeze. And, by God, I forgot all about it. I'm going to fire that manager. He's supposed to take care of details like that for the members."

Details like that? There were so many details her hands were becoming tired. "You count the little stuff awhile and let me count the big ones," she suggested.

The "little stuff" was $10's and $20's. The "big ones" were $100 bills with quite a few $500 and $1,000 ones included. Ann was exhausted when they finished. The total count was $219,000.

"Not bad," said Trigger Mike.

Big money was no longer a novelty to Ann as Mike supposed. Over the years she had become accustomed to it by counting Mike's hoard. He had given her large sums as well and even designed a special plant for her own use. But so much in one package was a little hard to accept. And to think Mike had been so preoccupied with a card game he had forgotten all about it.

Feeling well satisfied with the impression he had made, and perhaps as a reward for her help, Mike gave her $10,000 for Christmas. She put the money away and noted the amount in her little black book. As of the end of 1958, it listed some impressive totals:

In 1956—January, $2,000; February, $3,500; April, $2,000; May, $2,500; June, $3,500; August, $2,200; October, $2,500, and December, $5,000, for a yearly total of $23,200.

In 1957—January, $2,700; February, $5,000; March, $3,200; April, $7,500; May, $8,300; June, $5,000; July, $6,200; August, $4,000; September, $1,000; October, $5,000; December, $10,000, for a yearly total of $57,900.

In 1958—January, $3,800; February, $5,900; March, $3,600; April, $7,900; May, $10,000, June, $6,500; July, $7,500; August,

$9,700; September, $3,300; December, $10,000, for a total of $68,200.

The total might have been even higher in 1958, Ann decided, if Mike hadn't thrown away so much cash in Las Vegas. But it was nothing to sneeze at, even so. Once she asked Mike if she could put her loot in the bank so it could draw interest. "I'd be dead," said Coppola abruptly. To soothe her fears he assured her he was putting aside amounts equal to what he gave her for the future. The cash he kept in the house, she knew, was considered operating capital to finance shylocks, bookies, and other investments as they came along. It was good to know he was saving something as well.

Part of the money in the big package was used to pay Chesler's loan to Sleepout. Mike remarked to Ann when he paid it:

"Now Sleepout owes me."

A year later the shoe was on the other foot. Chesler owed Mike $50,000, and Mike was pressing for payment. The portly Chesler, "a tremendous bettor," had gambled foolishly on two races and Mike handled his bets. When Chesler's horses lost, Mike couldn't conceal his elation. In the ordinary course of business such big bets would have been placed with a bookie who might have "laid-off" part of the bet with Gil Beckley. Gil, in turn, if strapped for cash, might have passed part or all of it on to Mike. On the top levels of betting business, such men as Chesler had learned to deal directly with the top. Coppola was not a bookie in the usual sense: he was willing to do his friends a favor but he expected his friends to pay off promptly if they lost. Things were not always left to chance or the speed of the horse. Working through Screw Andrews, Mike occasionally fixed a race. Both jockeys and horse trainers were on his payroll and called him frequently.

When Chesler didn't pay up immediately, Mike called him at the Fontainebleau. They agreed to meet but Chesler didn't keep the date. A furious Mike called the three biggest bookies in the Miami area and ordered them not to take Chesler's bets until he paid off. Ann argued with him briefly:

"You're being sort of mean," she told him. "When you owed Lou money he didn't press you for it."

"This is different," replied Mike. "I want my money and that's that."

What Mike wanted, Mike got. Chesler paid up and apologized.

Soon the men were back on a friendly basis and the incident forgotten. Chesler, a real estate promoter who had built two cities in Florida, could not afford to anger a top man in the syndicate. Too much of his capital came from syndicate associates. Developments were even then occurring in Cuba which prepared the way for a huge new investment on Grand Bahama Island. Not only syndicate money but syndicate influence would be essential in that attempt to build a new Caribbean gambling center.

With money matters settled, the Coppolas could relax. Soon it was Derby time again, the social event of the underworld. Off to Louisville and the Brown Hotel they went. Gil Beckley and his wife, June, shared the excitement as Tomy Lee won the run for the roses, and the Beckleys then accompanied them to Cincinnati-Newport. They had dinner at the Beverly Hills Club.

Beckley had ended his long exile in Canada and was operating the biggest layoff betting business in the nation from the Glenn Hotel on Monmouth Street. Ann obtained a certain satisfaction in hearing that her old friend was living much of the time at Jimmy Brink's mansion on Dixie Highway. A handsome ex-football player, Tito Carinci, who wore his black hair in bangs and operated the Glenn Rendezvous on the first floor of the hotel, also lived there. It would appear, Ann decided, that the widow of Charley's old boss was operating a rooming house for hoods.

There was tension in Newport these days although no one appeared really worried. Those "sneaking preachers," as one gambler put it, were still trying to cause trouble. They had appeared before the October grand jury and, despite a brush-off, had returned in February. No one would have paid them much attention except that the *Courier-Journal* in Louisville sent a reporter up to cover both sessions and his stories created a degree of heat.

The reporter happened to be the author.

A very funny thing happened in December, Ann was told. The same reporter had gone with some preachers and a state beverage agent into the Flamingo. Fortunately, said Sleepout, he had been tipped in time. When the party arrived they found a sedate scene. Years before the Flamingo had lost its liquor license, so to prepare for the visit Sleepout had to clean out the bar. A vase of flowers replaced the row of bottles. All the customers were asked to cooperate. The preachers found them seated at the tables drinking milk—

or trying to down the stuff. The reporter tried to lead the way into the casino at the rear, but Kenny Bright—the Cleveland Syndicate representative—neatly blocked them.

"The back room is closed, gentleman," said Kenny, "but could I offer you a glass of milk?"

It was all very funny, Ann agreed. Fifteen minutes after the preachers left, the bar was open and the milk had been poured down the drain.

The reformers were undiscouraged. They continued to visit gambling joints and brothels despite a February grand jury report which had been specially written for them. The report said, in part:

"Our experience, reason and personal evaluation of human failings incline us to the oft-repeated belief that man's frailities and weaknesses cannot be completely legislated away. Mankind having been born in sin will ever be a prey to the temptations of sin."

If the gamblers were inclined to shrug off the ministers, Newport officials with an eye to the elections were not. The *Courier-Journal*'s stories, first of their kind in many years, had been widely read. If the stories continued, the Cincinnati newspapers would be forced to start crusading in self-defense. The situation was potentially dangerous.

In an effort to cool the zeal of the preachers, City Manager Oscar Hesch arranged a meeting with the Reverend Harold Barkhau, most influential of the ministers. Barkhau reported later he was told by Hesch:

"I asked you to meet with me because you have been here longer, you are older, and I think you know the situation better. Would you ask your group to withhold going to higher authority for a couple of months? Mr. Wise and I have had a conversation and we are determined to wipe out prostitution. You really don't want all the handbooks closed, do you?"

Reverend Barkhau, whose church had been once destroyed by fire and rebuilt with help of gambler's money, was willing to compromise. Other and younger ministers, such as Dudley Pomeroy of the First Baptist Church and George Bennett of the First Presbyterian Church were opposed. Ultimately they won the debate and with Chris, the patient postman, leading the way, the Social Action Committee continued its unhurried campaign. It soon became apparent even to Barkhau that any promise by Wise or Hesch to close brothels was an empty one—city officials could not control police who long before had made their own deals with pimps and madams. Reverend Bennett was able to write in his diary:

"Strange, how little we know each other, how different our backgrounds, our denominations, our lives—yet in one thing so solidly united and close."

That unity was the one thing the syndicate could not beat.

Ann listened to the gossip with only half an ear. Ever since her marriage she had been planning a big party for her relatives, a party to which everyone of importance in the Newport-Covington area would be invited. Her sisters and brothers would be able to see how important, how successful, she had become. Mike had not wanted to be bothered, but when Ann insisted he grudgingly gave his consent. The Beverly Hills Club as the location appealed to her though Beckley advised against it. With so many preachers and reporters snooping around, such a famous person as Trigger Mike might be recognized and featured in a newspaper story. Better go to some fine restaurant that didn't have a casino. There were a few, you know. Ann agreed and selected Retschultze's, a nice place outside Covington on the road to Louisville.

The turnout wasn't quite as large as Ann hoped. An ex-Newport city commissioner was opening a new joint over in Campbell and a lot of guests left early to attend. It was satisfactory, nevertheless, and the food was good. Even though it wasn't the Beverly Hills or the Fontainebleau, her relatives seemed impressed. As usual, however, when things were going well, the only bad chip in the game was Mike. He began drinking early and continued at a heavy pace. Her sisters avoided him, a fact that did not escape his attention and only increased his bad humor. Ann accepted the situation philosophically —it seemed that Mike never wanted her to be happy unless he was the cause of it. The bastard was so self-centered.

Noting his growing annoyance, Ann decided she'd better quit table-hopping and give him some attention. After all, she was just trying to show him off. But it was too late. When she returned to her seat beside him, Mike swayed toward her and leered:

"I'm going back to Miami on the next plane."

"You can't do that," said Ann. "You promised we would stay two more days."

"Can't help it," said Mike in a guttural whisper. "Got to get home. Joan needs me. She can't get her snow without old Trigger Mike, you know."

"Joan?" Ann could not comprehend. "Snow? What ever in the world are you talking about?"

Mike's snigger was obscene. He was very drunk. "You don't know your darling daughter, do you? Your princess takes drugs. She may get hooked soon."

"Hooked?" Ann was still fumbling for understanding, but her stomach was turning to ice. All those old fears, old suspicions. She had suspected something but, dear God, not this.

Pleased with her reaction but a bit impatient, Coppola snarled: "She could turn addict, you bitch. You've been too busy spending my money to notice."

With that he stood up. Ann sat stunned as he motioned unsteadily to Jelly Wehby.

"I gotta catch a plane," he said. "Drive me to the airport."

Emil "Jelly" Wehby was a huge fat man, a flunky of Screw Andrews, who sometimes used him as a bouncer-bodyguard. For him an order from Coppola was the same as an order from Screw. He obeyed instantly. Ann, sitting numb and motionless, watched the two men leave the room. All eyes followed them out, then turned back to Ann.

The noise of a motor starting outside the building penetrated the hurt and shame. Ann came suddenly to life. Mike had to be stopped. Whatever had happened in the past couldn't be changed, but he had to be kept away from Joan. He couldn't go back alone. She jumped up, overturned her chair, and ran toward the door. Only Gil Beckley intercepted her.

"What's going on?" he asked quietly.

"Give me your keys," said Ann. "I've got to stop Mike."

Beckley produced a car key. "It's the black Olds," he said. "I borrowed it from Roger Seith."

Ann didn't wait to hear more. Grabbing the key, she fled to the parking lot, her long gown pulled high to let her run. Mike had already vanished, but she knew Wehby's car—a new station wagon. Even though it was well after midnight Dixie Highway was still crowded. The night was young in Newport-Covington and a lot of suckers were still coming up from Louisville.

The Greater Cincinnati Airport is located, curiously enough, in

Boone County, Kentucky, southwest of Covington, on level ground which stretches to the very edge of the Ohio River gorge. It can be reached from the front by driving down Dixie Highway. A shorter but narrow and more dangerous approach is River Road and the side street which climbs out of the gorge to the rear of the airport.

Ann went down Dixie Highway, hitting eighty miles an hour when the traffic thinned. Riding with her were memories—memories of Mike insulting the young swain who came calling to take Joan to a football game in the Orange Bowl; of Mike arranging dates for Joan with Lefty Rosenthal and Chuck White, the handsome son of Charles "the Blade" Tourine; of Mike buying a new car for Joan; of the beatings that never took place when Joan was present.

She reached the airport and followed the long detour around the public parking lot to the front of the terminal building. There was Jelly's car, illegally parked with the motor running. She stopped behind it. Through the large window she could see Mike at the ticket counter. Wehby stood behind him, holding a suitcase. So the bastard hadn't acted on impulse after all; he had brought his bag along when Wehby drove him to the party.

Ann rushed into the building. What she said, she could never remember. It was insulting. It was vicious. Even Mike became embarrassed as the girls behind the counter stared in amazement. He told her to come outside. The air felt cool on Ann's flushed face and she renewed the verbal assault. This time Mike said nothing. As Wehby, who had followed along still holding the suitcase, watched, Mike knocked her down. She fell against a concrete bench. Mike bent over her and Ann kicked up with all her strength. The kick landed and Ann scrambled to her feet. She was an animal now, fighting for life and something dearer than life, her daughter. However she was no match for Trigger Mike Coppola, who learned the arts of gutter fighting in East Harlem before she was born. He struck her again and again until she lay dazed, blood trickling from her nose and mouth.

Coppola stepped back satisfied. He glanced inside the terminal. The girls on duty at the ticket counter stared back. One of them was holding a telephone. Not even Coppola wanted to face them now.

"I've changed my mind," he said to the impassive Wehby. "Let's go back to the hotel."

Jelly put Mike's bag in the station wagon, held the door for Mike, and climbed under the wheel. Without a glance at the bloody face of his wife, Mike rode away.

"Step on it," he snapped.

Ann pulled herself up, shook her head to chase away the red blobs, and got back into the Seith-Beckley car. Wehby's taillights were vanishing around the corner of the parking lot. Recklessly she followed, gunning the motor hard. They were just outside the entrance to the airport when she caught up with the station wagon and cut in front of it. There was a crash of glass as the right window of Ann's car shattered under the impact. Both cars came to a stop.

Cursing wildly, Mike got out to meet her.

"Look, you bitch," he said. "You've got to stop this shit. Move over. We'll go somewhere and talk."

Wehby watched them drive off in the Seith-Beckley car. Instead of taking Dixie Highway, Mike turned left toward River Road. It was a lonely area. Back in bootleg days a lot of people were taken there on their last ride. Jelly shrugged. It was none of his business. He would go back to the restaurant and try to find Screw. Let Screw worry about it.

At Retschultze's, a few people were still standing around discussing the incident. Screw had already left for the new opening in Campbell. Beckley was still there, waiting for his car to return. Wehby told him what had happened. The Brain swore softly to himself. There was nothing to do but wait. Wehby drove on in search of Andrews.

On River Road, meanwhile, Ann sat stiffly. She felt physically and emotionally exhausted. Having achieved her objective in turning back Mike at the airport, she felt incapable of further effort. Mike, sobered by the action, made the twisting descent into the gorge without difficulty. As they drove on through the blackness, Ann felt a surge of hope. Maybe this was just one of Mike's attempt at humor. The bastard was capable of telling such a lie just to hurt her.

"Oh, Mike," she said, grasping his arm. "Tell me it was just a joke. You didn't mean it, did you?"

Coppola braked the car to a stop. On their left the roar of the river was loud. The darker bulk of the mountain on the right could be felt rather than seen. Mike reached across his wife and opened the shattered door.

"Get out, bitch," he said. "I'm sick of listening to you."

Ann didn't move. With a curse, Mike shoved her from the car. She stumbled and fell into a ditch. Lights of an approaching automobile touched the scene. The oncoming car slowed, then speeded up and went by fast. Coppola slammed the door and drove off in the direction of the lights of Cincinnati far ahead. Ann lay whimpering in the ditch.

Reaction to hope so quickly born and so speedily dead left her weak. Fear came to give new strength as Mike's taillights vanished around a curve. The bastard might change his mind again and go back to the airport. She had to stop him. Joan's life might depend on her. Somehow she staggered up and started walking.

It was along River Road that Gil and June Beckley found her. Mike had returned to Retschultze's and given Beckley the key to the car. It took the smooth Beckley only a minute to persuade Mike to tell where they had left Ann. Someone volunteered to take Mike to Sleepout's house in Fort Thomas. Beckley got into Seith's car and started down River Road in search of Ann. He found her outside a fish house which was closed for the night. She was pounding on the door, hoping to awaken someone and borrow a telephone to call Joan in Miami Beach. When Beckley assured Ann that Mike had gone to Sleepout's home for the night, Ann consented to be taken to her hotel.

The evening wasn't over. Someone at the airport had reported the fight. And Covington police got an anonymous call from the driver who had seen Ann pushed from the car on River Road. A radio message alerted the two police cars in the area to watch for the Olds and the station wagon.

Fort Mitchell police spotted Seith's car on Dixie Highway and ordered it to the police station. Fort Mitchell was only a wide place on the road, but it had a station and it was there Beckley stopped.

The situation was complex enough but Beckley knew how to simplify it. The whole affair was simply "domestic trouble," he explained, and it was all settled. The officers knew Beckley by reputation and they remembered Ann as Charley Drahmann's widow. They wrote no names and made no detailed report. "Just routine," they said.

When asked about the episode later, the officers were vague. "Do you consider it a normal thing that a woman has been beaten up, thrown from a car, picked up, and later apprehended?" one officer was asked.

The man admitted it was not normal. He also agreed the report on the incident was "very incomplete," but he had an excuse:

"It was lack of prosecution," he said. "Nobody wanted to do anything about it."

Beckley was permitted to take Ann to her hotel. A doctor was called. He couldn't do much about the black eye but he treated her cuts and abrasions and assured her no bones were broken.

Next day the sophisticated Beckley assumed the role of peacemaker. He persuaded Mike to tell Ann he had "exaggerated" Joan's habit. She really wasn't on the heavy stuff—just a few "bennies" and "yellow jackets" like all kids try. And, promised Mike, he would see she didn't get any more. All he had to do was spread the word and Joan wouldn't even be able to buy, beg, or borrow a pep pill of any kind.

Beckley was successful in his appeal to Mike only because he knew his man was desperately afraid of the Internal Revenue Service. For years he had gone to elaborate extremes to conceal his income. He warned Coppola:

"Ann's not just another dame. She's tough and she's mean. You get her mad enough and you'll have an old-country vendetta on your hands. She'll go to the feds and talk. You can't afford that, Mike."

Ann accepted the truce for several reasons. It was good to believe that Mike had exaggerated. Not to think so would be too terrible. And she knew he did have the power to cut off Joan's drug supply. There was still hope if Mike would keep his word.

The couple, still not talking very freely, returned to Miami Beach and the stormy marriage continued much as before. Ann began a conscious effort to reach her daughter, to establish a better relationship, but Joan resisted. It would take time, Ann decided, a lot of time. Fortunately, Mike remained in a reasonable mood. Ann was able to postpone her date with reality.

Joan accompanied her on a trip to Cincinnati in November 1959. Ann hoped the visit would soften her daughter but she could note little change. The visit itself was unsatisfactory. Too many people had questions they were afraid to ask. It was almost a relief to return home. The women got in late. It was after midnight when Ann entered the master bedroom. Mike was asleep but stirred as she was undressing.

"I've got a headache," he complained. "Look in the dresser drawer and get me some aspirins."

Ann obeyed. There were no aspirins in the drawer but there was a small box that had not been there before. She picked it up.

"Open it," said Mike.

Inside the box was a pair of diamond earrings. They sparkled in the night-light's glow.

"Who are they for?" asked Ann.

"For you," said Trigger Mike.

"You darling," said Mrs. Trigger Mike.

*"I am more guilty than he.
It was my flesh and blood
who got hurt."* ANN DRAHMANN

Nine

IT HAD BEEN A PROFITABLE YEAR FINANCIALLY, ANN DECIDED, as she made a final entry in her little black book. Mike had given her $8,000 in January, $9,000 in February, $3,500 in March, $7,000 in April, $8,000 in May, $6,500 in June, $5,300 in August, $10,000 in September, $7,500 in October, and $13,000 in December.

The total for 1959 was $77,800, the best year yet. Grand total for four years of marriage was a neat $227,100 in cash. Add to that the furs, the jewelry, the clothes, and the cars, and she hadn't done too badly. In fact, a girl might be able to coast along for quite a while on the funds in hand if she decided to go it alone in the future.

Mike had not done too badly either. A check of his plants at year's end revealed a record total—$341,000. How much he had put aside in other hiding places, she could only guess.

Since that episode last May in Covington they had experienced a strange relationship. Mike had treated her with new respect, and been unusually generous, but both of them were conscious of a battle of wills over Joan. Ann had made some progress. Joan was a little more receptive, apparently appreciating the extra time and attention Ann gave her. With Mike on his good behavior, Ann had decided the only way to win Joan was by affection, demonstrated constantly but without pressure. Ultimately, she hoped, they would be able to talk as woman to woman. When that time came it should be possible to expose Mike for the monster he was without destroying Joan's respect for her mother.

Ann's position was much like that of Jack Thiem, the Newport detective who had lost his battle. To get the information he felt he needed to fight corruption, it had been necessary to compromise himself. To win the security Ann wanted, she had also compromised with evil. Thiem had been unable to win the support of the NCA and his enemies had used his tarnished badge to frame him. Ann hoped that Joan would understand her problems better when and if a showdown came. Meanwhile, it would be disastrous to tell her too much. Joan might very easily call a plague on both Mike and Ann and retreat from reality into the nether-land of drugs. On the basis of pure logic, Ann admitted, she had been as greedy, as amoral as Mike. Joan had to be made to see, somehow, beyond logic to comprehend the forces that drove her mother to the arms of a syndicate gangster.

Yet it was dangerous to wait. With Joan already using drugs—how much Mike had exaggerated, Ann didn't know—a showdown was needed. It would come soon, Ann felt. Mike's temper was growing shorter as he saw Joan respond to Ann's efforts. The cat-and-mouse game they had been playing with Joan was better suited to a woman's temperament. Luckily, Coppola had become preoccupied with Screw Andrews in a new project and Ann gained a little time.

Andrews, now boss of the numbers racket in greater Cincinnati, had developed illusions of grandeur. In a very real sense he had taken over from the late Pete Schmidt—Pete had died peacefully in bed in 1958 at the age of 72. Like Schmidt, Screw dreamed of a new gambling palace from which he could dominate the assorted rackets of the area and make politicians dance at his bidding.

Mike had no intention of challenging the Cleveland Syndicate's power in Newport, but he was willing to help Screw achieve local control that would enable him to organize the prostitution racket and take a cut from the hundreds of small independent handbooks. The field of narcotics was a possible area of development as well. The whores of Newport were all potential customers.

Key to Screw's plans was the new mayor of Newport, Ralph Mussman. Unique in local political circles, the rotund Mussman was an educated man. He held a master's degree and had taught in a Covington high school where he also coached the football and basketball teams. His interest in sports led him to the job of Newport recreation director and it, in turn, brought his appointment as city manager during one of those intervals when Oscar Hesch was out of favor with the ruling faction. His career struck a snag, however, when he ordered Newport police to enforce the laws relating to prostitution and gambling. Such a policy was obviously unthinkable—in fact it indicated a dangerous communist trend—so Mussman was promptly fired. It was later learned he had actually been cooperating with the Newport Ministerial Association and all good "liberals" knew what a bunch of "Reds" those preachers were.

But Mussman had friends who recognized that even a good man can be misled. An hour after he was replaced as city manager by that old standby Oscar Hesch, Mussman was appointed county juvenile officer. County Judge A. J. Jolly, the man who had defended Screw in the Clark murder case, made the appointment. Jolly recognized that Mussman could be useful once he understood the political realities. Under the judge's expert tutoring, Mussman soon learned the facts of life and in September 1959, he was elected mayor. As mayor he was frank about his policy:

"If you run for office and you think you know what the people want and they elect you," he explained, "you go along with the will of the people. If I run for office as a reformer, I should reform. If I run as a liberal, I should be liberal in office."

A "liberal" in Newport was someone who, as one candidate put it, believed that laws were made to be broken—especially laws prohibiting gambling and prostitution. Mussman considered himself elected as a liberal so he set out to be one.

Almost his first act was to form a real estate agency and buy at auction some city-owned property at the foot of Fourth Street near the Ohio River flood wall. He promptly sold it to Screw, who announced plans to build a glass-and-steel nightclub complete with penthouse overlooking the river and the skyline of Cincinnati.

Screw had taken advantage of his association with Trigger Mike, and the unlimited funds that association made available, to arrange some interesting deals. An urban-renewal program had long been underway in the "Bottoms" of Newport. For some reason it seemed unable to progress beyond the point of acquiring slum property and razing buildings. A square block stood vacant for four years in the heart of the Bottoms. Other buildings were purchased though destruction was delayed. The Newport Housing Authority—with Screw's old attorney, Morris Weintraub, as counsel—paid Screw

$475,000 in federal urban-renewal funds for the Sportsman's Club and two adjoining buildings. But since Screw had no immediate place to go, the authority rented the building back to him. The numbers racket, then grossing at least $8,000 a day, continued to be operated out of the old building while Mussman cooperated in finding Screw a new home.

The property purchased from the city by Mayor Mussman was ideal, but there were some minor problems—the site was too small for one thing. Aware that if he applied for a building permit, this fact would be apparent, Screw told his contractor to begin work without one. A snooping reporter discovered the omission, however, and a public hearing was ordered. It resulted in action. Under Mussman's direction, the City Commission made everything legal by trimming the minimum rear and side-yard requirements of the city building code to make them conform to the dimensions of the lot Mussman had sold to Screw. With that detail out of the way, the commission ordered a building permit issued.

Trigger Mike was pleased when Screw reported that everything was now legal and the new home of his illegal racket was under construction. For a brutal killer, Screw was demonstrating great political ability.

He was not so pleased, however, when late in January some non-racket friends of Ann dropped in from Cincinnati. Perhaps aware the airport incident of the previous year was still being discreetly discussed, Coppola refused to talk to the visitors and retired in a huff to examine his ivory collection. Ann was angered by the snub and from this rather trivial incident the long-delayed showdown developed. Ann went to bed angry after her guests left, and she slept late. When she awoke the sun was in the room. From downstairs came the sound of Mike's children clamoring for breakfast. She heard Mike's voice. Well, she decided, let the bastard fix the children's breakfast. If he could ignore her friends she, for once, could neglect his children.

Her attitude was "pure meanness," as she admitted later, but before she could think better of it, Mike was in the room.

"Get up, you bitch," he ordered.

"Go to hell," said Ann. "I don't feel well."

Coppola stared at her, his face contorted. She could almost read his mind. For once the argument centered on his children instead of Joan. Well, by God, two could play at that game.

Mike turned on his heel and walked rapidly to Joan's bedroom. The girl had been out late the night before and was sleeping soundly. Mike threw back the sheet that covered her and stared at the sleeping girl.

Joan awoke, blinked, and stared up at the swarthy face above her bed. Mike was unshaven. The scar on his chin was very pronounced. He grabbed her by the arm and yanked.

"If your mother can't get up with the kids," he shouted, "you get the hell out and fix their breakfast."

Joan, still half asleep, sat on the bed staring at her stepfather. He seemed like a stranger, an angry stranger. Mike jerked her off the bed and to her feet.

"Get downstairs, you bitch," he hissed.

Ann, who had been listening intently, followed her daughter to the kitchen. The children had taken advantage of Mike's absence and gobbled down their favorite cereal. Hurriedly they grabbed their books and went off to school. A storm was brewing and they wanted no part of it. Ann had been good to them but Mike was their father.

Joan began making coffee as Ann faced her husband.

"You swine," she began. "Why do you have to drag my daughter into our affairs? Don't you ever go into her bedroom again."

Mike, his face splotched with red, swung his fist. Ann fell against the table. Mike followed up his advantage, kicking her as she tried to stand. It was a savage beating, but halfway through it Ann glimpsed Joan's face. The girl was standing by the huge stove as if transfixed. Her face was white, her eyes enormous. Dimly, an idea stirred in Ann's dazed mind. Mike was showing his hand at last. He was proving himself to Joan as no words from her could ever have done.

Ann staggered up. "You yellow-bellied bastard," she gasped. Mike knocked her down again.

And abruptly Joan stepped between them.

Mike backed away as if suddenly aware he had an audience. His rage had been so complete he had forgotten the girl.

Joan helped Ann to her feet.

"Come on, Mom," she said, her voice tight. "You don't have to take this. Let's go."

The impact of the words struck Mike like a blow. His face went black with rage.

"Damn you," he snarled. "I'll teach you a lesson too."

Ann staggered forward, took the blow Mike aimed at Joan. "Go on," she screamed to her daughter. "Go to Joy's house. I'll join you later."

Joan hesitated, reluctant to leave her mother. But as Mike suddenly left the room, she allowed herself to be pushed out the door. Wearing only a thin robe over her pajamas, she went to her car. The sound of the motor starting was music to Ann, who slumped exhausted into a chair by the table and put her head in her hands. She had won, maybe. If so the beating was worth it.

Mike left the house, slamming the door behind him. There was now time to think, to plan.

An hour later Joan telephoned. Ann told her the coast was clear. She came home and packed a bag. Ann, battered and bruised, was too weak to help but she watched her daughter proudly. The girl had guts beneath that fragile beauty. Unlike Ann, she could face reality.

They talked for a few minutes. Joan made it clear that Ann had to leave Mike. There was no use in continuing the tragic farce. Ann thought of the cash she had won in exchange for blows. There had been a point to that. But she agreed with Joan. They would talk more later, decide what they were to do. Right now she needed to rest.

Later they did talk, long and frankly. Ann told Joan the truth about her married life, blaming herself along with Mike. Joan took it well. She understood. And in the warmth of friendship, she told of her addiction. Ann was shocked to hear the details. Later she was to write:

"The real tragedy I cannot nor will I ever speak of. The hurt and the damage is far too great."

Joan was willing to change herself and felt able to do it. The women discovered they could be friends. Ann was almost thirty-nine. Joan was twenty-one. There was plenty of time. Joan had never felt needed before. It was a welcome feeling. Somewhat to Ann's surprise she approved in principle what Ann had done in marrying Mike and was delighted to hear they had ample funds in reserve. With the money they could travel, build a new life together, forget the past.

Ann agreed, but privately she had some reservations. Mike must be forced to pay for what he had done to Joan. Besides, there was more money to screw out of him in divorce proceedings.

Allies now, mother and daughter made plans. Four days later, Joan returned to Alton Road. Mike was pleased, then baffled. He was treated politely by both women. The kids got their breakfast on time. Everything was as before and yet different. Sometimes Mike felt like an intruder in his own home.

Meanwhile, carefully, cautiously, the women removed most of their valuables from the house: clothes, cash, and jewelry. When the final break came there was no way to predict how Mike might react. Conceivably he would stay in the house he loved so deeply. There might be no opportunity to remove anything. The cash was the biggest problem—where to put it beyond the reach of Mike's long arms?

By February 16, all was ready. Joan wanted to stay with Ann and face Mike together, but Ann was afraid for her. Better to have Joan out of the house if Mike went berserk with rage. Ann could handle him alone. One more beating wouldn't hurt.

That evening when Mike returned for dinner, Ann went on the offensive. It was a pleasure. In his petition for divorce filed next day, Coppola gave his version of the night's events:

"Plaintiff further alleges that on February 16, 1960, the defendant [Ann] verbally abused the plaintiff and called him every vile name imaginable all night long and threatened to kill the plaintiff. That the police were called [by the neighbors] and in the presence of the police, the defendant asked the plaintiff for $100,000.00 as a settlement in divorce and then told plaintiff that she would use the money, if given her, to have him killed. That the plaintiff believes that the defendant would carry out her threat of murder upon the plaintiff and has therefore moved from his home and has taken his two children of a previous marriage with him."

Ann later gave a slightly different version of what happened when she asked Mike for a divorce. In her words:

"This man was so cagey that he decided to beat me but he said he could not afford to mark or bruise me since he knew my attorney was flying in from Cincinnati the next morning. The animal took and twisted my arms and legs until I lay wrenching with pain, and pulled my hair out by the handful. I wanted to die but I knew I finally was going to be allowed to live as he couldn't get a thrill out of hurting a ghost.

"He knew he had finally broken my spirit completely but he had to throw the very last punch, being warped as he is, in the divorce filings. Even though he has a notorious reputation—and I think he was notorious before I was born—he defied his very own code of life not to be a stool pigeon or tell anything a gangster has on anyone. This, I must repeat, is the underworld code, but the big man with the yellow streak down his back six inches wide had to lie and say— knowing it would get into the papers—that I was going to make juvenile delinquents out of his children who I loved very much."

While Ann was waiting for her attorney to fly in from Cincinnati, Mike consulted with Ben Cohen. Shortly after 3 P.M. on February 17, Cohen filed suit for divorce on behalf of Mike. Ann was charged with "extreme cruelty." The newspapers did pick up the story and Mike's allegation that he feared Ann's "vile and abusive language" would make delinquents of his children tickled the imagination of the most stolid editor. Mike had not received much publicity in the Miami papers during his years on Alton Road, but his nickname was known and it in itself was enough to make his charge seem funny.

Among the persons reading the newspaper story was Internal Revenue Agent Joseph Wanderscheid. Some months before he had been given Coppola's income tax returns to audit.

With the divorce suit already filed, Cohen and Coppola were ready to talk business. Mike, as Ann suspected, insisted on keeping the house. In return he was willing to make a cash settlement. Ann could keep everything he had given her including her latest car, a Lincoln Continental. There would be no alimony payments—it had to be a clean break.

The discussions continued long into the night. The visiting attorney slept in Ann's bed. She moved into the boy's room. All the children had been sent to visit friends.

That night as Mike snored peacefully, Ann made her final inspection of his plants. Two hours were required to count the money. It totaled $300,000 plus bonds and some star rubies and other jewels which had belonged to Doris.

Mike, decided Ann, must have had a couple of bad days since January. He had dropped $40,000 somewhere.

Next day, sleepy but alert, she watched Mike collect this booty and give it to Joey Morrison with whispered instructions as to where he should stash it. Joey took off in a hurry. Mike then packed his bags and moved to the Fontainebleau until the divorce became final and Ann could move out.

On March 10, Ann's local attorney—the Cincinnati one had gone home—filed a motion to dismiss Coppola's suit and a cross-claim for a divorce. In it Ann charged Mike with extreme cruelty but the overt acts she listed were but a pale reflection of the truth.

The cross-claim was filed after the attorneys reached an agreement on the property settlement. Mike was to get the house. Ann got $25,000 in cash and Mike waived any rights to property he had given her in the past.

There was also an under-the-table agreement which provided Ann with another $25,000 in cash. The deal represented an acknowledgment of realities. Mike was afraid a public record of the entire sum would attract the Internal Revenue Service. Ann realized that any such probe would bring attention to her finances as well.

Her cash hoard now totaled $277,100, and she was free of Mike. The final decree was signed March 25, after both sides waived the thirty-day waiting period. In handing down the decree, Judge Harold Vann ruled:

"The plaintiff and the cross-claim defendant, Michael Coppola, has been guilty of extreme cruelty to the defendant and cross-claim plaintiff, Ann Coppola."

The judge also restored Ann's pre-marriage name. She was now Ann Drahmann once more.

Victory was complete yet Ann wasn't satisfied. Mike still had much for which to pay. Money, although important to him, was something he could afford to lose. The next courier from New York or Las Vegas would restore his losses and there would be many couriers in the future. Had only Ann been involved, she could count the score even. Joan was another matter. Gil Beckley had been right when he warned Mike that Ann was capable of an Old World vendetta. She wanted revenge for Joan.

The daughter didn't share her feelings. Mike was a bastard, she agreed, but the divorce was final and the affair ended. She was happy to see her mother independent, but why look back all the time? There was so much in the world to see and do. They might begin by visiting Europe.

Ann was willing, but, as always, there were a few things to do first. Her money had to be hidden properly and that posed some problems. Ann knew the dangers. She had watched Mike take precautions for four years. While hunting a permanent solution she sent Joan off to Cincinnati to stay with relatives. Soon, she promised, she would join her and it would be off to Europe for the women and Mike could move back into his house.

Just as she had everything about settled, Joe Wanderscheid strolled around the side of the house. He rang the doorbell, then followed the path. Ann was wearing a one-piece bathing suit. She had been sunning herself on the patio beside the pool. Joe, a little dazzled by her beauty, managed to introduce himself. He was an Internal Revenue Service agent assigned to audit her ex-husband's tax returns. Could she help? Would she help?

Within thirty minutes Ann had promised to help on one condition —he would guarantee Mike would be sent to prison. Joe could only promise to do his best to send him there if the facts warranted. Ann looked at him calmly.

"I don't think you're the man to do it," she said, "You don't ask the right questions."

Ann, usually skilled at estimating people, greatly underestimated Joe Wanderscheid. Of medium height and weight, with brown hair thinning on his head, he was completely nondescript looking. As a teen-ager he had suffered badly from acne and had been given X-ray treatments with the result that his face was burned, leaving "pox-marks" and a ruddy complexion that gave him an "outdoorsy" appearance. It also made him look much younger than his fifty-one years and caused women to want to "mother" him.

A native of Lawler, Iowa, born and raised on a farm where he was one of seven children, Joe learned patience teaching for two years in a one-room country school. Seeking to escape the country, he studied accounting and business administration. A year before graduation he became desperately ill with goiter trouble. An operation was required and recovery took more than a year, but Wanderscheid went back to college and completed his studies. After a brief job as manager-auditor of a country club near Cleveland, he took a job with the Collections Division of the IRS as a zone deputy collector at Columbus and Zanesville, Ohio. In Zanesville he became involved in an investigation of a coal company. After entering the mine in search of evidence, he was nicknamed "the Ferret." More important, the case resulted in his promotion to revenue agent. Eventually he was assigned to Houston, Texas, where he soon was digging into the crime complex that was Galveston, Beaumont, and Port Arthur. The area was wide open, ranking close to Newport and Hot Springs in illegal gambling and prostitution. As an acting special agent he cracked cases against cops, madams, and gamblers. He made headlines when along with Special Agent Matthew P. Harris, he secured the indictment of the former police chief of Galveston, Fred M. Ford. A special prosecutor from the Justice Department, Fred Ugast, presented their evidence and the jury took only nineteen minutes to convict. Ford was sentenced to four years in prison.

Joe was reassigned to the IRS inspection service at Atlanta but soon wangled a transfer to Miami, where he was handed Coppola's tax returns shortly after he arrived in 1959. The proposed probe had resulted from an FBI tip. Back in October 1958, Coppola's Las Vegas gambling spree had been duly noted; however, in those days, the FBI had no jurisdiction in gambling cases. There was then no central federal agency to which such tips could be given. Ultimately the wheels turned a little and the IRS was given the hint. If Mike could gamble so heavily, odds were he had more income than he had reported.

When assigned the tax returns for audit, Joe moved slowly. He noted that Mike had reported income of $15,000 in 1957 and $31,087, in 1958. What was responsible for the huge increase? The 1959 returns might give a clue. Joe decided to wait until Mike filed his new returns. But one day a colleague, Special Agent Richard E. Jaffe, showed him the newspaper story of Mike's divorce suit and Joe decided to wait no longer. At last he had a starting point. If Ann would talk, he might have much more. He drove immediately to Alton Road.

Ann told Joe very little in that first interview. All her life she had automatically assumed that "the feds" were foes. To be asked to cooperate with them was something of a shock. After thinking about it, she decided she might cooperate if the probe was on the level. First she had to make sure of Wanderscheid. He seemed nice enough

—a little slow, careful, but much too cautious. At any rate, a girl wouldn't have to worry about him making a pass. Not with that face and manner.

If Ann still had her reservations about Joe, the revenue agent was nevertheless satisfied. He had made contact. It was obvious Mike's ex-wife was full of hate. She would cooperate eventually. Women always did. Joe wasn't exactly sure why.

Upon returning to the office, Joe hunted up Jaffe and told the tall, balding younger man that the case looked promising. Ann had hinted a lot of money was involved and the rumors about Trigger Mike being a top gangster were not exaggerated. Jaffe, one of the brightest intellects in the service, was intrigued.

"Keep me informed," he told his friend. "When the case is referred to intelligence, maybe I can wangle it."

Joe was pleased. Dick was the best and he had the feeling the best would be required. Besides, Ann would like him.

*"I went to his house every
evening wanting the jewelry."* ANN DRAHMANN

Ten

FIVE DAYS AFTER HIS FIRST MEETING WITH ANN, JOE WANDERscheid made an appointment and returned to the house on Alton Road. Ann took him into the Florida room and they talked for more than two hours. She gave much general information, but Joe had difficulty in making her be specific. Ann explained that for her own protection she wanted to be served with some kind of official paper making it mandatory that she talk. Joe tried to make her understand that at this stage the probe was preliminary. If she could give him something specific a referral could be made and a special agent assigned.

Vague as they were, Ann's replies whetted his appetite.

Yes, she knew how much money Mike had when they were married and how much he had when they were divorced. It was a whole lot more.

Yes, she had a record of expenditures over the years, including the cost of the pool, but she would give no details.

Yes, she knew of trips they had made and how much Mike lost in Las Vegas, but again no figures.

Some agents might have felt frustrated. Wanderscheid was confident he was making progress. Meanwhile, he made an appointment with Coppola. Ann gave him the name of Mike's accountant, Emanuel Kramer, and through Kramer the appointment was arranged.

The meeting took place at the Cynthia Hotel Apartments on Miami Beach in Kramer's apartment. In answer to Joe's question, Coppola said he kept no financial records, that his income was earned at the racetracks, that he didn't believe in banks, and kept all his winnings in his right trouser pocket. At year's end, he said, the money left in the pocket was reported as income.

Coppola refused to give the revenue agent his telephone number or current address. If wanted, he said, he could be reached through his accountant.

A few days later Ann called to say she had traded places with Mike. He had returned home from the Fontainbleau and she had moved there from the house. She also made certain suggestions.

Joe conferred with Jaffe. Since no referral had been made, the matter was still outside the jurisdiction of the Intelligence Division and Dick could only advise and observe. But his advice was good.

At 11:20 A.M. on April 8, Jaffe and Wanderscheid entered the plush reaches of the Fontainebleau and crossed the curving lobby to the office of Comptroller Frank Margulies. The "Season" had just ended but many of the "snow-birds" remained to sit beneath the crystal chandeliers and enjoy the luxury of America's most elaborate hotel.

Wanderscheid produced a "Commissioner's Summons" and told Comptroller Margulies he wanted to inventory the safe-deposit box of hotel guest Ann Drahmann. Primly, Margulies refused. He could not permit such an inventory without permission from the guest. After some talk he consented to check the records and thus confirmed Ann was indeed a guest in Room 672. She also had rented safe-deposit box 537. At Jaffe's insistence, he called Ann, who—while pretending surprise—had been waiting for the call. She promised to come right down.

The situation had its curious aspects. Ann, while in sympathy with the IRS agents, was afraid to give the appearance of cooperation and even unsure as to how far she wanted to go in helping them. They might take her own money and jewelry instead of trying to get Mike. There was also the very real fear of what Mike might do. She was prepared to brave his wrath but only if she was sure he would be convicted in the end. Neither Wanderscheid nor Jaffe could give that assurance. So the game proceeded on a highly tentative basis with the agents striving to push as far as they could without scaring off their potential key witness.

Ann arrived, beautiful as ever in a new dress. Since the divorce she had shopped wildly for both Joan and herself. After all, what was freedom if it couldn't be celebrated?

Playing the "dumb broad" role to the hilt, Ann asked the comptroller if she could refuse to open the box. He suggested she call her attorney. In the presence of Margulies and the agents, she called Jerome Greene, who had handled the divorce. After some discussion, Greene told her to open the box and let the agents inspect the contents.

Margulies suddenly vanished as Ann got the safe-deposit box and took it into the comptroller's office. In the box was a green lock-box approximately fifteen inches wide and long, and six inches deep. Ann opened it with a key from her purse. Jaffe, who had taken unofficial charge, peeped inside and noticed a number of $100 bills and several small jewelry cases. He asked Ann to count the cash. She obeyed. There were 225 $100 bills and thirty $50 bills for a total of $24,000.

"Living expenses," said Ann in a whispered aside to Joe.

Also in the box was a letter to Ann on the stationery of Botts & Greene, attorneys at law, with a check for $25,285. The letter explained the check represented the proceeds of the divorce settlement with Michael Coppola. The only other document in the box was a last will of Ann, leaving the check to Joan Drahmann in case of Ann's death.

Jaffe then began examining the jewelry cases and recording a description of their contents. He heard the door to the office open. Assuming it was Margulies returning, he paid no attention as a man walked across the room and halted behind Margulies' desk where Jaffe was working.

"Whatta you doing?" demanded an angry voice, and Jaffe looked up into the narrowed eyes of Mike Coppola.

"We're inventorying the contents of this box," said Jaffe quietly.

"You've got no right," shouted Coppola. He pointed to the pile of currency beside the box. "Dat's my money."

Wanderscheid and Jaffe said later they could scarcely contain their glee. Trigger Mike had lost his cool—and claimed possession of the under-the-table part of the divorce settlement.

"Right then I knew we had a case," said Wanderscheid.

As the agents stood silent, Coppola began gathering up the jewelry cases.

"This ain't Russia," he shouted. "You got no right to be persecuting my wife."

Coppola placed the jewelry boxes back in the strong box and slammed it shut. The advantage of surprise was still with him.

"What's that you've been writing?" he asked. "You got no right to put down what's in this box."

He reached across the desk and grabbed the pad of yellow paper upon which Jaffe had been listing the jewelry. The special agent reacted instinctively—he grabbed it back, turned to his briefcase, and slid in the pad.

"Look," said Jaffe. "Speaking of rights, you've no right to come barging in here and interfering with our work."

"Like hell I don't." Coppola snarled. "I'm representing my wife that you've been persecuting. Don't think I don't know. You've been bothering her for weeks. I won't stand for it."

Jaffe fought to control his temper. "Mr. Coppola," he said quietly, "our presence here is no concern of yours. This box belongs to your former wife. She's divorced—remember? We gave her an opportunity to consult her attorney and he told her we had a right to examine this box."

Coppola spun around. "Is dat true?" he asked Ann.

She nodded, keeping her face unsmiling but unable to control the amusement in her dark eyes. Mike was up against something bigger than a woman now—he couldn't bully Uncle Sam.

Mike demanded and received the phone number of her attorney and started to go out, but Jaffe followed up his advantage.

"How did you know we were here?" he asked.

"I'm not going to tell you," replied Mike, anger thickening his speech again. "If you want to know dat you'll have to get me before a federal grand jury."

"Did someone from the hotel call you?" persisted Jaffe.

"No," said Mike, veering from dangerous waters. "It was just a friend. Nobody from the hotel."

With that he left the room to call Greene. Jaffe noticed that Margulies had returned and was standing silently just inside the room.

"Did you tell Coppola we were here?" Jaffe asked him.

The comptroller became indignant. "I'll report you for such an insinuation," he blustered. "What's the name of your superior and his office number?"

In some amusement Jaffe told him his supervisor was Richard Wallace and gave Wallace's number. A veteran supervisor, Wallace was a nephew of the fabled Elmer Irey, the man who as head of Treasury intelligence agencies had helped convict Waxey Gordon and Al Capone. Margulies would get little satisfaction from talking to him.

Meanwhile, Coppola finished his phone conversation with Greene and was suddenly conciliatory. He returned to the office as Jaffe and Wanderscheid were collecting their personal belongings in the belief the episode was finished.

"You might as well go ahead with it now that you've started," said Mike unexpectedly. Recognizing an opportunity, Ann protested. She didn't want the agents to continue. Mike began arguing with her. Ann pretended to bow. She reopened the lock-box and emptied its contents.

"I was wrong about that money being mine," Coppola said to Jaffe. "It's hers. I gave it to her and anyway," he added in a careful afterthought, "it'll be on this year's taxes."

Jaffe restrained a smile and returned to the desk. The inventory resumed:

- 1 platinum ring with 4 rubies, small diamonds.
- 1 diamond heart pendant with pear-shaped diamond center.
- 1 pearl and diamond ring.
- 1 pearl and diamond pin.
- 1 double-strand pearl choker.
- 1 pearl and diamond bracelet.
- 1 solitaire engagement ring.
- 1 diamond and platinum wedding ring.
- 1 pair of pearl and diamond earrings.
- 1 gold ring with rubies.
- 1 pair of diamond earrings with pendant.
- 1 gold watchband.
- 1 man's gold ring with diamond.
- 1 blue sapphire with diamond pendant.
- 1 blue sapphire and diamond ring in platinum setting.
- 1 platinum ring with 3 small diamonds.
- 1 gold ring with small diamond.
- 1 gold ring with diamond.
- 2 gold watch cases.

1 gold I.D. anklet.
2 gold and pearl bracelets.
1 diamond brooch.
1 pair of blue sapphire earrings with diamonds.
1 pair of gold and pearl earrings.
1 gold heart locket with name "Ann" engraved.
1 gold cross on chain.
1 gold telephone charm with pearl.
1 pair of gold earrings—no stones.
1 gold pendant with diamonds—letters I LOVE U

Coppola kept up a steady stream of conversation during the inventory. That diamond brooch—it really didn't belong to her. Some guy borrowed some money and left it as security. . . . That item is twenty years old. I got it cheap. . . . That piece only cost $500 and that one $700. . . .

When Jaffe was finished he asked Ann to sign the bottom of the page to indicate she had witnessed the inventory. Coppola told her not to sign. She refused, then turned to wink at Joe.

It was 12:45 P.M. as Joe and Jaffe picked up their briefcases and started out. Coppola pointed his finger at Ann.

"Stay here," he ordered. "I want to talk to you."

He followed the agents through the lobby and watched them descend to the hot street. Then he called his accountant by telephone as Ann waited. The delay was short. Miami Beach is not a large city and few people there kept Mike Coppola waiting long. When the accountant arrived, they moved out to Ann's Lincoln Continental, which waited on the street. She turned on the air conditioning.

"I want your jewelry and that money," Mike began.

"No," said Ann.

They argued. Coppola promised he would not keep the jewelry himself but would turn it over to a mutual friend to hold.

"Why?" said Ann, playing dumb again.

"I don't want that jewelry appraised," said Mike. "I haven't accounted for it on my tax returns. Those bastards are after me."

Ann agreed to compromise. She would keep the money but she would give the jewelry to a mutual friend with instructions to give it to no one else. Mike was satisfied. He had reason to be. Apparently he had more influence with the friend than Ann. She soon learned Mike had taken the jewelry from the friend. Indignantly she called on her former husband.

Coppola said he had sent the jewelry to New York to have the precious stones replaced with some cheap ones. When everything blew over, he promised, he would give her back the pieces with the original stones restored. How long will that be? Ann demanded. Two or three years, said Mike. It would be sooner but he couldn't trust her not to wear the jewelry in public.

Ann remained angry and immediately began to conspire with Joe to recover the jewelry. They tailed Mike around town for days trying to determine if it had returned from New York. When no clue was obtained Ann resorted to direct harassment. At intervals during the early summer she would park in front of the big house on Alton Road and blow the horn loudly. If Mike appeared at the door, she would shout:

"I want my jewelry, you cheapskate."

Exasperated, Mike would yell back:

"I don't have it, you bitch."

The neighbors found it rather funny.

Meanwhile, on April 19, Wanderscheid arranged another interview with the taxpayer. It was as inconclusive as the first. Coppola said he was retired from business in New York, but he refused to name the business. However, he boasted the New York office of the IRS conducted an investigation of him in the 1950s and found he was clean.

Wanderscheid was able to confirm the truth of that statement. A probe had been conducted. It was very superficial in many respects though it provided one essential point—Coppola had signed an affidavit stating that as of December 31, 1946, his net worth was not in excess of $7,500. The affidavit had helped get Mike off the hook in the first probe—made at a time when the IRS was saddled with a lot of political appointees and outright crooks—but it gave Wanderscheid a valuable starting point in 1960.

A starting point had become essential. As a result of the jewelry inventory and Mike's claim to the money in the lock-box, a formal recommendation was made that possible tax fraud on the part of Coppola be investigated. The recommendation went up the chain of command and returned approved. On May 2, a file number was issued and a case-jacket prepared. Jaffe was designated the special agent in charge and Wanderscheid was assigned as the revenue agent. The value of the team had already been demonstrated and would soon be demonstrated again.

The first move, Jaffe decided, was to get Ann's jewelry appraised. In an effort to protect her, Joe went to the Fontainebleau and served Ann with a formal summons to produce the jewelry. Ann explained that Mike had the jewelry. Joe told her the summons would remain in force and she agreed to obey it as soon as she got the jewelry back.

A formal interview was arranged with Ann on May 17. She said very little for the record but when the court reporter left the room she relaxed.

"When the time comes," she said, "I'll testify against Mike regardless of how dangerous it is. But right now I might be sticking my neck out for nothing. I'm still not sure you boys are smart enough to trap Mike."

Jaffe didn't push. He had great confidence in Wanderscheid's ability to win a woman's confidence and Joe believed he was still progressing. Ann was permitted to leave but Jaffe warned her to be careful and to watch her words when she called the IRS.

The growing confidence Ann felt in Uncle Sam as represented by the two agents—despite her expressed doubts—was proven a few nights later. Ann watched her former home until she was sure Mike was away and the children in bed. Using her old key, she entered the house and went up to the master bedroom. Joan's old room had been converted into a den, she noticed. She opened the plant with trembling hands. If Mike returned unexpectedly, he could shoot her and claim he thought she was a burglar. There was a lot of money inside, but for once she didn't count it. Yes, here was the box and her jewelry was inside. There were also a lot of loose stones. She didn't stop to examine them—just took the box and ran.

Wanderscheid was preparing to leave next morning when Ann called. She had her jewelry back, she said. Would Joe assure her it would be returned if she brought it in for appraisal? Many of her friends had said the IRS would confiscate it.

Joe reminded her of all the weary hours they had spent together tailing Mike about Miami in an effort to learn where the jewelry was hidden. During all that time she had trusted him. Why get cold feet now? As yet there was no lien against Mike's property. Neither Joe nor Jaffe had any authority to keep her jewelry.

Ann took a deep breath and agreed to bring it in. Joe, who knew how much the decision represented, took a deep breath and called Dick Jaffe.

It was July 4, a holiday, and that complicated things immensely. Jaffe called his supervisor, Dick Wallace, who recommended he contact David Rabinowitz of the Miami Diamond Center. Rabinowitz agreed to serve as appraiser and, since the matter was urgent, to reopen his store for that purpose. The men agreed to meet there at noon. Another special agent was drafted to help. Jaffe went to his office and obtained guns, handcuffs, and two rolls of color film. A skilled photographer, he had his own camera.

Ann was no longer living at the Fontainebleau. Considering it too much the domain of Trigger Mike, she had moved to the Blair House, a plush apartment building on Bay Harbor Island. It had been built with Teamster Union pension funds and Jimmy Hoffa maintained an apartment there when he wanted to get away from it all and come to Miami Beach. June Beckley had recommended it to Ann. Gil also had an apartment there for use when business brought him down from Newport.

On the way to the apartment, Jaffe stopped and called Joe. The revenue agent said Ann wouldn't be ready to leave until 12:30 P.M. Another complication! Jaffe told Joe to call Rabinowitz and change their rendezvous to 1 P.M. A few minutes later he called back to see if Joe had succeeded. New complications! Rabinowitz, a wary businessman, had become fearful he was about to be the victim of an elaborate robbery plot. He had called his attorney and the Miami police.

Fast talking by Jaffe was necessary to get matters straightened out. The other special agent, who had not been on the case and thus presumably was not known to Coppola, went up to Ann's apartment. Jaffe parked down the street. At 12:35 P.M. he saw Ann and the anonymous special agent drive by. He followed, making sure no one else was tailing Ann. The trip to downtown Miami and the store was uneventful.

A still worried Rabinowitz admitted the party. Jaffe set up his camera, photographing each piece of jewelry in living color. The appraisal took two hours. The jeweler was very interested in the imitation stones which had replaced the originals. They represented good workmanship. Ann produced the loose originals. Four perfectly matched diamonds from one piece of jewelry had a weight in excess of ten carats and were valued at $15,000. Total value of the jewelry was $40,995.

There was a tense moment when the appraisal was completed and the jewelry replaced in its box. Very slowly Wanderscheid presented the box to Ann. A smile of relief lighted her dark eyes and her body visibly relaxed. The return to the Blair House was made without incident. As Ann prepared to leave the car she placed a hand on Joe's arm.

"I never really expected to get them back. Now I have full confidence in you."

For a holiday it was a good day's work, Wanderscheid and Jaffe agreed as they went home to their wives.

For Ann, it was an education. She had lived among men all her life who at best were amoral and at worst little different from animals. She had accepted almost without conscious thought their premise that law-enforcement people were little different despite their badges. Only the "feds" got a measure of respect, and it was assumed that even they were corruptible if the price was right. Ann, whose revolt had been against Mike rather than the system he represented, was beginning to put Coppola and his friends into perspective now that she had someone honest with whom to compare them.

The investigation began to roll as Ann became more cooperative. Joe was in touch with her every day. They developed code names for specific meeting places—church parking lots, modest bars, small restaurants. Ann would call Joe each morning. If her information of the previous day had checked out, Joe would say: "Looks like a nice day." If only part of her data had been confirmed, he would comment: "There's a few clouds." Ann would reply: "Meet me at Station B." Joe would be waiting and the status of the probe would be reviewed. Ann might suggest a new angle. Joe would call Jaffe.

Much of the conversations concerned the next step—the production of cash. Joe argued that such evidence was essential, the heart of the case. Ann finally agreed, but she insisted on certain precautions. Mike knew she was cooperating with the probe but he assumed she was doing it under legal compulsion. Let him continue to think so. It would be safer.

On July 22, Wanderscheid formally served another summons on Ann at the Blair House. Failure to comply, he solemnly warned, could result in a contempt citation. Under those circumstances, Ann replied coldly, she had no choice.

In insisting on such dialogue, Ann was simply assuming her apartment was bugged. It was a logical assumption in Miami where scores of "private eyes" made a living bugging people. Ironically, and despite the later ravings of Senator Edward Long, the only bugging in the Coppola case was ordered by Coppola. Ample evidence was developed later that Ann's phones were tapped. Both Joe and Jaffe assumed from the beginning that their phones were security risks—thus elaborate codes were used. But the IRS was careful to keep its evidence from being tainted—its men used no electronic shortcuts.

Five days after the summons was served, Ann was ready to take her cash to the City National Bank in Coral Gables, a suburb just south of Miami, where under the alias "Ann Osborne" she would pretend to deposit it. Jaffe and other special agents took up stations near the Blair House and followed Ann's white Lincoln as she headed south. She drove at high speed and the agents lost her several times. They caught up with her in time to see her halt in the bank's parking lot.

Jaffe followed Ann inside the bank, watched her talk to the safety-deposit clerk. After waiting ten minutes, he called Wanderscheid and another special agent into the bank. Jaffe strolled over to the clerk and asked to speak to the dark-haired woman who had just rented a box. The clerk hesitated. She would have to get permission from higher authority. She called the bank president. Jaffe showed his credentials and explained he only wanted the woman notified that they were there. The president agreed and the clerk was sent to get "Miss Osborne." She returned with Ann.

"You know me, don't you?" asked Jaffe politely.

Ann nodded coldly.

"Do you want to comply with the terms of the summons you received?"

Ann sighed. "Well, you've got me cold. We might as well get it over with."

The bank president, who had heard everything, nodded his approval and Ann and the agents entered the booth reserved for safety-deposit box holders. Ann opened the oversized handbag she had been clutching and dumped stacks of bills on the table. They were $100 bills in packets of $5,000 each. The agents took turns, one reading the serial numbers while another wrote them down. The process took six hours. Near the end, with the bank ready to close, they decided to speed their working by recording the Federal Reserve prefix number only on a batch of $10 and $20 bills. Even so, it was a very boring business, Joe decided. Ann didn't agree—she enjoyed counting money and had more experience.

The total was $180,110.

When the job was finished, Ann put the money back into her handbag and left the newly rented box empty. She explained:

"I don't want to take a chance of dropping dead with all that money in a box under a fictitious name."

The special agents rode shotgun through the gangster-infested streets of Miami and Miami Beach—where for $20 you could get a man's legs broken and for $50 you could have him killed—to the Blair House, which also was full of hoods along with honest citizens. They watched in some anxiety as she vanished inside with her heavy handbag. To get the kind of money she was carrying, someone might very well arrange for her to "drop dead."

On August 5, Ann met the agents in the Fort Lauderdale IRS office—by now there were fears the Miami office was staked out by Mike. She produced an additional $40,000 in cash. Part of it, she explained, had been in her pocket that day in Coral Gables—in her pocket as a reserve in case the special agents doublecrossed her and held on to the cash in the pocketbook. The rest represented what was left of the $50,000 she had received from Mike in the divorce settlement. It was a little short, she said, because she had spent $15,000 of it since leaving Alton Road. It was expensive to live in the style to which she had become accustomed as a syndicate wife.

The special agents recorded the serial numbers of the additional money and gave it back to Ann. They discovered later she was still playing it safe. June Beckley told of accompanying Ann to various banks where Ann exchanged $100 bills whose serial numbers had been recorded for bills of smaller denominations. Ann had decided she wanted revenge first, but she also wanted to keep her money if she could.

Ann prepared a balance sheet: total gifts from Coppola, plus the divorce settlement, was $277,100. From other sources such as the sale of her house in Kentucky she had received funds that brought the total to $290,100.47. Expenditures which she was able to help the special agents confirm totaled $60,924.88. This left cash on hand of $229,175.59. The agents had actually counted $220,100, leaving only a little more than $9,000 in unaccounted expenditures.

Jaffe and Wanderscheid were very well satisfied. The case against Trigger Mike looked very good indeed. But, if Ann Drahmann suddenly dropped dead there would be no case.

"One of them said: 'If you testify against Mikey we'll kill you.'" ANN DRAHMANN

Eleven

ROBERT F. KENNEDY, A MAN WHO WAS TO PLAY A DECISIVE role in the investigation of Trigger Mike Coppola, visited the Cincinnati–Newport area on September 14, 1960. The author, then a *Courier-Journal* reporter, happened to be there at the same time.

Kennedy was campaigning on behalf of his brother, the next President of the United States. The author, while interested in the campaign, was more concerned at the time with the battle plans of the Newport Ministerial Association. That the two campaigns were related soon became obvious.

The ministers had earlier won a promise from Governor Bert T. Combs—wangled when he was running for election against Happy Chandler—to take action against Newport officials if and when he was presented with solid evidence of corruption. A meeting in September was called to discuss how that promise might be implemented.

Debate was spirited. Some of the ministers were discouraged, ready to quit. For three years they had been fighting and nothing more than a few indictments against minor figures in the prostitution racket had been achieved. Others, such as the Reverend Dudley Pomeroy, felt that the groundwork had been laid for a showdown in 1961.

The issue boiled down to surrender or a new offensive headed by legal counsel. Willing to serve as counsel was Jesse K. Lewis, that old war-horse who as assistant attorney general in 1943 had led the biggest raid in Campbell County history. Later Lewis had been successful in getting the commonwealth's attorney of Kenton County, Ulie Howard, disbarred in federal court. The heat from that action, plus the Kefauver Committee's revelations about the syndicate, had led to the closing of the Lookout House.

Lewis's star had dimmed somewhat in 1955 when he ran for governor as an independent on a pledge he would end organized gambling in Kentucky. This seemed too much of a good thing in a state where the beloved Alben Barkley had boasted: "An attack of virtue could ruin us." Lewis not only lost but in the eyes of many "reasonable men" he had become a zealot, a champion of hopeless causes.

Nevertheless, only such a person would be willing to tackle the syndicate in Newport. The big problem was how to pay him. Lewis, for all his zeal, couldn't work for nothing. Reverend Barkhau suggested a fund drive be launched at the proper psychological time. Meanwhile, he said, the individual ministers could pledge their personal credit to raise funds.

When the vote came, to hire Lewis or quit, the optimists won easily, but there was agreement that if at the end of a year no progress had been made, the ministers would resign en masse and let the devil keep Newport as an annex of hell.

After conferring with their new counsel, the ministers voted to turn Chris Seifried and his team of laymen loose to gather evidence of gambling and prostitution. To permit him time to gather it, they agreed no mention would be made of the decision to hire Lewis. The author was told that when time came for an announcement he could break the story.

Meanwhile, the author learned Kennedy was arriving in town that night. His source was James Lukens, a Cincinnati Teamster Union official who had defied Jimmy Hoffa and worked with Kennedy when he was counsel to the McClellan Committee. Lukens, who was in charge of arrangements, also disclosed that a group of Newport gamblers had offered to pay the costs of a dinner meeting of Kentucky politicians Kennedy was scheduled to address. Luckily, at the last minute, he learned about the sponsors and made new arrangements.

When asked, Lukens promised to arrange a press conference the following morning. He set it up in a hotel room atop one of Cincinnati's tallest towers. The author intended to ask Kennedy about organized crime, but the hostile Cincinnati reporters who crowded into the room had other things on their minds.

Robert Kennedy was winding up a long campaign tour and he seemed on the point of exhaustion when he entered the room. It was a shock to see how small he was, and his frailness was accented somehow by the circles under his eyes and the lines of strain. Politics took its toll and Kennedy was a politician of the most active type. From somewhere he produced a smile and seated himself in the middle of a large couch. The questions came fast and hard.

Only the night before his brother faced a group of Protestant ministers at the Rice Hotel in Houston, Texas, and answered all their questions about the "religious issue." Cincinnati newspapers that morning were full of the story and it seemed there was little left to ask on that subject. But prejudices growing out of that ancient conflict between Catholic and Protestant were still strong in the Cincinnati-Newport area and local reporters were eager to replow the field with Robert Kennedy.

Patiently he answered the old questions with answers that seemed to come automatically and without conscious thought. Almost he seemed to be talking in his sleep. When the newspaper reporters finished, he had to repeat the routine for the television cameras.

Outside the window, Newport was bathed in morning sunlight and seemed somehow in another world. Distance concealed some of the drabness of that town whose population of 30,000 was less in 1960 than it had been in 1910.

When the religious issue was exhausted, there was a pause. The author fired some questions of his own—about Newport and organized crime. Kennedy seemed startled at the abrupt change of subject, then pleased. He sank back on the couch. A little color warmed his face.

Instead of worrying so much about religion, the next Attorney General of the United States declared, the public and the press should give thought to certain other matters of which organized crime was one of the most important.

"How can an Administration handle Khrushchev and Castro when it can't handle Hoffa?" he asked.

Yes, he was familiar with crime conditions in Newport. If his brother was elected President there would be effective action taken against syndicate hoods in Newport and everywhere else. Possibly a national crime commission would be formed. Something had to be done quickly. Organized crime had been too long neglected.

The news conference broke up as an aide reminded Kennedy he was due at another meeting. There was silence as he started from the room, pausing only to shake the author's hand. Next day the *Courier-Journal* had a scoop—the Cincinnati papers made no mention of Kennedy's remarks about organized crime. They headlined the religious issue.

Despite their indifference, however, crime was becoming bigger news in Newport. A weird situation began developing in September, a few days after Kennedy's visit. Circuit Judge Paul Stapleton—appointed to relieve Judge Murphy of the burden of civil cases—was hearing a routine divorce matter. The wife casually mentioned that her husband worked at the Snax Bar—that huge casino next to the Playtorium which represented Pete Schmidt's last effort at empire building.

"What does your husband do at the Snax Bar?" came the routine question.

"He's a dealer of craps," was the routine reply.

Suddenly Judge Stapleton bestirred himself. Times had indeed changed in Newport. In Stapleton's reaction was the proof that the minister's long campaign had aroused public opinion.

The Judge stopped the hearing and summoned Sheriff Norbert Roll, a tall and aging political hack. He orderd the sheriff to go to the Snax Bar "and arrest anyone connected with it if there is evidence of gambling."

Reporters noted a flurry of action. A little later Roll reported that after "a thorough investigation we could find no evidence of gambling."

This was a little raw even for the Cincinnati papers whose editors were beginning to smart a little over the *Courier-Journal*'s repeated scoops. Three hours later two reporters visited the Snax Bar and found a hundred people busy making bets. The reporters dropped $5 of expense money.

The story caused a lot of people to laugh loudly. When the laughter was loud enough, Stapleton ordered the sheriff to try again. He came back to report that "people were eating in the bar part and the door to the back room was locked. We had no search warrant so we left."

An hour later a reporter walked into the back room unchallenged and found the casino in full operation.

Stapleton later disclosed to the author that within minutes after he had ordered the second raid, Charles Lester came into his private office and demanded:

"How long are you going to keep annoying my clients?"

Stapleton said he told Lester "as long as necessary." The silver-haired attorney then picked up the judge's phone, called the Snax Bar, and warned that the sheriff was coming. He listened a moment and hung up with a laugh.

"They knew all about it," he said. "The sheriff is just leaving the courthouse to go down there."

Under the circumstances, Judge Stapleton can perhaps be forgiven for not continuing the effort. An uneasy calm settled over Newport, broken only by news that 420 slot machines shipped from Newport had been seized by the FBI on the docks of New York. They had been intended for England, where gambling had become legal and syndicate hoods were moving in to exploit the opportunity. The exporters had made the mistake of hiring a local company to pack the slots in crates for shipment. The company was headed by Henry Hosea, an honest man and future leader of the reform drive. Hosea had managed to befuddle the gamblers into mislabeling the crates, thus giving the FBI an excuse to seize the machines.

And then came an Act of God—at least that's what the ministers called it. Judge Murphy fell ill. The regular October grand jury was in session and it had no one to whom it could report. The Kentucky Court of Appeals, the state's supreme court, had the duty of appointing a substitute and for reasons no one quite understood it selected Judge Edward G. Hill of Harlan County.

Known as "the Tamer of Bloody Harlan," an area that had known mountaineer feuds and coal mine violence for decades, Hill was a handsome, dark-haired man in his early forties who, outside of court, could drink a hardened hillbilly under the table but who, inside court, insisted on stern decorum. Furthermore, he had attended law school in Cincinnati and knew Newport well.

Arriving in town, the judge accepted the grand jury's routine report which included this passage:

"We dismissed two homicides which resulted from shootings, which upon a mature evaluation of the evidence appeared as manifest cases of justifiable homicide by reason of self-defense."

The law of the frontier still had appeal to juries led by Commonwealth's Attorney Wise.

Hill accepted the report without comment, dismissed the grand jury without thanks, and entered an order convening a special grand jury on May 10. As an afterthought, he ordered some long-stored slot machines destroyed on the courthouse steps.

It was all quite shocking, unprecedented, but the ministers were first to recover their wits. At a special meeting they authorized Seifried to appear before the special grand jury and ask for the indictment of Sheriff Roll for failure to enforce the gambling laws.

Newport was in an uproar. A tentative effort to bribe Judge Hill was made in vain. He was tipped that an effort to frame him with a woman was planned so he moved from a Covington motel to a Cincinnati hotel. All was set for a showdown when on May 10 Judge Murphy rose from his sick bed and literally pulled himself up the stairs to the courtroom where the jury panel was waiting to be selected. He was resuming his duties, he said, taking over from Special Judge Hill. He had no idea why they had been called, he told the jurors, but he gave them his routine charge. They retired to figure out their reason for being.

Again chance favored the reformers. Chosen foreman of the special grand jury was Carl A. Giancola, a retired druggist and a man of honesty and intelligence. Ordinarily the job of foreman went to a gambler's friend but Judge Hill had upset the routine.

With Giancola providing leadership, the grand jury decided to hear the ministers. Four representatives of the Social Action Committee appeared and presented evidence. Officials were called to give their side of the story. As Giancola told it in sworn testimony later:

"Sheriff Roll maintained 'there is no gambling in Newport,' and the jury didn't like that statement very well. We were all sitting on the edge of our chairs and when he said there was no gambling you could just see the jurors flop back. That sunk them. We had no alternative but to indict the sheriff."

Giancola also disclosed that after the indictment had been voted, Wise "came in and tried to talk us out of it." He didn't succeed.

On December 1, the case was scheduled to be tried. Defense attorneys filed notions for dismissal and on the evening before the trial Judge Murphy was still considering them. The author, arriving late in Newport to cover the story, noticed the lights were still burning in Murphy's office at 8:30 P.M. A minister had been assigned to accompany the author—a routine practice—and the pair proceeded up York Street, where a crowd could be seen outside the Yorkshire Club. About fifty people, mostly men, were milling about, complaining loudly that moments before they had been abruptly evicted from the club. No new customers were being admitted either. A man in evening clothes blocked the door with the words:

"Sorry, bub, the joint's closed."

Up and across the street the scene was being repeated at the Flamingo, but no one was guarding the door of Sleepout's joint. Inside the bar the unlicensed liquor was on display and the way to the back room was open.

Incredible confusion existed in the huge casino. Dice tables, blackjack tables, roulette wheels were being dismounted by perspiring men. Wall boards showing results at every major horsetrack in the country were being taken down in the handbook at the rear. The inch-thick carpet was being rolled up. Workmen scurried about in frantic haste, oblivious to the presence of strangers. One was asked:

"What's going on?"

"The sheriff's in trouble," was the reply.

The order to close had been unexpected, coming well after the night's action had begun. But the orders were being obeyed instantly at casinos all over town. At the Snax Bar, which Sheriff Roll had been unable to penetrate, the door to the casino was open and the dismantling process well underway. Not only gaming equipment was being removed and shuttled out a back door, but huge strips of gold wallpaper were being taken down.

Again came the word from a harried supervisor: "The sheriff's in trouble. We hope we won't be closed long."

In the midst of the activity sat two men at a little table. They were playing cards and paid absolutely no attention to repeated requests that they hurry and finish. Intent on their cards they sat there while the room was stripped.

Outside on the streets, cabs from Covington and Cincinnati had hurried to the scene. Disappointed customers were offered alternate entertainment. The cabbies competed at the top of their voices.

"Here for the hottest girls in town," one cabby bellowed.

"Girls, cheap and clean," shouted another.

Not a policeman was to be seen.

Newspapers on street racks bore banner headlines indicating there might not be a trial tomorrow if Judge Murphy accepted the defense motions. The evidence, however, was unmistakable. Someone had decided there would be a trial and had prepared the way for Roll to declare there was no gambling in Newport.

The trial next day was a strain on Wise, who had to give the appearance of prosecuting a political friend. On the basis of the evidence he permitted, the jury had no choice but to acquit the sheriff. The night the trial ended, all Newport joints reopened as usual. Even the gold wallpaper was back at the Snax Bar. Chris Seifried, in a statement that reflected his infinite patience, said:

"I think it is possible that the gamblers have won a victory today and lost a war."

Events were to prove the validity of that appraisal, but any gambler inclined to dismiss it soon had something else to ponder. On November 8, 1960, John F. Kennedy was elected President. Author Theodore H. White has described the scene as the Kennedy clan waited for the returns from Campbell County to come in. Since records had been kept, the county had always been on the side of the winner. The first returns were favorable, but ultimately the county gave Richard M. Nixon 54.2 per cent of its votes. Those appeals to religious prejudice had paid off. And perhaps some of the gamblers remembered Robert Kennedy's pledge at that press conference a few weeks earlier.

One person who remembered it was Ann Drahmann.

It had been a long hot summer for Ann, a period of growing tension and impatience. The first warning had come on July 21 when "two good friends" called to suggest she'd better leave town "if you don't want to get hurt." On August 25, she met with Wanderscheid and Jaffe, signing a long statement about her life with Mike and giving answers to questions she had earlier declined to answer. She told them that Mike had managed to hide from her a $10,000 diamond necklace. She had called the house repeatedly but Mike had refused to give it back. Finally she had used her key again and entered the house while Mike was away. Unable to find the necklace, she had taken $9,700 from his plant. When next she called Mike for the necklace, she told him she had taken the money and would keep it until the necklace was returned. Mike didn't believe her. She told him to check his plant. He returned soon to the phone and almost fused the line in his rage.

Later, said Ann, Mike sent a hood to the Blair House with orders to get his money. She told him to get out when he didn't produce the necklace. The situation was now a standoff. Did the agents think Mike might go to the police and charge her with breaking and entering? He had her apartment under watch, she said, and any car that lingered near the building was checked out by Mike's men.

Jaffe asked her if she wanted a guard, warning her that Mike might try anything. Ann refused. Joan, who had been sent to Cincinnati, was back with her in the apartment. She thought she was safe with Joan there.

The daily meetings with Wanderscheid continued and the pressure on Joe increased with every meet. Ann was, in his words, "a living doll," and constant association was a strain as it would be with any normal man. He tried to head off trouble by warning Ann they must keep their relationship impersonal. If it became anything else they might blow the case.

Ann accepted the argument. Winning had become an obsession. Her fears for Joan and the plans to travel had become secondary. Mike had to be punished. She had gone too far to stop now. After he was convicted, as she put it to Joe, "we'll think of the future." Wanderscheid wasn't too sure what she had in mind for him and he was afraid to ask. He formed the habit of arriving early when the meeting place was a church parking lot. A few minutes of meditation inside the church restored his sense of balance. Once he asked Ann if she didn't want to go inside with him. "It might help the case," said Joe. Even this bait was insufficient. Ann had traveled a long road since that day in school when Sister Arcadia punished her for not becoming a stool pigeon.

About 8:30 on the night of October 20, both telephones rang in her apartment. She picked up one phone. The party at the other end breathed loudly and said nothing. The same was true of the other phone. She hung both up but when she tried to make a call neither line worked. Somehow the callers had tied up both her phones.

Suspecting that Trigger Mike was up to something, Ann leaned out of the window and asked the doorman-guard below to call the telephone numbers of the Midtown Social Club. He soon reported that both lines there were busy. Suspicion became certainty—Mike was pulling a fast one.

Never thinking the trick might be designed to get her to leave the apartment in order to make a call, Ann decided to take a ride. She got into the white Lincoln and drove out of the parking lot. Suddenly there was movement in the back seat. A man who had been hidden there climbed into the front of the car and ordered her to drive north along Collins Avenue.

"You think you're a real smart whore, don't you." said the man, making conversation.

"Whatta you mean?" asked Ann. She had never been afraid of hoods and wasn't now.

"You're not going to hurt Mikey," replied the stranger. "Just yourself. You can't hurt Mikey—he's in the clear."

"If he's in the clear why are you bothering me?" asked Ann.

"Because we don't like stoolies. We'll teach you to get out of town and leave Mikey alone."

Ann noticed another car was now following them. She stole a glance at her companion. He resembled Chuck White, Charles "the Blade" Tourine's son, but it wasn't Chuck.

They drove north to the area known as Eastern Shores, and turned off to the right. Beyond she could hear the pounding of surf. It was a black night and the spot in which she was ordered to stop was even blacker. The car behind stopped too and a man got out. It was too dark to see his face. They pulled her bodily from the car and onto the beach.

"You got to let Mikey alone," said the first man. "If you don't we'll kill you."

The beating began. Over the years Ann had learned much about avoiding punishment. She managed to turn, taking many of the blows on her hip and thighs. These bums were hitting below the belt. She fell and absorbed a few kicks. Consciousness was fading when at last the men finished with her. She lay there, moaning softly, as the men returned to their car. When she was sure they were gone, she tried to stand. Her right leg was stiff, unbending. Somehow, she pulled herself to the car. Luckily they had left the key. She got the motor started and managed to drive back to the street. But the effort was too painful to maintain. She stopped and began blowing the horn. Consciousness came and went as the horn shattered the stillness. After what seemed an eternity, a North Miami Beach police car pulled alongside. The officers drove her to their station. She told them the beating was "a federal matter."

At 2:30 A.M. FBI Special Agent Bob Fetzner called Joe Wanderscheid and told him he had been contacted by the North Miami Beach police chief, who reported Ann Drahmann had been beaten by hoods and was in a state of shock. She had been found, Fetzner said, at Northeast 22nd Avenue and 163rd Street.

Joe called the chief and confirmed the story. Mrs. Drahmann was being sent home in a cab, he said. Joe suggested she should have some protection. The chief agreed to follow in a car and promised to ask Ann to call Joe when she reached her apartment.

At 3:30 A.M., Ann reported she was safely back in the Blair House. She felt awful, she said, but had not called a doctor. No, there was nothing else to do at the moment. Just get the goods on that yellow-bellied bastard, Mike Coppola.

Wanderscheid debated calling Jaffe but decided his friend needed sleep. Next day the two agents drove to the Blair House and spotted Ann limping out of the parking lot. She got into the back seat, assisted by Joe, and said the pain was getting worse. It was decided to take her to a doctor. She named the man she wanted and when contacted he suggested the examination be conducted at a hospital. When X-rays revealed no broken bones, Ann insisted on going home despite the doctor's advice that she stay in the hospital. Joan was alone in the apartment, Ann explained, and Mike might strike next at her.

On the ride back, Ann disclosed that in the early morning hours she had received three calls from Coppola. He accused her of being on the telephone all night in the first call. In the second he elaborated—she had been making nuisance calls to his friends. The third time he called, he began:

"Well, you whore, I hear you've been laying guys in your car up on Eastern Shores."

The gangster had been in a good humor. He continued by accusing her of seducing the two agents who were investigating him and assuring her that if the case went to court he would produce witnesses to prove she got all her money from prostitution.

"I guess that would make me the highest-priced whore in history," said Ann with grim humor.

Next day Ann was sufficiently recovered to hold a press conference. She accused Coppola of arranging the beating. Responsible newspapers gave her good and sympathetic coverage—after all, she was a pretty woman and Mike was notorious—but a Miami Beach scandal sheet took a different line. Under an unflattering picture of Ann on the front page, it ran these cutlines:

"TROUBLES—Ann Drahmann (or Ex-Mrs. Mike Coppola) unhappily contemplates her various mounting problems as her latest occurrence is disbelieved by the Police Department. After being arrested on May 8, of this year, for drunken driving in Miami Beach, and now this, certainly doesn't give her too much to smile about."

The drunken driving rap, one of several charges, had long before been taken care of by Ben Cohen, who had his own reasons for maintaining a friendly relationship with Ann. But the underworld got the message. On October 27, Ann reported that because of the beating and the publicity, even her friends would no longer accompany her. She was beginning to feel very much alone and a little frightened. She was staying in the apartment all the time now, leaving the shopping to Joan. Word from sources had it that Mike would kill her if she tried to testify.

Again and again she asked Jaffe to speed up the probe, cut the red tape, get Mike indicted. Patiently, the special agent explained that certain procedures had to be followed. Accuracy, not haste, was the theory on which the complicated route a case had to follow was based. There was no way to hurry the process unless someone on the top level ordered it done. Jaffe didn't add that one top IRS official frowned on using a man's wife as the key witness in such a case. She had enough troubles without that, but it was something that bothered both Joe and Jaffe.

A few days later, when John F. Kennedy became President-elect, Ann suddenly had a bright idea. At the proper time she would appeal to Robert Kennedy. He would get things moving.

By late January 1961, the investigation seemed virtually complete. With Ann furnishing the leads, the agents had gathered ample evidence to confirm her testimony. Without her help many of Mike's concealed expenditures could never have been found. In many cases, Ann called the merchant or tradesman personally to refresh his memory.

An incident in December increased Ann's impatience. Joan, who had been given an allowance of $100 a week and left to her own devices, was picked up by Miami Beach police and charged with driving under the influence of barbiturates, possession of narcotic drugs, and abusive language. Ann produced a doctor who said he had prescribed the drugs for Joan, and the charges were ultimately dismissed. This reminder of Joan's problem increased her eagerness to get through with Mike's case so she could begin the already delayed process of rehabilitation.

The letter to Robert F. Kennedy, now Attorney General, was written at the end of January. Ann said she feared a long waiting period might result in her murder. She was ready to testify—why couldn't the red tape be cut?

Aware the letter was being sent, Wanderscheid brooded over the next problem that would arise—the prosecutor. Much would depend on him. One night he happened to call his old friend of Texas days, Fred Ugast. Fred became interested in the Coppola case and suddenly Joe had a bright idea—Ugast was just the man for the job. He was pleased when Fred said he would ask for it.

Quick action was needed for suddenly all systems were Go. Within hours of receiving Ann's letter, Kennedy sent word to Miami. He wanted the final report completed and approved and on his desk by the following Monday—six days away.

Ordinarily, at least six weeks would have been required.

Under Supervisor Dick Wallace's direction, Jaffe and Wanderscheid buckled down to work. District and regional officials whose approval was required were brought to Miami by plane. In an unprecedented burst of speed, the report was finished and on Kennedy's desk by the day specified.

Only one disagreement marred the project. Jaffe included in the report a recommendation that Ann be given around-the-clock protection. The then district chief of intelligence objected and pressured Jaffe to delete the item. Knowing full well he was risking his chance for promotion, Jaffe refused. One day after the report reached Washington, Kennedy ordered the recommendation implemented.

Wallace and Jaffe carried the word to Ann at the Blair House. When told men would be guarding her night and day, Ann—who had become rather lonely—smiled broadly and commented:

"Well, as the governor of North Carolina said to the governor of South Carolina—it's been a long time between drinks."

The handsome nephew of Elmer Irey turned beet red. Jaffe, who had become accustomed to Ann's humor, laughed loudly.

"Operation Baby-sit" began.

Ann was taken to Homestead Air Force Base near the Florida

Keys and installed in VIP quarters. Two special agents were ordered to guard her at all times and additional Air Force Police equipped with dogs were assigned to protect her from the vengeance of Trigger Mike. She left the base only to testify before the federal grand jury.

On April 21, 1961, the grand jury indicted Coppola on four counts of income tax evasion. Fred Ugast was assigned to prosecute, assisted by the brilliant Lawrence K. Bailey.

Kennedy really meant what he said that day in Cincinnati, Ann decided.

"You know how greatly I admire the Attorney General." ANN DRAHMANN

Twelve

EVEN AS ROBERT KENNEDY INTERVENED IN MIAMI TO SPEED the case against Trigger Mike, events began in Newport that would shortly give the aggressive Attorney General a chance to act against the syndicate there.

One thing led to another as the syndicate and its political allies sought to counter the growing influence of the ministers. Every countermove failed, however, and triggered still another development until some gangsters decided that maybe God was on the side of the preachers after all. It was safer to blame God than their own stupidity.

Taking advantage of the indignation created by the acquittal of Sheriff Roll, the ministers began a fund drive which was climaxed on February 12, 1961, with a "United Sunday" in area churches. Newport ministers were joined by colleagues in neighboring Kenton and Boone Counties, Kentucky, and in Hamilton County, Ohio. Each minister participating preached on the evils of vice and crime, hitting hard not so much at the moral aspects but at the practical results of such conditions. Contributions poured in as the *Courier-Journal* carried the story, and they came from all parts of Kentucky, Indiana, and Ohio. Suddenly there was ample money to pay Attorney Lewis to push ouster proceedings against those officials who had tolerated crime.

In an effort to offset the propaganda of the preachers, the Campbell grand jury issued a report just four days after United Sunday. It was an amazing document, declaring as it did the jury's belief that conditions in Newport were no worse than in other cities, and belittling the efforts of the reformers. This technique had been used to good advantage in the past. The jury also declared:

"A Community in many ways chooses its way of life as do individuals. Its choice is reflected in the voice of the electorate. If that way of life be distasteful to some, let it be submitted to a plebiscite. Some, of course, will find any way of life distasteful."

Such an argument might have appealed to former Governor Happy Chandler, who once proclaimed his belief "in the right of the people to have it dirty," and it certainly echoed the sentiments of Mayor Mussman. But times had changed in Newport and there were plenty of people, encouraged by the minister's stand, who didn't buy the argument that Newport was the kind of place they wanted.

Using the grand jury report as a club, the *Courier-Journal* began demanding action from newly elected Governor Combs. Taking advantage of the editorial support from the state's largest newspaper, the ministers and their attorney descended on Frankfort on March 2 and presented a thirty-one-page affidavit demanding the ouster from office of eight Newport and Campbell County officials for failing to suppress gambling, prostitution, and illegal liquor sales. The governor hesitated, promising to study the matter.

Now the ministers had allies. A group of Campbell County businessmen formed themselves into a "Committee of 500" and sent a long letter to Combs in support of the ministers. One of those signing the letter was George W. Ratterman.

A native of Cincinnati, Ratterman at age thirty-four had already a varied career behind him. With brawn to match his brains, he had played quarterback at Notre Dame behind the great Johnny Lujack. Leaving school without getting his law degree, Ratterman married his childhood sweetheart, Anne Hengelbrok, a native of Newport, and began playing professional football. During the ten years that followed he played pro ball in the daytime and attended night school until he obtained his law degree. Coming at last to the Cleveland Browns he found himself second to the great Otto Graham. Ratterman, one of the highest paid players in the game, was content to let Graham get the glory and the bruises. In 1956, he got into a game long enough to be injured badly enough to end his career. He returned to Cincinnati to work for an investment firm. His home was in Fort Thomas, however—that exclusive suburb where such men as Sleepout Louis and Charles Lester lived.

As a boy and as a man Ratterman had well understood conditions in Newport, and as the father of eight children he wanted to do something about them. Some of his friends, he discovered, such as Jack Cook, were members of the Social Action Committee. Ratterman attended a few sessions and was disturbed to discover he was the only Catholic there. He began a personal drive to bring more Catholics into the reform movement.

The Committee of 500 gave him his chance. It quickly became the political arm of the do-gooders. As one wag put it: "The ministers carry the Cross while we carry the Flag." Catholics who shunned the Social Action Committee were persuaded to join the businessmen. Ratterman even convinced the Bishop of Covington to issue a statement in favor of reform and the ouster from office of those who had failed in their duty.

In the heavily Catholic community of Newport proper, the bishop's statement had tremendous impact. The Committee of 500 began to grow so fast it was decided to sponsor a reform candidate for sheriff in the upcoming election. As chief law-enforcement officer, the sheriff had, in theory at least, wide powers. He could go anywhere in the county, inside Newport and outside. In practice over the years the sheriff had confined himself to tax-collecting and a county police force had handled law-enforcement outside municipalities. At least it did in theory—in practice the county force did little more than chase traffic violators who didn't have any pull with the syndicate.

The problem was to find a suitable, and willing, candidate. When no one else would volunteer, Ratterman consented. On April 4, at an overflow meeting in a hall above the Newport Public Library, Ratterman took the plunge.

"I am willing to run for office if you people are really serious," he told the crowd. "Let the battle be joined now for I shall not accept one penny of their foul money nor shall I be influenced by their cheap threats. . . ."

The only person who did not stand in applause at the end of the speech was Red "the Enforcer" Masterson. The man who once boasted to the author that he got his "first square meal in a Newport whorehouse," sat as if stunned as cheers thundered defiance to the casinos down the street.

But others were quick to accept the challenge. They framed George Ratterman.

First plans called for Henry Cook, counsel for the Committee of 500 and long a thorn in the side of Charles Lester, to be framed. A former Beverly Hills Club dancer who, when she got too tired to dance, had taken a business course and found a job as one of Cook's secretaries, was to be used. A local gambler with whom she was in love suggested her name and Tito Carinci, that pal of Gil Beckley, made the proposition.

Carinci operated what was now called the Tropicana Club in the old Glenn Hotel. The name, Glenn Rendezvous, had become too notorious. Suckers were afraid to visit it so Carinci installed some neon nudes on the marquee and put up a new sign. The suckers returned in droves. A handsome ex-football player, Carinci lived much of the time at the old Lookout Stud Farm, which was still owned by the widow of Jimmy Brink.

The dancer flatly refused to help Carinci trap Cook in a compromising situation, but when fast-moving developments made Ratterman a more logical target, she was approached again. When her gambler boyfriend promised to marry her if she would help, the girl agreed. At the last minute, however, loyalty to Cook and the cause for which he fought caused her to back out and Carinci was forced to find an understudy in a hurry. The original choice later slashed her wrists on the eve of a trial and was hospitalized. Her part in the complicated affair never became public knowledge.

The plot was basically simple, containing as it did ingredients from two successful frames of the past. One of the models was the manner in which detective Jack Thiem was run out of town. Many of the witnesses against Thiem were to be used against Ratterman. The second model involved a Catholic priest who, several years earlier, had been ruined when pictures of him were taken with an unclad girl.

Ratterman had somehow to be lured to the Tropicana Club where pictures would be made under compromising circumstances. He would then be blackmailed into withdrawing from the race at a time when it would be too late for the reformers to field a substitute. As things turned out, it became necessary to use an alternate plan.

That old friend of the Coppolas, Gil "the Brain" Beckley, was present during the early stages of the affair. Ratterman was asked by a friend, Thomas Paisley, to meet Carinci at the Tropicana. According to the naïve Paisley, Carinci had decided to quit the rackets and move to New York. He needed help in making the break. Assuming that if Carinci was sincere he might have much information of value to the reformers, Ratterman agreed to meet him at a Cincinnati restaurant. He had no intention of going to the Tropicana, having learned the nature of that joint in the days when he was a happy-go-lucky football player. The meeting took place about 10:30 P.M. in a small foyer outside the Gourmet Room of the Terrace Hilton Hotel.

Beckley sat just inside the Gourmet Room where he could see the action. With Carinci, he had attended the Kentucky Derby a few days earlier. Unfortunately, Trigger Mike didn't make the Derby that year. He was having domestic trouble.

Ratterman, Carinci, and Paisley ordered drinks and discussed football, politics, and Tito's plans for leaving Newport. At one point, Carinci left the others and consulted with Beckley. After the third drink things suddenly became hazy for Ratterman. It was later discovered, and pinpointed by scientific analysis, that chloral hydrate had been placed in that third drink. The schedule didn't call for Ratterman to be knocked out by the dose. A state line lay between the Terrace Hilton and the Tropicana Club and Ratterman had to be conscious when he crossed it. The boys told themselves they were too smart to give the FBI a kidnapping angle to use for an investigation of Newport.

When Ratterman was sufficiently groggy as to be unaware of what he was doing, Beckley left the hotel and checked with the reception committee at the Tropicana. Then, satisfied that all was well, he caught an early morning plane for Miami—the one Trigger Mike had tried to catch two years before.

Carinci, meanwhile, managed to steer Paisley, who was rather drunk, and the drugged Ratterman to the elevator and then to a car. They stopped at a friendly bar near the river to assure themselves of witnesses who could testify Ratterman was willingly accompanying them. Then Ratterman, by now aware of things only in flashes, was loaded in the car and taken across the river to Newport. He kept ordering the driver to "Take me home" but the driver had other plans. The Tropicana was entered through the back door and Ratterman was hustled up to a bedroom on the third floor which Tito maintained for the benefit of special guests who might desire a quick roll with a show girl.

It was then that original plans began to go astray. Thomas

Withrow, a man who played a key role in the Thiem frame, was supposed to be on hand to take a picture. He didn't show. Neither did the dancer. Carinci met the latter problem by going to the first floor where the nightclub was located and ordering stripper April Flowers to cut short her act and report to the third floor where he was entertaining a "friend." Returning upstairs, Carinci found a dazed Ratterman on the second floor looking for an exit. The muscular Carinci turned him around and marched him like a broken puppet back to the bedroom.

In the photographer's absence—and repeated efforts to find him failed—the alternate plan was put in motion. Marty Buccieri, boss of the casino, which was also on the third floor, closed down abruptly and ordered all customers out. There was no need to embarrass the cops who soon would be coming. April met the shills and stickmen as she went upstairs. Briefly she wondered why they were leaving so early.

Waiting at the police station was Detective Pat Ciafardini, another man who had played a part in the Thiem frame and who had "investigated" the Screw Andrews' killing of Melvin Clark. A handsome, flashy man, Ciafardini had been at the Tropicana early in the evening waiting for his girl friend, waitress Gay Fine, to finish. When word came that Ratterman had arrived, he left to await a call if needed. The call came at 2:30 A.M., and the man making it was the lover of the ex-dancer who had refused to cooperate.

Although off duty at the time, Ciafardini called in a cruising police car and ordered the two officers inside to take him to the Tropicana Club. "Ratterman's there," he explained. Carinci was waiting on the first floor by the camouflaged elevator. No one had warrants but when Tito put up token resistance, the men "arrested" him and he went up in the elevator to make sure they found the right room.

April, who had no idea of her duties, had shed her scanty costume and was wearing only a red and rather transparent gown. She was sitting on the bed attempting to awaken the fully dressed Ratterman when the cops came charging in. Earlier, a second stripper had been assigned to get Paisley out of the way, and Ratterman had been given a fully loaded drink which knocked him out.

The cops headed for Ratterman on the bed. April slipped into the next room. A few seconds later Ciafardini entered. She had known him for a long time.

"What's going on, Pat?" she asked.

Ciafardini, not realizing girls had been switched, winked and took her by the arm. "We're going to jail," he said.

Ratterman was half awake—his slumber interrupted when the cops began pulling off his trousers. They wrapped him in a bedspread and took him to headquarters. The entire raid, from the time Ciafardini received the original call, had taken only seventeen minutes. In that time, he had called in another police car from some blocks away, driven six blocks to the Tropicana, crossed the street, arrested Carinci at the elevator, gone upstairs and arrested Ratterman and April, descended to the street and driven back to the station where it was necessary to climb a long flight of steps. Quite an achievement, everyone agreed.

Bond was set at $5,000 each. A local bondsman who knew the score conferred with Charles Lester, who suddenly arrived, and made bond for April and Tito. He refused to post bond for Ratterman, saying the candidate lacked security.

By 3:15 A.M., after several bungling attempts to dial, Ratterman called Henry Cook, who managed to get the candidate released on bond. They drove to Ratterman's home in Fort Thomas where Anne Ratterman was waiting. Along the way, Cook remarked:

"This will make you or break you."

The night wasn't over for the conspirators. The police officers, Lester, Carinci, and Buccieri met again on the third floor of the Glenn Hotel—presumably to compare notes. Ciafardini left at 4:15 A.M. to go to the home of Police Court Judge Joseph Rolf, the man who would be judge and jury at the trial of Ratterman. Another conference followed at the Flamingo Club, where Sleepout Louis was briefed.

It had been a busy night for a lot of people.

The news hit Newport with the coming of daylight and the impact was that of an atomic bomb. Gamblers were beside themselves with delight and reformers were angry as never before. It was soon apparent that in one respect, at least, someone had miscalculated. Newport had become too sophisticated—it knew a frame when it saw one. The Reverend Donald Baker, a pioneer in the reform drive, was downtown where he heard the news.

"In one-two order," he said, "the word came down the street: 'Ratterman's arrested' and 'It's a frame.'"

Instead of shock and disgust on the part of the do-gooders, there was sympathy for Ratterman, his pretty wife, and their eight children—sympathy and the conviction that this was the last straw.

Ciafardini, meanwhile, was holding a continuous press conference, though he got his story so confused reporters were ordered by his superiors to stick to the original police report.

Late in the afternoon, a tired Ratterman called a press conference of his own. Scores of reporters arrived, for by then the story of a reformer allegedy caught in bed with a stripper had tickled the fancy of editors all over the country. Newport was national news now. George began his statement with the remark:

"A funny thing happened to me yesterday on the way home from the office."

He then read a prepared statement, charging bluntly he had been drugged and framed and detailing the events of the evening before as well as he could remember them. Father P. H. Ratterman, his brother and dean of men at Xavier University where Carinci had played football, gave substance to the charge by reading aloud the results of blood tests conducted earlier in the day at a reputable Cincinnati laboratory. Chloral hydrate in massive amounts had been found in Ratterman's blood.

While the press conference was in session, the Newport Ministerial Association was holding an emergency meeting in the next room. Reverend Pomeroy, president of the group, presented a statement to the assembled reporters. It asserted the belief that Ratterman was framed and reaffirmed "our intention to support George Ratterman's candidacy for Campbell County sheriff."

The ministers were acting on more than faith alone, as later events proved. But flashbulbs lighted the room as Baptist minister shook hands with Catholic layman. For once the old hostility dating to Know-Nothing days were forgotten. The moral stalemate which Ratterman had tried to break by his appeal to the Bishop of Covington was now ended—and the underworld had only itself to blame.

That night April Flowers played to a small but select audience at the Tropicana Club. She almost missed the show entirely. When released from jail, she had found her bags packed and stored in her red convertible parked outside the club. Still bewildered, she had protested. Someone decided she would be useful as a witness, and Carinci ordered the bags taken upstairs once more.

Her act consisted of a dance featuring dots of light reflected on the walls and ceiling from tiny mirrors attached to her costume. As she stripped, the lights decreased in number and the act was over when the last light went out. The audience, consisting entirely of federal agents and the author, applauded politely.

Cook secured a one-day delay in the trial which began on May 10. So great were the crowds it was deemed necessary to move from police court to a larger courtroom—the one used for so many years by Judge Murphy. Even so, the place was packed, and people filled the halls outside. A standing woman fainted from the heat and had no place to fall.

Lester, faint color showing in his pallid cheeks, represented April and Carinci. Cook was Ratterman's attorney. Mayor Mussman, who smilingly dismissed the affair as a "ten-dollar police court case," sat at the table with prosecutor Thomas Hirschfeld.

The first three days were bitter medicine for the reformers. Judge Rolf, who had met with Ciafardini in the hours after Ratterman's arrest, ruled that the three cases be tried separately and called April's case first. Ratterman was called as a witness against April and for the better part of two days, Lester and Hirschfeld battered him back and forth while Cook stood by helpless to interfere. Witness after witness lied—they were to admit the lies later in federal court—and Ratterman's reputation was smeared again and again. Watching him was his wife, wearing a white hat and a string of pearls against a dark dress. Without a conscious gesture she made a striking contrast to the two strippers on the other side of the room.

At the end of April's "trial," the judge took motions for dismissal under advisement, and Ratterman became the official defendant. The prosecution began once more with the lying witnesses and looked forward to Ratterman's testimony in his own defense. Carinci became so bored he began blowing bubble gum into huge balls, and an alert photographer snapped a picture using natural light. At the end of the third day the prosecution rested. Henry Cook would now have a chance to present the other side.

With the gamblers assuming the fun and games were over, the crowd thinned as court opened on Saturday, the fourth day of the trials. Committee of 500 wives finally got a chance to sit down.

Lester didn't even bother to show up, assuming the rest was routine. Opinions were divided as to who had put on the best show—Carinci with his appeals to Ratterman from the witness chair to "be a man," or Ciafardini with his exhortations to God "to strike me dead if I'm not telling the truth."

April had put on a good act too, all agreed, but she was just a little too skinny. The other stripper who had entertained Paisley had the edge for looks and had come up with the best line: "The couch was too narrow to make love."

Slowly Henry Cook stood to call his first witness. The ex-United States Attorney had a flair for the dramatic. Everyone stared at each other as the name of the witness was called—Mrs. Nancy Hay. No one had heard of her.

She proved to be the sixty-eight-year-old grandmother of Mrs. Thomas Withrow, and she held herself proudly as she entered. A hush settled over the courtroom as she told of receiving a call from Lester on April 14. Lester had asked her to have Withrow, with whom she lived, to call him. She passed on the message, she said, and was present when Tom returned the call.

Hirschfeld wasn't sure what this was leading to, but he asked the witness why she had come forward to testify. The grandmother replied evenly but with telling scorn:

"Because I pride myself on being a good Christian and a good citizen."

"No more questions," said Hirschfeld.

"Call Thomas Withrow," said Cook.

Withrow, short and stocky and more than a little scared, took the stand. Lester, he said, told him to go to the Tropicana Club and see Marty Buccieri about taking some pictures. He quoted Lester as adding:

" 'You will be well paid for this. I got your name from Bill Wise.' "

A sign went around the courtroom at the mention of the commonwealth's attorney.

Obeying instructions, Withrow said, he drove immediately to the Tropicana Club. The meeting took place in what he called "the old casino," and "Marty started talking like I knew exactly what was going on. I guess he figured Lester had this set up already."

" 'Now we want you to take this picture,' " Withrow quoted the casino manager as saying. " 'It'll be of a man and a woman. It'll be in a room. We'll open the door. You take the picture and jump out. We'll protect you.' "

The photographer said he pretended to agree, but asked himself: "What in the hell am I getting myself into here?" Upon request, he gave Buccieri his card with his home number. When he got home, however, he told his wife:

"If Marty calls tell him I'm not here."

A lot of things had happened since the time Thiem was framed—and perhaps the most important was his marriage to a wife with a strong-minded grandmother. She had persuaded him, it developed later, to take his story to a minister in the hours following Ratterman's arrest.

Another sign went around the room as Withrow finished. Hirschfeld looked bewildered. Lester was not present and Mayor Mussman, no longer chuckling, was no help.

The next witness was Mrs. Thomas Withrow. She completed the chain of events, telling of a telephone call to her home at 1:35 o'clock on the morning of Ratterman's arrest. The call came, previous testimony indicated, exactly five minutes after Ratterman entered the Tropicana Club and Ciafardini left for the police station. The caller asked for Withrow.

"He said he needed Tom right away," Mrs. Withrow testified. "He said he wanted a picture taken and how soon could I reach him? I said that it would be approximately ten minutes. I asked him who was calling and he hesitated and said, 'This is Marty. Have him call Marty at the Glenn Hotel.' "

Remembering her husband's instructions, Mrs. Withrow made no attempt to find Tom. At 2 A.M. the phone rang again. It continued to ring at intervals until 3 A.M. Mrs. Withrow and her grandmother let it ring and stared silently at each other. What kind of devilment was going on at the Glenn? Next morning they found out.

Hirschfeld had no questions on cross examination. He sat as if stunned. Cook, sensing the man needed time, moved the court recess for lunch. Judge Rolf, who looked like a ghost despite his polka-dot bow tie, was quick to grant the motion.

Federal court records tell what happened next. Hirschfeld called Lester, told him what had happened, and asked, he said, for information to counter the damaging testimony of the Withrows. Lester replied, "I'll think of something," and urged him to delay the trial until Monday.

Unaware of this byplay, reporters scurried back to the courthouse eager to see if Henry Cook had yet another bomb up his sleeve. Others who had heard radio bulletins came flocking to the scene. Strangely absent, however, were the gamblers, pimps, and prostitutes who had attended the first days of the trials.

When Rolf tapped his gavel, Hirschfeld stood up. "I know Thomas Withrow," he said, "and I'm inclined to believe his testimony. This is not a Police Court case. I think it should be investigated by the grand jury."

"I agree," said Rolf. He tapped the gavel again. "Case dismissed; court's adjourned." And he literally ran out of the room.

The crowd broke into no wild applause. It was a quieter, more solemn kind of joy. Men shook hands . . . women kissed and cried. Mrs. Ratterman stood on her toes to kiss her husband. "I've always been proud of George," she said, "and I have always considered it an honor to be his wife."

Far away, Ann Drahmann read those words a few days later and wept.

Carinci, the only principal present—he had just come from Lester—lowered his head and made a line plunge through the crowd. In his days at Xavier, it would have been a touchdown.

The Rattermans vanished into the offices behind the bench. The crowd surged out into the second-floor hall and waited. When George and Anne reappeared, the applause began. It came in waves, louder and yet louder. It followed him down the grimy stairs, past the mural of civic virtue on the stairwell, to the first level of the courthouse. Ratterman moved slowly, accepting kisses, returning handshakes. And still the applause continued. Out the door and into the bright May sunshine went the procession. Lester, from his office up the street, could see it. Sleepout Louis at the Flamingo could hear it.

Echoes of that applause were heard in New York, Miami Beach, and Las Vegas. Some of the more intelligent gamblers packed their bags and caught planes immediately, thus assuring themselves the first shot at available jobs in other cities. Most gamblers waited, however, unable to believe the revolution had arrived.

Action and reaction . . . the gamblers had tried to counter the ministers' appeal to the governor by discrediting Ratterman. The effort had boomeranged and now the Governor had no choice. He stalled a few weeks as public indignation mounted across the state, but on June 7 he ordered ouster hearings against four top law-enforcement officials—Sheriff Roll, Newport Police Chief Gugel, Newport Detective Chief Leroy Fredericks, and Campbell County Police Chief Harry Stuart.

The big heat was on, and would get hotter. A federal grand jury began probing the possibility Ratterman's civil rights had been violated by his arrest. The FBI was ordered to assist. Robert Kennedy now had the handle he needed in Newport.

"I'm not as brave as I thought I was." ANN DRAHMANN

Thirteen

MIKE COPPOLA WAS FIGHTING BACK. ANN WAS OUT OF HIS reach temporarily but secure in the belief that every man has his price, Mike began probing for a weak spot in the enemy's organization.

Utilizing mutual friends, he hired persons alleged to have "influence" in Washington and asked them to help him get the case dropped. He explained to the individuals that the government had no real case against him. His only mistake, he said, had been to marry the widow of a rich Newport gambler. When his wife, the ex-widow, discovered he was planning to leave her, she conspired with various federal agents to frame him.

The money the government was trying to charge to him, he continued blandly, was really the widow's dough. Everyone knew how profitable the rackets in Newport were—and that's where the money came from.

All of this, Mike continued, he had personally explained to officials in Washington. He had even told them the location of a safe-deposit box near Newport where his ex-wife kept all her money. As additional proof of his story he had given the government some tape recordings which proved conclusively in her own words that she was trying to frame him. Nevertheless, Bobby Kennedy wanted a quick kill in his alleged "War on Crime" and no one paid any attention to the evidence.

Coppola was being persecuted just like Hoffa, the sob story continued.

Part of Mike's story was true—he had told officials in Washington the tale. Perhaps rememberejng that in the corrupt days following World War II, he had talked federal officials out of prosecuting him, Mike had sought to repeat his performance. It was an almost fatal mistake.

Experts examined the recording Mike submitted and found it a jumble of phrases and sentences from a dozen conversations with Ann. Mike had taken what he wanted out of context, rearranged them to give the impression of one continuous conversation, and rerecorded it. For the agents it was confirmation that Ann's telephone had been bugged. And for Ann it was the answer why Mike had continually called her and baited her into losing her temper and returning threat for threat.

The charge that Ann's money came from Charley Drahmann was harder to disprove. Jaffe was dispatched to the Newport-Covington area to seek the truth. Special Agent Earl DeVoto, a veteran campaigner there, was assigned to help him. They ran down every lead in a town where rumors of Ann's wealth were still alive. Screw Andrews was one of many gangsters they interviewed, and he provided some comic relief. Accompanied by his attorney, Morris Weintraub, Andrews gave a statement which contained several lies. Months later, as the trial date drew near, Weintraub called Jaffe in Miami and demanded a copy of the statement. Apparently Screw had forgotten which lies he had told and wanted to refresh his memory before testifying. When Jaffe refused to send a copy, Weintraub "raised hell" and even protested to Bill Hummel, district chief of intelligence in Louisville.

A conscientious investigation disclosed that there was no foundation to the story. In the process of hunting, the special agents were able to shatter another potential defense—that Ann's money came from loans to Mike. None of the boys in Newport, however friendly they might be to Mike, wanted to call attention to their own finances by perjuring themselves on Mike's behalf. They had troubles enough of their own, what with the Ratterman investigation and the continuing pressure of the ministers. Newport was alive with federal agents —it was no time to stick one's neck out.

Thus the heat in Newport had a definite negative effect on Trigger Mike's efforts to mount a defense. In the old days the boys would have given him anything he needed, but not now. And in his eagerness to avoid a trial, to settle out of court, he had tipped his hand too soon. Had he waited until the trial was under way to produce the fake recording and present his allegations about Drahmann's wealth, Ugast might have had trouble disproving them in the limited time available.

So Mike was left to contemplate news stories he received from Los Angeles, where Mickey Cohen was on trial for income tax evasion. Cohen was the Brooklyn-Cleveland transplant who had taken over for the syndicate on the West Coast after the boys executed Lansky's old partner, Bugsy Siegel. Lou Rothkopf, a charter member of the Cleveland Syndicate with whom Ann had dined shortly after her marriage to Mike, had installed Cohen despite opposition from Jack Dragna, the so-called "Al Capone of Los Angeles." But the IRS had proven a tougher foe than Dragna, and the clippings Mike read offered him little comfort. Cohen's career as a crime boss was near an end. Mike could hardly be blamed for wondering if his days of glory were also numbered.

Meanwhile, Ugast was working hard. William H. Karo, appellate division conferee, attorney, and certified public accountant, was designated as the "expert witness" who would interpret the complicated facts and figures other witnesses would supply. Karo spent many hours studying the mountain of information that had been collected while Ugast made certain Ann had been pumped dry of all the facts she was willing to give. Some things Ann didn't want to discuss. In vain, Jaffe warned her that her failure to talk about other gangsters associated with Mike only increased the possibility she would be killed to ensure her silence. Ann didn't agree. The other hoods would react only if she threatened them. Not even Robert Kennedy could guarantee that all the big wheels of organized crime would be put behind bars or that she could be protected from them for the rest of her life.

Operation Baby-sit was becoming boring. It was nice to have sophisticated men about at all times, but a girl needed a little privacy. Too many men were almost as bad as too few. Perhaps remembering Ann's crack about the governors of the Carolinas, Supervisor Wallace had made certain she would never be alone with one agent. Why subject a man to such strain? So, as the weeks dragged by, there was endless talk, jokes that became threadbare, and Scrabble. Never any strip poker—just Scrabble. Ann became an expert at the game.

Moreover, there was the problem of Joan. In pursuit of her vendetta, Ann had neglected her daughter. Like the tumor which gnawed at her, Ann's sense of guilt increased. Now that her part was finished until the trial, why not give Joan that long-promised trip to Europe? It would get the girl out of the glittering rut that was Miami Beach, and perhaps give her a chance to meet some new and decent men.

Ugast reluctantly agreed. The trial was still months away. While no one doubted Mike had friends abroad—Lucky for one—it might be safer. Let Ann and Joan tour Europe if it would make them happy. Precautions could be taken.

Ann decided to sail on the S.S. *United States* from New York on May 25. She would land at Le Havre, France, and go from there to Paris where she promised to contact Harold Moss, Revenue Service attaché at the American Embassy. She would keep Moss informed of future travel plans and he could arrange protection wherever she went. She agreed that she would check twice weekly with the nearest American consul. To keep her absence from the country a secret, it was decided she would send all mail to relatives to Post Office Box 3896 in Miami. Special agents would pick it up there, remove the outer envelope, and remail the letter to its destination. Arrangements were made for her to cash checks abroad if necessary.

It seemed as foolproof as any scheme could be under the circumstances. Everything would depend upon how well Ann and her daughter followed instructions. Greatly elated, the women left for New York to catch their boat. It was like getting out of prison, Ann remarked. The special agents who had guarded her were also happy. The duty had been a strain in more ways than one. Now they could go back to their families, resume a normal life.

And then from the FBI "word" came in.

Confidential informants in the underworld—informants considered "usually reliable"—reported that a decision had been reached. Ann Drahmann was marked for death. She would not return from Europe to testify, but would "disappear" while abroad.

The information was considered doubly reliable because it disclosed the underworld had full details of the trip—details which were supposedly top secret. Such intelligence could not be disregarded, yet the ship sailed in less than twenty-four hours.

The assistant chief of intelligence at the IRS office in New York received an urgent message at 5:20 P.M., May 24. Fred Ugast was arriving from Washington by the next plane. The A.C. was to assign special agents to meet him at LaGuardia Airport and arrange to protect a witness who was sailing next day.

The order came at a bad time. Most special agents had departed for the day. The A.C. called the U.S. Treasury's pistol range at 90 Church Street and located two men and a Coast Guard intelligence agent. They were ordered to meet Ugast immediately. Ugast, delayed by last-minute emergencies, arrived at 9:30 P.M. The agents were waiting. Wasting no time, Ugast drove with them to the Hotel Navarro, 112 Central Park South, where Ann was staying.

A quick conference was arranged in the cocktail lounge. Special agents stood guard in the lobby as Ugast tried to persuade Ann to cancel the trip. She would be in danger aboard ship and at all times in Europe. Ann, only a little shaken by being told her death warrant was signed, refused to believe it. Mike had more sense than to put out a contract for her, she insisted. If only she were involved, she would agree to stay, but for her daughter's sake the trip had to go on as planned.

When asked, Ann could not explain the security leak that had given the underworld knowledge of her plans. Perhaps it resulted from loose talk by her daughter. Joan wasn't aware of how deeply her mother was involved in the case, Ann said, and she didn't want her alarmed by talk of murder.

It was an impasse. Ugast told Ann that Jaffe was flying up from Miami and would talk to her next day. Ann promised only to listen.

Special agents were assigned to spend the night in the corridor outside Ann's suite and instructed not to approach Joan or Ann and not to interfere with their movements. The waiting agents were startled at 12:30 A.M. when Joan and a male companion arrived. They had assumed the women were inside. Joan identified the man as her boyfriend and the couple were permitted to enter the suite. Ann was found in the bar with another man. After Operation Babysit, Ann was enjoying her freedom. The agents watched carefully but discreetly until Ann at last retired and Joan's friend left. The rest of the night was uneventful.

Ugast, meanwhile, checked the FBI to see if that agency was taking any steps to protect Ann. Kennedy's "Coordinated War on Crime" was still largely a theory and the FBI had done nothing and planned to do nothing. Deciding the IRS would have to do the job alone, Ugast began the task of finding the proper security people with the steamship company. By midnight he located James Ryan, security manager for the United States Lines. Luckily he was a former supervisor of narcotics in New York and was known to local agents. Ryan agreed to meet them on the dock at 8 A.M.

Jaffe arrived during the night and met early with Ann. Again she refused to change her plans. Ryan also had bad news. There was little, if any, possibility of arranging protection for an individual passenger aboard the S.S. *United States*. Ugast boarded the ship and conferred with the executive officer. He agreed with Ryan.

It was 10:25 A.M. In one hour and thirty-five minutes the ship would sail. The local chief called his office and was told Robert Manzi, assistant director of IRS intelligence, was trying to reach him from Washington. It took fifteen minutes to make contact. Manzi informed him that a decision had been made on the national level—meaning Robert Kennedy—to place a special agent on the ship to accompany Mrs. Drahmann to her destination.

Standing beside the chief as he talked to Manzi from a phone booth on Pier 86 was Special Agent Wallace Musoff of the Manhattan IRS office. The chief hung up the phone and turned to Musoff.

"You're elected," he said.

Manzi had given instructions to contact Lawrence Fleischman of the New York office of the Customs Service for help in getting a special agent aboard the ship. Fleischman was something of a legend. Years before as a young undercover agent he had trapped Peter Licavoli—a leading associate of the Cleveland Syndicate in rum-running days—and sent him to prison. In the present emergency he responded quickly. Two customs agents were dispatched to the pier. Arrangements were made with Kenneth Gautier, vice president of the United States Lines, to obtain a first-class ticket and stateroom for Musoff. Credit, so that the special agent could buy additional clothing aboard, was established.

An agent called Musoff's home and asked his mother—Musoff was unmarried—to pack a suitcase. Another call to Inspector John J. Shanley at the Police Commissioner's Office resulted in a police car being sent to Musoff's home in the Bronx to pick up the suitcase. It was 11:10 A.M.

There was no time to get a passport or a medical clearance but the cooperative Customs men arranged to have that done aboard ship. Meanwhile, Jaffe and Ugast briefed the special agent about the case and the nature of the danger threatening Ann. He was promised additional instructions upon landing. To provide Musoff with pocket money, all agents present emptied their own pockets—and came up with $450, a revolver, and ammunition.

At 11:59 A.M., the police car with siren screaming arrived with the suitcase. One minute later the ship sailed with Musoff, Ann, and Joan aboard. As yet the harried special agent had not time to meet the women he was to guard. He reported next day by radiophone that he had established "amicable arrangements" and Ann was cooperating fully.

Jaffe, the amateur photographer, had a memento of the frantic episode. As he led Ann and Joan through the building toward the gangplank, a flashbulb blinded them. Instantly other special agents seized the man with the camera. He proved to be only a free-lance photographer hoping to make some cash from carefree vacationers by shooting first and selling later. He had no idea, he insisted, who the women were but had assumed from their clothes they were wealthy enough to afford his prices.

The photographer was left in the dark as to the identity of his subjects, and his negative was confiscated by Jaffe, who soon climbed wearily on a plane and headed south.

A few days later Jaffe checked Post Office Box 3896 and found a letter addressed to him. Dated May 30, it had been written aboard ship—

Hello Boys:
Just a few lines to let you know I am so happy I didn't allow you to talk me out of making this voyage.
We are having a perfectly divine time. I am so completely relaxed I sort of wish I could stay on this ship a month.
Wally is a perfect doll and he, Joan, and I have become real buddies.
We land at La Havre tomorrow so I will write from there. Don't worry as I do not intend sticking my neck out.
Incidentally I am so happy I know you boys, as we have been treated as Royalty. The Commodore, the Chief Purser, and a number of other important personnel have entertained us at cocktail parties and such, and I know it is only because of all you boys.
Wally is sitting here and said to tell you the only trouble we are

having is fighting the men away from Joan. You notice he didn't say he had to fight anyone because of the old lady, but take it from me I don't have any trouble. Will write later.

Ann

Upon landing, and after some confusion, Wally Musoff was ordered to return home. Harold Moss, the Internal Revenue Service attaché at the American Embassy in Paris, took charge of security. A bodyguard in constant attendance on two young and foot-loose women seemed impractical. Instead, Moss was directed to keep in touch with Ann and to make arrangements with local police for protection in whatever city or country she decided to visit.

After a few days in Paris, the women decided to take a look at Switzerland. While in Geneva an incident occurred that enraged Ann. A call came from Swiss police who said they had been informed her life was in danger. Would she come to the station at 10 A.M. and supply details?

It was only 8 A.M. when they called and Ann had been out on the town until 5 A.M. Angrily she hung up. The call represented a slip somewhere since plans had been for local police to stay in the background and not make direct contact. To hell with them, decided Ann. She went back to bed.

Moss called later in the day and only made matters worse. Ann was out and Joan took the call and received the apology. Ann was more angry than ever. She had been trying to keep her daughter ignorant of the shadow under which they moved—and now she knew the truth. To hell with security. From now on she would ignore Moss and his bungling allies.

The hotel clerk recommended a nightclub just across the border in France. They decided to go there for dinner. Ann liked it immensely. The club featured a bar, a dining room, and a casino which reminded her of the old Lookout House back home—only here gambling was legal. There were also "two charming men," one about twenty-eight and the other forty-five. Ann commented to Joan that it was a bit peculiar these two unrelated men should be traveling together, but they certainly danced well and the food and liquor were good. When it became time to return to Geneva the men produced a new Cadillac and drove them to their hotel. This saved Ann $10 in taxi fare and she was pleased to ride in a large car again. They were scarce in Europe, she had discovered.

The charming strangers got down on their knees to persuade Ann and Joan to linger awhile in Geneva, but they had already planned to move on next day and refused to change their minds. Four days later in Zermatt Ann was signing the hotel register. The clerk said she had already received a phone call. She assumed it was from Moss, who had her schedule and would be frantic since she had not talked to him since the incident in Geneva. But when the call came again it proved to be from the gentlemen of the casino. Joan admitted she told the younger man where they were going.

At dinner that night they had a wonderful time. The men—Felix and Rene—invited them to go to the top of the local mountain next morning and they accepted. Upon meeting the women at breakfast, the men broke into laughter at seeing Ann in high-heeled shoes. She replied she didn't intend to do any walking. They would go up and down by cable car. Nevertheless, Rene insisted on taking Ann to a store and buying her a pair of heavy mountain shoes that "weighed a ton."

Walking was in order, Ann discovered, when they reached the top. For two hours they wandered around looking at the breathtaking view and eating lunch at a quaint inn. When Joan at last suggested they get back to the cable car, the masterful older man objected. He wanted to descend by foot. After an argument, Joan and Felix went off to the cable car and Ann and Rene were left alone on the mountaintop. They started down. Ann had concealed her exhaustion—life on Miami Beach had not conditioned her to Swiss mountains—and now she regretted her attempt to be as young as Joan. Her feet were blistered as well. She began cursing herself for letting Rene persuade her to hike home and "suddenly the dawn came."

"I realized for the first time," Ann said later, "this whole setup stunk. I remembered how we had met, how they followed us to Zermatt, their ages, our ages, and I froze in my tracks. I just knew without a shadow of a doubt he was going to push me to my death."

As always when faced with physical danger, Ann rallied. She called herself "a complete idiot, a damned fool," and then began figuring how she could survive the trip.

Every few minutes her companion would pause on the brink of a cliff to point out some landmark of interest. "If I go," said Ann to herself, "you're going with me," and she clung desperately to Rene's arm, knowing that if he pushed "I would take him with me."

When Rene told her to look at something, she closed her eyes. "I didn't see anything but me at the bottom of the mountain."

The descent continued with Ann becoming so exhausted she could scarcely maintain her hold on Rene's arms. It began to rain, an icy drizzle falling on the deep snow. "I was freezing and I thought, 'If he's going to push me why prolong the agony?' He acted so peculiar."

Whatever Rene's intentions, he didn't shove Ann over the edge. They reached town about 8 P.M. Wet, muddy, and ready to collapse, Ann found the strength to stop in the bar for a drink and persuade Rene to write a card to "friends" in Miami. She immediately mailed the card to Jaffe with a letter of explanation. If something happened now, the "boys" would have a clue.

The moment she reached her room Ann called Moss in Paris. She felt better after talking to him and apologized for her breach of security. Two days in bed were necessary before she felt able to walk. Rene was waiting—he wanted her to climb a still taller mountain, this time by chair lift. Ann laughed in his face. Next day they moved on to St. Moritz and this time Joan didn't tell Felix their destination.

Italy was the next country on their schedule. Joan had insisted on seeing it despite warnings from Moss to stay away. As they neared the border Ann began to think of Lucky Luciano. Imprisoned years before, and then deported after allegedly helping U.S. Navy Intelligence protect shipping during World War II, he was still considered active in the international affairs of the Syndicate. An old friend of Trigger Mike—Ann could remember sending him Christmas cards—he lived in Naples. It was one city, she decided, they wouldn't visit.

Back in Miami, Jaffe kept Ann informed by letter of the progress of the case. He also tried to keep her out of trouble. It was an agonizing business, this attempt to influence her by mail but the entire case against Coppola depended upon Ann being alive and willing to testify.

Ben Cohen moved for a "Bill of Particulars," which, if granted, would disclose to Coppola the degree to which Ann was cooperating. In arguing his motion, Cohen said of Ann:

"We understand that right now she's gallivanting all over Europe."

The motion was denied and the trial date set for November.

Meanwhile, Cohen disclosed that he too was planning to do some gallivanting about Europe.

Cohen's plans were revealed at a hearing for another client—Gil "the Brain" Beckley. The "Kennedy heat" was beginning to be felt over the entire country. In New Orleans a federal grand jury, advised by Robert Peloquin, who was transferred to the case from the Ratterman probe, indicted Beckley and twelve other nationally known bookies. They were charged with defrauding the telephone company of long-distance telephone tolls and the government of the excise taxes that should have been charged to the calls. From his headquarters in the Glenn Hotel, Beckley had been able to make daily conference calls to bookies about the country without charge and without records. He had bribed telephone company employees, known to the underworld as "cousins," to plug him into the long-distance circuits.

Beckley was at the Blair House, where Ann had lived when the indictment was returned. Jaffe was assigned to arrest him and bring him in for booking. During the ride to the Federal Building they discussed the Coppola case.

"It's going to be messy," said the Brain.

Cohen was retained to defend Beckley but soon announced he was turning the case over to another attorney because of his pending trip to Europe. Jaffe instantly gave the alarm. His concern was heightened by reports from informants that Trigger Mike was suddenly in a good humor after a long period of depression. Obviously he knew something, or thought he did. An air mail warning was sent to Ann which said in part:

"It occurs to me that perhaps the coincidence of your arrival in Italy and Cohen's arrival in Europe—perhaps to arrange certain matters—may be the cause of Mike's merriment. I would therefore advise you and Joan to be exceedingly cautious in Luciano's territory.

"You ask if I really think they intend doing away with you. My answer is 'Yes,' if they can do it in such a way that it looks accidental or if they can cause you to vanish without a trace. The implication would then be made that it was a voluntary absence. So please be exceedingly cautious with strangers and stay alert."

Shortly after arriving in Rome, Ann received an invitation to Naples to meet Luciano and another deported gangster, Mike Spinella. The latter had lived in south Florida for years and at the time of his deportation was a partner with Meyer Lansky in an exotic yacht club and casino in the Florida Keys. Ann had been very upset when a friend told her Spinella had arranged to have his picture made with a visiting Kennedy. Investigation revealed it was Edward and not Robert who had been tricked into posing with the gangster.

Despite all the warnings she was tempted to accept the invitation out of sheer curiosity—Lucky was such a legend—but U.S. Embassy officials became almost hysterical at the thought and she reluctantly turned down the opportunity.

She was to hear of Lucky again. Meanwhile, the affable Ben Cohen arrived in town.

"I was sick when Cincy blew the series." ANN DRAHMANN

Fourteen

BEN COHEN WAS NOT THE ONLY DISTINGUISHED ATTORNEY traveling abroad. On July 24, 1961, Charles E. Lester checked out of the Waldorf Astoria and boarded the S.S. *Leonardo da Vinci*. His passport was stamped for Spain and Switzerland.

Federal agents who had reports that $500,000 was in transit from Newport to safety in Swiss numbered bank accounts gave Lester's new sports car, which he was taking along, a thorough inspection. Nothing was found but other agents in Europe were alerted to keep a close watch on Lester as well as Cohen.

If, as was suspected, the money allegedly being shipped from Newport came from the numbers racket bankrolled by Trigger Mike, the decision to move it was very timely. For Coppola's lieutenant, Screw Andrews, was scheduled for trouble.

Less than a month after Lester sailed, IRS special agents led by Earl DeVoto—the man who had helped Jaffe explode Coppola's contention that Ann's money came from Charley Drahmann—raided the Sportsman's Club in force. The joint was the only major operation still running in the stricken city. Heat from an assortment of federal, state, and local probes had closed all casinos including the Beverly Hills Club on July 18.

Negro Shriners, ten thousand strong, were holding a convention in Cincinnati and several hundred of them had followed the example of their white brethren and crossed the river to Newport in search of entertainment. A huge banner welcoming the Shriners stretched across Central Avenue in front of the club as thirty-three special agents from several states surrounded it about 11 P.M. On signal they lifted sledgehammers and smashed their way into the ramshackle frame building which Andrews was still renting from Newport housing authorities while his new steel-and-glass palace was being constructed a block away.

Newport police, less than a block away at City Hall, were not notified of the raid. The IRS had no illusions despite the fact that an alleged group of "Young Turks" from the department had attempted a raid a few days earlier and confiscated a few slot machines.

Screw was not in the joint when the raiders entered the gaudy interior, but six operators, including his son, "Junior" Andrews, were arrested. The visiting Shriners were processed and released as the agents got down to the real business of the evening—a search for numbers racket records.

Eleven slot machines were the first find. They were hidden behind a secret panel and mounted on metal frames which, in turn, were fastened to wooden turntables. When the panel was lifted the slots turned themselves out of the wall and ready for action. Andrews had purchased the required $250 tax stamps for each machine so the IRS agents couldn't touch them. But they could pass the word to the "Young Turks" in the police department who had overlooked them earlier. The cops arrived and confiscated the machines, which were illegal under state law.

Other secret panels were discovered. Some concealed financial records and others hid big safes. In one such safe, which hired experts opened after a long struggle, the agents found $51,000, guns, and more records. Not all the cash had been sent to Europe.

A long narrow room in the heart of the building was found. Entrance was by way of a concealed door. Inside was space only for a narrow table and some chairs. But twenty telephones were on the table and all of them were ringing. They continued to ring softly for hours as uninformed customers called to learn the winning number of the evening. The agents answered until they were tired—and supplied numbers at random.

A complicated gadget was found which by means of compressed air blew numbered ping-pong balls into the air until one of them spilled over into a chute. This was the Newport version of bolita. Instead of a drawing, Screw offered the suckers who came to the club a chance to see a "blowing." The device required considerable study before the agents learned how the operator could arrange to have the ball with the desired number pop free. Like the numbers racket everywhere, the game was rigged.

When the search was completed, DeVoto was unsatisfied. A tall, rangy man, he had spent years in the Newport-Covington area and learned much about the personalities of the gangsters. While many records had been found, the key ones were still missing. It was unlikely they had been destroyed. A man backed by Coppola and the Eastern Syndicate would want records to protect himself in case some cynic questioned his profit totals.

Another search was ordered. By using tape measures the T-Men discovered some leftover space. Finding the entrance to it was the problem. While re-searching a closet in which earlier records had been found, the shoe of an agent scuffed against a piece of wire on the floor. He picked it up. About ten inches long, the wire had exposed ends where insulation had been cut back from the copper. Intrigued, the agent sought the function of the wire. He noticed two nail heads about eight inches apart, shoulder high, in the very back of the closet.

Acting on a hunch, the agent placed the ends of the wire against the nail heads. A buzzing sound came from within the wall and the back of the closet swung open. Inside was a small room literally packed with minute details of the numbers racket. The secrets of Screw Andrews were exposed. Months later, after those records were analyzed, Screw would be convicted in federal court and sent to prison. The records showed he had been reporting for tax purposes only one-seventh of the true total of his multi-million dollar business.

Morris Weintraub provided some comic relief for the tired raiders. He appeared and demanded to be admitted. The agents asked in what capacity he was making the demand—as counsel for the housing commission which owned the building or as attorney for Andrews, who rented it? Visibly shaken, Weintraub finally acknowledged he was there to represent the racketeer. Once inside, Weintraub demanded the agents throw the author out on the grounds reporters had no right to be there. The agents declined.

The raid on the Sportsman's Club, dramatic as it proved to be, was but one incident of many in Newport's long, hot summer. Following the Ratterman police court fiasco, events had followed one another in bewildering sequence. Ratterman had again been put on the rack when the Campbell grand jury, advised by Wise, indicted Carinci and Ratterman's hapless friend, Paisley. The trial that followed provided another opportunity to smear Ratterman and the inevitable "Not Guilty" verdict was supposed to destroy the idea he had been framed. Again the bright boys misjudged public opinion. With a federal grand jury probing the case, no one paid much attention to Wise's feeble efforts. The candidate frankly admitted he would not cooperate with the prosecution and reformers everywhere applauded. Legal hypocrisy no longer fooled many in Newport.

The spotlight shifted to Frankfort, where the long-sought ouster hearings began. Kentucky Attorney General John Breckinridge elected to prosecute the officials. He was aided by John Anggelis, a young and able associate of the aging Jesse K. Lewis. The hearings began slowly. Chris Seifried and his laymen presented evidence of gambling and prostitution gathered during their four-year fight. Jack Thiem returned from the past to tell of his battles with Schmidt and Chief Gugel. But the climax came on the third day when former madam Hattie Jackson testified.

She wore a black hat with a narrow white brim and veil, a striped dress with wide collars which showed her neck, and dainty white gloves. Trim and still shapely, she might have been a suburban housewife making a call. Her voice was low—so low Chief Gugel and Detective Chief Fredericks used it as an excuse to move their seats nearer. They sat there, Gugel glaring from behind his eternal dark glasses, and Fredericks impassive but never moving his eyes from her face.

The story Hattie had threatened to tell in 1957 now poured out in all its sordid detail. She listed officials who she said had received payoffs—Gugel, Fredericks, Wise, Siddell, Judge Murphy, Pat Ciafardini, and others. As she talked, rumors circulated around the Capitol and the conference room in which the hearings were held became crowded and overflowed. When at last Hattie came to her arrest and Gugel's action in turning loose rats in her cell, she broke into tears.

For several minutes she sobbed into a lace-trimmed handkerchief. Absolute silence gripped the room. It was the dramatic high spot of the hearings. Attorney General Breckinridge, who had located Hattie, commented later:

"She looked down the table at Gugel and said, 'For what I gave you, you should have put me in a penthouse,' and there wasn't a man in the room who didn't know what she was talking about and didn't feel like beating Gugel to death. She made the case."

On cross-examination, Gugel's attorney sought only to show the rats were loosed because the sewer in the cell was under repair. The basic truth of Hattie's account was not questioned.

If Hattie had made the case, that fact was not immediately apparent. At the end of the day Commissioner John L. Davis recessed the hearings until September to give the defense a chance to get ready. Meanwhile, news of Hattie's testimony rocked Newport.

It was then the town closed down.

The author in his capacity as a *Courier-Journal* reporter played a key part in what followed. He dropped in on Judge Murphy and found him still seething over Hattie's charge he was on the payoff list. It was an "unmitigated lie," he said. When the author suggested that such "lies" should be exposed, the judge agreed. He might just call a special grand jury to investigate. A little discreet needling by the author and Murphy lost his head—he picked up the phone and called Breckinridge in Frankfort.

"I'm calling a special grand jury to meet—let's see, August 14 is the soonest it can meet. I want Hattie Jackson up here to testify. Will you deliver her?"

Breckinridge promised and promptly put his head together with Henry Cook, counsel for the Committee of 500. The moment Murphy signed the order calling the special grand jury, Breckinridge demanded that Murphy disqualify himself. After all, he could hardly preside over an investigation of himself. Murphy, who by now was having second thoughts about the whole business, had no choice but to step down. In a triumph of irony, Ed Hill, the tamer of Harlan, was appointed special judge.

A year before, Hill had called a special grand jury and Murphy had returned to guide it. Now Murphy had called the jury and Hill was coming back to take up where he left off the year before. Chris Seifried had an explanation—it was God moving in His mysterious ways. The gamblers had other words for it and Murphy was the target of most of them. It was a helluva time for Charles Lester to be gallivanting about Europe.

The Cleveland Syndicate held a policy meeting at the Beverly

Hills which soon adjourned to Miami Beach where their arrival was duly noted. Three days later, Chiefs Gugel and Fredericks announced they were retiring. If anyone thought the announcement would cool the flames in Newport, they were again mistaken.

On August 14, the special grand jury panel met at the courthouse. Judge Hill, wearing his black robes—a custom not followed by Judges Murphy and Stapleton—was a handsome, impressive figure. He made no excuses to the prospective jurors.

"This court," he said, "feels the necessity of a thorough examination of this grand jury."

Quietly and confidently he began asking questions of the jurors—and hit pay dirt the first time. A woman acknowledged that she had a relative who worked "in a place where they make book." She was excused.

Suddenly other members of the panel pleaded they were "too nervous" to serve. Others said their health was bad. Some freely admitted associations with gamblers that disqualified them in Hill's eyes. When the panel was exhausted, nine jurors had been tentatively seated and twenty-two others excused. Judge Hill drew fifteen additional names from the jury wheel and continued his inquisition.

Ultimately a jury consisting of five men and seven women was selected and sworn in. And it was then Judge Hill dropped his bomb. He wanted the jury not only to investigate Mrs. Jackson's charges but he wanted a probe of a "possible conspiracy by all officials who are charged with the duty of enforcing the laws of Campbell County and Kentucky."

Speaking slowly, impressively, without notes or prepared text, the handsome judge in the unfamiliar black robe, commented:

"It has been my behavior in the past to instruct on those things which have been most prominent in a community in regard to law violations, and I don't think the court is required to be any more stupid than anybody else. . . .

"I don't know what your personal feelings may be about laws against vice and gambling and prostitution, but it is not for the court to question the wisdom of the legislature which passed these laws. . . .

"You will have scars here for years as a result of the nefarious practice of openly operating gambling places. . . . I ask this jury to consider whether or not children could be raised in an atmosphere of wholesale, wide open violations and corruption without being tainted in some manner. . . .

"I did not come here to preach a sermon. I didn't ask to be sent here. I was ordered here by the Chief Justice, but since I am here I hope you will feel I am not a foreigner in your midst come to tell you how to run your business. . . . I hope you will find I am a kind person, but I do insist on doing what I am supposed to do under the law and I hope this community will accept me in that light."

Four thousand miles away Ann Drahmann read newspaper clippings sent by relatives in Cincinnati. As the account of Hattie Jackson's testimony had moved her, so did the words of Judge Hill. Even on paper they had power, the power of sincerity. For almost the first time Ann was able to put life into perspective. What had happened to her with Trigger Mike had happened to others in some degree. The evil was not the doings of one man, however vicious, she decided, but the inevitable product of a system. Generations of children growing up in the Cincinnati-Newport area had been tainted, as Judge Hill said, and she was but one of them. Joan had also been tainted by the same corruptive influences. So also, perhaps, had been Trigger Mike in his youth. Newport, Miami Beach, East Harlem—no matter the physical differences, the evil was the same.

The effect of the judge's words was more immediately apparent on the grand jury. As Breckinridge put it:

"I felt we were at a considerable disadvantage with that grand jury. It was selected from the old jury wheel. That meant it was a run-of-the-mill jury, the kind that generation after generation had refused to find anyone guilty. It was exactly the kind of jury you'd expect to find in that kind of a community. Judge Hill took this jury and converted it before our eyes. The men started shaving, wearing neckties. The women wore their Sunday best. They began to take on the appearance of a responsible section of middle-class people. Right before our eyes they were converted by Judge Hill's most remarkable statement."

Commonwealth's Attorney Wise watched from the rear of the courtroom as Hill gave specific instructions that the conduct of the commonwealth's attorney should be investigated. And, he added, the jury was to report to him the moment the probe of Wise began. He would then appoint a commonwealth's attorney pro tem to advise the jury.

The ministers and their laymen were ready to proceed. At first there was some confusion about the position of Wise—could he advise the jury during the investigation of other officials? Cesare Bernardini, long a member of the Social Action Committee, put an end to it. He told the jurors he wanted to testify about Wise and demanded the judge be notified. Hill ordered the jury to recess until a substitute could be found. The search for an honest man in Newport legal circles took several days, but a young attorney, Frank Benton III, was ultimately selected. When the jury reconvened under his leadership the author was the first witness. One day later indictments began coming out of the grand jury room in batches. Almost every active gambling operator in Newport was named in one or more of them. Benton called the indictments "incidental" to the major probe.

The jury finished its preliminary work and recessed until August 31 to give Benton time physically to prepare scores of felony indictments based on wagering-tax data secured from the IRS. Under law, all holders of federal wagering-tax stamps had to make monthly reports listing under penalty of perjury the gross wagers accepted by them. The evidence had long been available to law-enforcement officials all around the country. In Newport, Wise had been repeatedly asked by reformers to secure the data but had refused. As far as could be determined, Benton's action in obtaining the records marked the first time in the country they had been requested by local officials in a gambling probe.

During the recess, IRS raiders kept things hot by hitting the Sportsman's Club. And Governor Combs did what every governor had refused to do—he signed an executive order declaring a state of emergency in Campbell County. State police, who in the absence of such an order were powerless inside Newport, now were free to act. They were assigned to help the grand jury. Among other duties they began serving subpoenas on witnesses when Sheriff Roll reported he was able to find but a couple. Roll displayed his aching feet to photographers to prove how hard he had tried.

With the additional evidence the state police provided, the grand jury swung back into action, returning indictments totaling sixty-five counts against fifteen "name" gamblers.

But once more Hattie Jackson provided the dramatic highlight. She returned to Newport. Photographers gathered as she climbed the stairs of the grimy courthouse where once she had been convicted of pandering. On one side was the attorney general of Kentucky and on the other was the largest man the state police possessed, Sergeant B. L. Sherrard. Another trooper guarded the rear.

Hattie held a newspaper in front of her face as the flashbulbs flickered like summer lightning. Sherrard said privately that she was "scared to death." Scared or not, Hattie entered the courtroom where the grand jury was sitting and talked for ninety minutes. A huge crowd gathered, including many well-known hoods. Sherrard sent for reinforcements and Judge Hill ordered the windows in the courtroom door covered. When Hattie left the room she was surrounded by guards who plowed a path through the crowds and escorted her to the street where a state police car waited.

A few days later another visitor from the past returned—Big Jim Harris, former marshal of Wilder and operator of the now defunct Hy-Dee-Ho Club. He talked for more than an hour and settled some old scores.

Wise, obviously upset by the return of skeletons from Newport's history, demanded to appear before the grand jury to testify in his own behalf. Benton permitted him to do so. Wise emerged, more shaken than before, and announced plans to sue every newspaper which had carried Hattie's charges. Mayor Mussman decided he should explain "the facts of life" to the jury and was also permitted to testify. He came out a much subdued man.

The end for the jury was near. It was running out of time. Judge Hill had already granted it the one extension permitted by law. On September 12, the jury voted ninety-three felony indictments against top gamblers and Benton told the press the jury had begun to vote on officials.

Newport waited, gripped with tension. Ratterman's campaign was forgotten in the excitement of the immediate crisis. Even the hot pennant race being run by the Cincinnati Reds became a side issue. For many years the gamblers, madams, and assorted riffraff of Newport had looked forward to a World Series in Cincinnati. Suddenly one was a possibility but no one could feel happy about it.

The Newport ministers took note of the date. Exactly one year before they had voted to fight on for another year and then quit town if no progress had been made. None were leaving now but the exodus of gamblers had begun in earnest. Every plane heading west toward Las Vegas or south to Miami Beach was loaded.

On September 13, the big wind swept through Newport. Indicted on charges of conspiracy to obstruct justice were Mayor Mussman, City Manager Hesch, ex-Police Chief Gugel, ex-Detective Chief Fredericks, four city commissioners, and a varied lot of police officers including Ciafardini.*

Wise escaped indictment but the jury denounced him in strong terms for not making better use of his powers. It also noted that the majority of jurors favored the indictment of additional officials "but the required nine votes were not received."

Later it was learned that the seven women on the jury had been unanimous in demanding indictments. Two "liberals," who somehow had survived Judge Hill's scrutiny, opposed any indictments. The three remaining men held the balance of power, two of their votes being needed to achieve the necessary three-fourths vote. The three split on certain officials.

As reporters gathered around Wise in the aftermath of the jury's final report, the commonwealth's attorney pointed suddenly at the author.

"I will not talk in front of that man," he shouted.

Judge Hill and Breckinridge were watching from the front of the room. Hill called the author to his side. "Let's get out of here," he said. "Our job is done." We walked out together.

The spotlight shifted back to Frankfort and the ouster hearings. Despite the resignations of Gugel and Fredericks, Commissioner Davis refused to dismiss the charges against them as moot. On October 6, he announced his findings—the two men were guilty as charged.

"It is utterly incomprehensible that open gambling establishments could flourish within the city of Newport to the extent described in the record without the knowledge of the two respondents here involved," Davis declared.

Governor Combs promptly concurred in the verdict and ordered full penalties. Since the men were already out of office, the penalty meant they could not be reappointed and could not hold any public office for four years.

The charges against County Police Chief Stuart and Sheriff Roll were settled a little later. Davis found Roll guilty and Combs invoked the penalty. The case against Stuart was different. He had defended his inaction by citing a written order from County Judge

---

* Two years later all of the defendants were acquitted.

Jolly—the man who got Screw Andrews off the hook in the murder of Melvin Clark. The order provided that county police were to patrol the unincorporated areas and enter into municipalities only if their help were requested by local officials. Davis had strong words for Jolly, but he concluded Chief Stuart had been justified in not interfering with gambling joints inside the cites. Even the Beverly Hills Club had been protected by the order—after the syndicate arranged to incorporate the area surrounding it into the city of "Southgate." It was a good place to live—the club paid most of the taxes.

Governor Combs, now full of "piss and ginger" as one gambler described it, overruled his commissioner and ordered Stuart ousted anyway. After having made the gesture, he quickly pardoned the chief, who immediately went back to work—or what passed for it.

Despite all the uproar, all the indictments, the gamblers had not given up hope. The knew from experience that such attacks of virtue were usually short-lived. Public indignation could not be sustained indefinitely. The heat would pass in time. Ratterman was the big danger. If he won in November, the game would indeed be over. If he lost, the situation would eventually return to normal.

Thus tension continued to grow as the election approached. All stops were pulled to inflame old prejudices and create new ones. The sacred principle of "Local Self-Government" was invoked and proclaimed from hundreds of bumper stickers which were worn alongside the slogan: "Root The Reds Home." Exactly how the liberals planned to eliminate such "outsiders" as John Breckinridge and Robert Kennedy, they didn't explain.

New "interference" came from Washington. It achieved little from a practical point of view, except to increase the heat, but it did demonstrate how far from reality a Senate investigating committee can be removed.

Senator McClellan opened a series of hearings on organized crime. Layoff betting was one of the major topics explored. Inevitably Gil Beckley was mentioned, but the committee's investigators seemed unable to grasp one minor point—that all telephone calls to Newport went through the Covington exchange. As a result they referred constantly to Covington when the telephone numbers they were putting into the record were in Newport.

On the second day of the hearings, General Counsel Jerome S.

Alderman was questioning IRS Special Agent Harold R. Wallace. The subject of "Covington-Newport" came up and Wallace reported that "the town is strangely silent."

Senator McClellan immediately wondered if the committee's subpoenas had anything to do with the silence, but Alderman said the IRS deserved the credit. This was too much for Senator Ervin, who asked:

"Is it not a fact that one of the Cincinnati newspapers has been conducting something of a crusade against gambling operations?"

When Wallace said "That is correct," Senator Ervin fired another:

"Is it not also a fact that a state grand jury in Campbell County, Kentucky, has been conducting investigations into gambling?"

Wallace said that was true too, and Ervin asked:

"Do you not attribute part of the apparent cessation of lack of interest in Covington to these factors in addition to the work of the Internal Revenue Service?"

The special agent agreed Ervin was right.

It boiled down to the fact that Senator Ervin had the wrong city, Covington, in the wrong county and the wrong newspaper in the wrong state, but at least he knew a grand jury was operating in the general area.

Nevertheless, the McClellan Committee carried on and had the privilege of meeting Morris Weintraub. He appeared as counsel for two Snax Bar gamblers who were selected on the grounds they were operators of a "typical medium sized" handbook. A committee investigator reported they handled $1,165,022 in wagers over a twenty-one-month period.

Both gamblers took the Fifth Amendment and refused to talk. Weintraub more than made up for it. Finally Senator McClellan, who could hardly get a word in, commented sourly:

"These are the most silent witnesses and most talkative attorney we've had in a long time."

The hearings were useful in that they helped put the area into perspective on a national level though some folks in Covington and Kenton County were annoyed at being confused with Newport.

In Newport, the strange silence deepened. Gamblers and their allies attempted to make the city into a ghost town in the hopes of convincing the voters it would become one if Ratterman was elected.

Casinos closed first, and then the corner handbooks, the bust-out joints, and the brothels. York and Monmouth Streets were empty where a few months before it had been almost impossible to find a parking place. The prediction that without gambling the town will die seemed confirmed when Cincinnati won the National League pennant and the World Series began across the river. Thousands came to see the games but few, if any, of those thousands came to Newport for entertainment afterward. Tito Carinci reopened his Tropicana Club in the Glenn Hotel just for the Series but reporters who checked found the floor show cancelled when no customers showed up. The reputation of Newport as a bust-out town was now national in scope and the suckers stayed away in droves.

As the election neared, the gamblers tried one final fling of the dice. A federal grand jury had been investigating the Ratterman case since May and had not acted. If Ratterman really had been framed, the gamblers began asking, why didn't the grand jury do something? There had been ample time to investigate. Obviously, the argument continued, they had found nothing because there was nothing to find.

Unlike most of the syndicates' propaganda, this made sense. It made even more sense after April Flowers reappeared.

April had been subpoenaed to the federal grand jury in June and had waited in the halls for several hours without being questioned. While waiting she showed reporters a scroll proving that on September 6, 1960, she had been commissioned a Kentucky Colonel. The commission was signed by Lieutenant-Governor Wilson W. Wyatt, then serving as acting governor. Informed of April's disclosure, Wyatt promptly signed an order stripping the stripper of her commission. April, still unheard by the grand jury, vanished into limbo.

On October 13, she reappeared—and under rather strange circumstances. She was arrested in a Cincinnati hotel room with Charles A. Polizzi, Jr. And the syndicate experts in Newport scratched their heads.

Young Polizzi's father was an early member of the Cleveland Syndicate and at one time owned pieces of the Beverly Hills Club, the Lookout House, and the Yorkshire Club. Yet here was young Chuck, armed with a pistol for which he had a permit, allegedly escorting April to Lexington, Kentucky, to squeal to the federal grand jury.

A lot of people wondered if the syndicate had decided the quicker Newport was cleaned up the better for its other operations. Others simply dismissed young Polizzi as a rebel against authority—in this case, syndicate authority.

Police let them go on to Lexington where they talked at length to the United States Attorney and the FBI. The grand jury, then in recess, didn't hear April, who vanished again.

The episode only contributed to the gambler's cry—if Ratterman was framed, why doesn't the jury act? The rumor spread that Frank Sinatra, the old swinger and member of the "Rat Pack," had persuaded Peter Lawford to intervene with his brother-in-law, Robert Kennedy, not to act in Newport. The lie made sense to some citizens who daily read Cincinnati newspaper editorials which generally considered that anything left of Barry Goldwater was anti-Taft.

Ratterman's forces were worried. The "liberals" had come up with something that hurt. Investigation revealed that in taking such a propaganda line, the gamblers weren't gambling. Someone in the Justice Department had decided that action in the case prior to the election would leave the department subject to criticism that it had meddled in local politics.

It was here the author obtained his greatest scoop. With help from Frank Staab, the brilliant FBI special agent who had headed the probe, and from Mitchell Meade, an equally brilliant young assistant United States Attorney, April Flowers was located in St. Louis and persuaded to talk. Her story appeared in the *Courier-Journal* on October 24 and was picked up by the wire services and splashed on the front pages of the Cincinnati papers. The story gave details of the frame of Ratterman and quoted April as saying she had given the information to the FBI. It also quoted her as believing her life was in danger unless and until the federal grand jury took action.

Ann Drahmann in far-off Rome knew what she meant.

One day after the story was published, the Justice Department reversed itself and announced the grand jury would meet within a few days. Once again the "liberals" had outsmarted themselves by demanding a grand jury report in the belief the jury wouldn't meet.

A candidate for City Commission appeared on television to declare:

"Laws? To hell with them. There's not one that wasn't made to be broken."

With the federal grand jury returning, outright defiance seemed to be about the only course left.

The jurors met in a defiant mood themselves. They had been eager to return to work, knowing as perhaps federal officials in Washington didn't know, that indictments after the election would mean little if Ratterman was defeated.

April appeared and testified. Under heavy guard she was slipped away. Several other witnesses including Ratterman were heard and then the jury assembled in front of District Judge H. Church Ford and asked permission to read a final report—a practice usually frowned upon in Federal Court. The judge gave them permission and the blistering report went into the record. It contained such sentences as this blunt statement:

"The foul odors of vice, corruption and bribery cover Campbell County officialdom like a pall."

With the report came an indictment charging six men with conspiring to frame, and with framing, George Ratterman, thus violating his civil rights. Named as defendants were Charles Lester, Marty Buccieri, Tito Carinci, Pat Ciafardini, and the other two officers who had accompanied Pat on his ill-starred expedition to the Glenn Hotel.

It was October 27, 1961. Ten days later Ratterman was elected sheriff of Campbell County in a landslide victory of the "Switch to Honesty" Party.

At a victory party that night in Fort Thomas, Catholic priest rubbed elbows with Protestant minister. Republican shook hands with Democrat. Wealthy suburbanite ate from the same buffet as women from "the Bottoms."

On December 28, 1961, in his annual report to the President of the United States, Robert Kennedy stated:

"Wagering has virtually ceased at a major gambling center, Newport, Kentucky."

And in Rome, a former syndicate wife went down to the bar and drank a toast to Ratterman.

*"One must have compassion,
love, and a conscience to
break."* ANN DRAHMANN

Fifteen

ANN HAD ALWAYS LIKED BEN COHEN, WHO CONCEALED HIS sharp intelligence beneath a fumbling, sometimes corny version of a Southern gentleman. He had done favors for Ann before and after her divorce, knowing that someday a friendly relationship might be to Mike's advantage.

They met twice in Rome. During the first meeting Cohen pointed out certain advantages for Ann if she remained in Europe. She could not be extradited, he said. On the other hand, if she did return, a desperate Mike would stop at nothing to discredit her. He could easily produce witnesses to swear she was a prostitute. At the second meeting there was talk of some additional reasons why Ann should not return—two hundred thousand reasons.

Ann's reply was instinctive. She chased Cohen through the lobby of the Excelsior Hotel, screaming curses at his retreating form. But later there was time to think. Miami Beach was a long way off. Joan had fallen in love with Europe and wanted to stay forever. It might be best if she did. The girl remained impassive. They were of two different generations, Ann concluded, and the damage Mike had caused Joan might never be repaired. Even so, she was much better off touring Greece or Spain than dating gangsters on Miami Beach.

So Ann was tempted.

Ultimately she turned Mike's offer down cold and refused to tell why. Let him assume it was Vendetta—Mike could understand that.

Much more was involved, and even Ann was not certain she fully understood. For months she refused to admit to federal agents that Cohen had approached her. They might have asked why she rejected his advice. Had Joe Wanderscheid been in Europe, she might have talked to him, but somehow it sounded silly when she pictured herself talking to anyone else.

Ann had become a patriot.

Self-educated, sophisticated in a superficial sense, Ann had never given much thought to God and Country. Money, and the security it represented, had been her adult goal. But now that she had all the money she needed, the rather trite discovery that money was not enough came to confound her.

In Italy, the birthplace of her parents, she made another discovery—she loved America. In repeated letters to "the boys," Wanderscheid and Jaffe, she elaborated on this theme:

"I wish you boys would do me a great kindness. Please write to me. Tell me anything about the States. What I used to think dull and uninteresting would be music to my ears. I get the Paris edition of the New York paper which consists of five sheets and I actually devour every single word. I once thought geography had nothing to do with one's happiness, but that isn't true. I am so homesick I could die. How I would love to be in Cincinnati this moment. And wouldn't it be wonderful if we could re-live certain parts of our lives?"

The news from Newport in the summer and fall of 1961 was another factor in her conversion to patriotism. She began to understand for the first time how gangsters such as Trigger Mike can corrupt a community and downgrade the lives of thousands. Her feud with Mike took on a different meaning when one considered it in that perspective. Her hatred of Mike grew deeper, if possible, but no longer was it based only on the beatings he had given her or the harm done to Joan.

Contributing to these thoughts and giving them urgency was her belief she had not long to live. Other doctors had confirmed the truth about her "tumor," and the truth was somber. Under the circumstances, what did $200,000 mean? What would $2,000,000 mean? God had given her a chance to serve her country and she was grateful. When at last she sat in the witness chair she would hold back nothing. People would have to listen and believe.

"I can't be bought for any amount of money," she told Ben Cohen. And she meant it.

Despite her new purpose in life, Ann did not lose her sense of humor. In one letter to "the boys," she described Italian men:

"The Italian men I have gone with have one object in life which is to take a girl out, buy her *one* Scotch, a plate of macaroni and a bottle of cheap wine—and then comes the payoff. Everything he has put into this girl, he is most bound and determined to squeeze out. If an Italian dances, he has at least one sensation with each dance. And do you know something, boys? Before I leave it has become some sort of an obsession with me to find out what the hell these Italians are capable of doing after five dances. They have to be dead in bed. I'm really not crude not vulgar. These are true facts."

Despite the research on Italian men, Ann found the wait long. In late August came a break. She flew back to Miami Beach for pretrial conferences with Ugast and used the opportunity to close her apartment in the Blair House. Whatever happened, she would not be returning there.

The visit was supposed to be a secret but informants reported Mike knew all about it. Again there were threats and again Customs Service and IRS special agents teamed up to make sure she had a safe departure. "Operation Shakedown" was instituted at Idlewild International Airport. All baggage and cargo aboard the outgoing jet was examined and the passenger lists checked. One of the passengers was Richard Burton, en route to Rome where he was filming the movie *Cleopatra*, but Burton was too preoccupied with thoughts of Elizabeth Taylor to notice the real-life drama that delayed his flight for twenty minutes.

Back in Rome, Ann found Joan missing. She contacted Moss and a frantic search of Europe began. Five days passed before Joan returned—she had been on a cruise.

"I didn't know how to greet her—whether to kiss her or spank her," Ann said.

Moss had feared Joan kidnapped to prevent Ann from talking, but Ann, after considering the matter, decided it wasn't likely to happen. As she put it:

"I know Mike wouldn't hurt Joan for the simple reason Mike knows he has half a chance as long as Joan is alive. I can't open up and tell all I know about the rats as long as Joan lives."

Calm returned. Ann was sitting one day in her favorite cocktail lounge "drinking my tonic," when three men struck up a conversation with her. Two were Americans. The chat was resumed next day. The men said they were television producers and they were in Italy to film a new series on "the Mafia."

If word was intended as bait, it worked. Ann became intensely interested.

"My big ears perked up and in my stupid little way I asked why and whom they intended to find in Italy as I, along with most Americans, was under the impression the majority of the Mafia were in the United States. I wouldn't think it necessary to come all the way to Italy."

It was the "dumb broad" act. Ann had been a syndicate wife for most of her adult life. The "Mafia," in her experience, was something you read about in Sunday supplements and paperback thrillers. The name La Cosa Nostra, which soon was to be famous, she never heard.

The men smiled at her ignorance and asked if she had never heard of Lucky Luciano. Ann kept a straight face. Yes, she had heard of Lucky. Everyone who had read the book *A House Is Not a Home* had heard of him. Furthermore, she added, the book made it clear that Lucky had been framed on the prostitution rap by Prosecutor Tom Dewey.

The Roman member of the television trio became very dramatic and Ann heard with amusement that she was so right. He had talked to Lucky on many occasions and found him an extremely charming and nice gentleman.

It seemed to Ann the conversation was leading up to something, but abruptly it was interrupted. A porter came rushing in, warning the men their cab and their plane were waiting.

The Roman waxed dramatic again and Ann had difficulty understanding him. "I got the impression that Lucky was either on his death bed or was about to go to jail. Joan laughed at my expression as they left at the most crucial moment."

Ann never learned what was going on, but the incident was strangely prophetic. Four months later Luciano was arrested by Rome police. After being questioned for hours about the international narcotics traffic, he persuaded them to take him to the airport where he was to meet a friend—a motion picture executive who was flying in to see him. The friend arrived and as they started out of the terminal, Luciano staggered and fell. In seconds he was dead from a heart attack.

Not all of Ann's barroom adventures had underworld overtones. One day as the trial date neared, she was sitting alone with her "tonic" when in walked "two perfectly gorgeous men." A conversation developed and a dinner date followed. The men were English and spoke in the clipped British manner. Ann was startled.

"I had heard English people talk on TV and in the movies," she said, "which is one thing, but to actually hear them in person is quite another. I decided they just had to be a couple of queers. It wasn't what they said; it was how they said it. I liked these two men, however, and I wanted them to feel at ease so I thought the best way was to ask them how long they had been going with each other.

"They informed me that if I was a man—no, a bloke—they would knock my bloody head off."

It developed the men were in the French Foreign Legion "and are really rough and tough in a good way—not the underworld way. We are the very best of friends. They kid me constantly about the fact I had 'the bloody guts' to ask them such a question."

But the time for flirtation in bars was ending. The trial of Mike Coppola for allegedly evading $385,000 in income taxes was at hand. The special agents had been very conservative in arriving at the figure—they believed it to be much higher. Ann estimated Mike's income as at least $1,000,000 a year.

Some agents were surprised that Mike was going to trial. They had felt the syndicate would not permit him to chance his ex-wife appearing to testify about underworld secrets. From Rome, however, Ann had warned:

"Don't overestimate Mike's sense of duty to his friends. Don't forget—he is the big wheel. He doesn't give a damn who he might hurt if he can save his own hide."

It seemed that Ann was right.

The trial began November 27. Ann was flown to New York and kept in hiding there under heavy guard. According to plan, she would reach Miami only an hour before she was to testify.

Ugast began slowly. A swimming pool contractor swore Mike paid him $9,500 for a pool in 1956—a year Mike reported his income as $10,800.

Suppliers of other merchandise ranging from cars to shoes at $33 a pair testified as to Mike's lavish scale of living and his habit of always paying in cash. But the big hit was Mike's former "housekeeper," the dazzling blonde. She waved a diamond ring Mike had given her and testified she lived in the Coppola home for three years prior to his marriage to Ann.

On the third day as Ugast was preparing to unlimber his big guns, trouble developed. Defense Attorney Jacob Kossman, who was serving as trial lawyer—Cohen's talents lay in other directions—won an admission from two jurors that they had read newspaper stories describing Mike as a gangster. Two previously selected alternate witnesses replaced them. All seemed well but suddenly a third juror admitted he had watched a television news account of the trial the night before. He was excused. There were no more alternate jurors. Reluctantly Judge David Dyer ordered a mistrial and reset the case for February 12, 1962.

The word reached Ann in New York. She at first refused to believe it. For months she had waited, steeling herself for the ordeal that had been promised on cross-examination. And suddenly, at the very last moment, the trial was postponed.

If the agents wondered about the three jurors, Ann wondered about everyone, from the judge on down. Had Mike put in a "fix"? It seemed very possible. Anger replaced disappointment. She went into a tantrum. To quiet her, agents put through a call to Ugast in Miami. The disappointed prosecutor was given a bitter tongue-lashing by Ann, who spared no adjectives in describing her feelings. Ugast finally had enough. He hung up.

Wanderscheid and Jaffe moved hurriedly to soothe his feelings and soon persuaded him to carry on. By 3 P.M., New York reported that Ann's rage was increasing. Moreover, she was taking a plane to Miami to finish her conversation with Ugast in person. She was also threatening to kill Trigger Mike.

Crisis! Ann was capable of doing anything, even to shooting Coppola if chance offered. Somehow she had to be made to listen to reason and accept assurance the battle would continue. Everyone agreed the only man who could handle her was Joe Wanderscheid. The problem was to get him to New York in time to intercept Ann. On the plane ride back there would be time to talk sense to her.

Ann's plane was scheduled to leave at 8:45 P.M. Joe could take a flight out of Miami which reached Idlewild fifteen minutes earlier. Time enough if all went well. A weary Wanderscheid was rushed to the airport and put aboard.

The plane moved heavily onto the runway and was almost in takeoff position when abruptly the motors stopped. The pilot announced a forty-five-minute delay due to a minor engine malfunction. Wanderscheid looked at his watch. The delay would cause him to miss Ann. Something had to be done. There was no way to reach his colleagues, who, by now, had left the terminal. It was up to him.

A hostess, bright and cheerful, came by. Joe grabbed her arm, produced his credentials, and turned on all the mysterious charm that had a way with women. He asked the girl to have the pilot radio Idlewild and tell them to hold the 8:45 o'clock plane to Miami. It was a matter, Joe said, of vital national interest.

The hostesss believed him instantly, and rushed to do his bidding. She returned to say the message had been sent. The plane would wait in New York.

When Joe landed, the hostess asked all other passengers to remain seated until he could deplane. He rushed through the terminal to a cab stand. The cabby refused to make the short run down the road—and risk losing a profitable fare to Manhattan. Joe called the dispatcher, flashed his badge, and got his cab. At the gate, people were waiting to tell him the plane was waiting. Breathing hard, Joe ran to the plane and climbed aboard. The plane was moving in an instant.

Ann was in the tourist section at the rear of the plane. Joe had a first-class seat. He asked the hostess if Ann could move up front with him, but there was no room. He moved to the rear and sat with Ann at the very back of the plane.

"Within minutes she was holding my hand," Wanderscheid recalled later. "I soon had her in a good humor."

Jaffe, in a high state of tension himself, was waiting when the plane landed at Miami. Three leading gangsters got off from the first-class section and his heart sank. The very last passengers to deplane were Ann and Joe. Jaffe embraced his friend. Ann gave him her pistol.

After a quick breakfast at the airport, they drove south to Homestead Air Force Base where Ann had spent so many months. "Operation Baby-sit" was resumed until, after many conferences, Ann was able to return to Rome with renewed confidence. Or so Jaffe thought. He learned differently when a letter arrived from Ann:

> I have a confession to make. When I left the States eleven days ago, I had definitely decided to forget the entire mess and start living my life anew. I had no intention, whatsoever, to return and testify. However, when I thought of all the money, time and hard work the U.S. Government has put into this case—not to mention that I am alive, I think, only because of all the protection that was given me—I felt very much ashamed and selfish. I decided I couldn't be a quitter. If I quit now I'll certainly be as bad as the gangsters and actually reach their level. You might convey to Mr. Ugast my intentions. Please tell him not to worry about me making a good witness.
>
> You see, boys, I know pretty much what I will be hit with in court. It won't bother me a bit. What it will do to me afterwards is more important, but I'll think about that after I testify. I'm terribly sorry for the way I acted to the boys in New York, Mr. Ugast, Joe and you. But it was such a shock when I heard it was a mistrial. I hope you all forgive me....

Looking ahead to the next time, Ann said she hoped Coppola's attorney would ask her why she was willing to testify against a man who had given her so much money.

> You see, boys, everything is relative. If Mike had been a hundred dollar a week man who had to do without lunch or cut down on cigarettes to buy me a bottle of perfume, I would say he was the very best. But considering the amount of money he makes, and will make for the rest of his life, I do not think his generosity was anything fantastic. You have heard the expression—easy come, easy go.

Jaffe replied the same day: "I have never doubted for a moment you would return for the second trial," he told her.

Tension mounted as the weeks passed and the trial date neared once more. Coppola was reported to have developed a bad case of shingles. Ann flew again to New York, leaving Joan in Italy. But this time she determined to wait out the final hours in Cincinnati. George Ratterman was now sheriff of Campbell County and "For Sale" signs stood in front of the Beverly Hills Club. The gambling equipment, she heard, had been shipped from the club to Miami for eventual use in the Bahamas where Lansky was rebuilding the empire Castro had crushed in Havana. Louis Chesler, Mike's old friend, was taking an active part in the land-development program that accompanied the gambling boom and such flunkies as Jelly Wehby had found work there.

Her brother, long an employee of Sleepout's Flamingo Club, had followed hundreds of other gamblers to Las Vegas. There, despite the competition from other unemployed gamblers, he got work with Ed Levinson at the Fremont. Sleepout sought to buy a piece of the action, but Nevada authorities had rejected him as "notorious" and he was reportedly wandering the Caribbean. Ed and Cliff Jones, former lieutenant-governor of Nevada, had a deal going with Bobby Baker, a big shot in Washington, to operate casinos on some remote island and Sleepout had been assigned the preliminary work.

Screw Andrews, his new $250,000 club completed, was waiting trial in Federal Court. The new club was padlocked—Andrews had neglected to pay his contractor when he realized the heat.would make it impossible to operate. Cincinnati's convention business was cut in half—many groups had cancelled reservations and few were making new ones. Without Newport, the Queen City was as dull as the first name given it—"Losantiville," which was supposed to mean: "City opposite the mouth of the Licking" River.

Ann took comfort in the sight of York Street. The Flamingo was now a rock-and-roll joint for teen-agers. "For Sale" signs were plastered on the windows of the Yorkshire. Over on Monmouth, the Glenn Hotel was dark and soon would burn completely in a mysterious fire that smacked of arson. The few remaining gamblers, men too old and rich to move, were pessimistic about the city's future, but inspired reformers were making plans to attract industry and get the urban-renewal program into the construction stage.

Newport was evidence for all to see, Ann decided, that the syndicate could be beaten. Perhaps if that vast gambling empire could be destroyed, the conviction of Trigger Mike could also be achieved. Her family was worried—Mike had subpoenaed everyone. He would stop at nothing to discredit Ann.

In Miami, Ugast and his associates made final preparations. More than two hundred witnesses were under subpoena. The judge planned to lock up the jury and selected a number of alternates. No more chances would be taken. There would not be another mistrial. It was now or never.

Crowds gathered in the old federal building at Third Avenue and Third Street. Rumors of sensational testimony to come had excited the imagination. The courtroom was a short distance from Biscayne Bay, whose blue-green waters lapped against Palm Island, where Al Capone had spent his last years in a drunken spree that ended only with his death. Beyond the island were the white towers of Miami Beach, where the syndicate ruled in garish splendor and Trigger Mike Coppola had for so long been untouchable.

Wanderscheid, delayed by a last minute crisis, arrived five minutes before court was to convene. Lounging there in the hall, short and swarthy in a dark suit, was Coppola. He motioned to the Internal Revenue Agent to come to him.

Ugast, leaving the courtroom, froze in horror as one of his key witnesses walked up to the gangster. Joe noticed that Coppola's mouth was covered with fever blisters. The man had been sweating it out.

"Joe," said Mike, his voice a guttural whisper. "You can thank me for pleading guilty. We've got enough on you to cost you your job if we'd gone to trial."

It was a last act of bravado from a beaten man. Wanderscheid turned on his heel and walked away without a word. Ugast called to him. They walked together inside the courtroom and stopped.

"What did he say?" asked the nervous prosecutor.

"He's pleading guilty," replied Joe. "Can you believe it?"

"Yes," said Ugast, after a long pause. "I can believe it. I don't think he had much choice."

Word had reached the intelligence division of a "Little Apalachin" meeting a week earlier at West Palm Beach. The assumption was the assembled gangsters discussed the Coppola case. Had they passed judgment on Mike—ordered him to take his medicine? It seemed very possible.

Court convened. Attorney Kossman asked permission to change his client's plea to guilty. There was a second of stunned silence. Judge Dyer, a solemn figure in his black robe, ordered a brief recess.

Within minutes, the session resumed and Coppola stood before the judge to hear his sentence. He was ordered to serve a year and a day on each of four counts, the sentences to run concurrently. He was also ordered to pay a $40,000 fine, and was placed on four years' probation when his sentence expired.

It could have been worse, the agents knew, but Mike was visibly shaken. He had not expected to go to prison. There was to be no delay. He was given one day to attend to his personal affairs.

A stroke of the gavel ended the case. Reporters crowded around Trigger Mike, who spat on the floor.

"I ain't been in prison since I was twenty-two," he growled.

When other questions were asked, Mike turned away. "I'm a sick man," he said. "I just want to serve my time in peace."

He left the room a lonely figure.

In a rare burst of candor, Attorney Kossman put his arm around Jaffe and commented:

"Nobody could have done it but you, Jaffe," he said.

The special agent thought of Wanderscheid and smiled. "Us," he corrected.

When queried by reporters Kossman would give no reason for the guilty plea. The reason he didn't want to name arrived on a plane from Cinicinnati at 2:30 P.M. Her first question to Wanderscheid, who met the plane was—

"How's the case going?"

"He pleaded guilty," said Joe.

"You mean it?" asked Ann. "You're not kidding?"

"I mean it. He's already sentenced to prison."

Ann was silent as they entered the building. She broke the long silence to say:

"Now I'll never get to tell all I know."

Joe, recognizing that Ann had nerved herself for a showdown battle, understood the feeling of anti-climax, of journey's end, that possessed her. They headed out the airport expressway en route to the downtown office. Ann spoke again, her voice gentle.

"Do you remember that time when I was trying to get you boys to hurry up with the case?" she asked. "Remember, I told you there wasn't any time to waste because I had cancer of the throat?"

"I remember," said Wanderscheid. "We thought you were trying to scare us."

Ann smiled. "I was trying to scare you, but it's the truth. I do have cancer only it isn't cancer of the throat."

Just before they reached the office, she spoke again. "If I'm found dead don't believe it's suicide. They'll be after me as an example to others."

Six months later she was found dead in Rome. All available evidence indicated she was not a victim of violence but of a more subtle form of pressure. In giving evidence about Coppola she had violated the underworld's code of ethics—a code she had outgrown. But more was involved. Coppola was still alive, still capable of revenge. Ann was a marked woman, and quickly she became an outcast. All people, the squares as well as the hoods, avoided her—afraid even to speak. It was as if she wore a scarlet letter on her face—"S" for Stoolie.

Joan might have helped, but Joan had developed into a harder, colder version of the girl Ann herself had been. As Ann lay dying she tried to apologize in a final note:

"My dear, I think you know (although unfortunately I didn't show it) how much I love you. You were the only bright and wonderful thing in my life. I can't put into words how extremely sorry I am for having hurt and hindered your life. But perhaps it may have helped you to be a bigger and better person."

She wrote of Coppola: "One must have compassion, love, and a conscience to break. Such people as Coppola have none of these. I suppose in a way they are very fortunate—they can't be hurt."

And so she died.

Dick Jaffe in a personal memo to Special Agent DeVoto in Covington put his sentiments on record:

"Do me a favor, Pal. If she's buried in Cincinnati, please go to her funeral and pay your respects for both of us. She may not have been a perfect lady, but she had more guts than most men we know."

There have been worse epitaphs.

*"Mike Coppola, you
yellow-bellied bastard."* ANN DRAHMANN

Epilogue

TRIGGER MIKE COPPOLA SERVED HIS SENTENCE IN THE FEDERAL prison near Atlanta where, years before, George Remus, king of the bootleggers, had lived royally with the help of a warden who was later convicted. Doing time with Coppola was an old New York colleague considered by some to be Costello's successor—Vito Genovese.

Prison life was enlivened by the presence of Joseph Valachi, a minor hood who killed a fellow inmate after Genovese allegedly gave him the "kiss of death." With nothing left to lose, Valachi decided to sing and—unlike Ann Drahmann—he was permitted to give a public performance. Millions watched on television as he testified before the McClellan Committee, but his worm's eye view of ancient history added little information of value to what was already known.

Indeed, by giving organized crime a new name—La Cosa Nostra—and attributing to it responsibility for the misdeeds of all ethnic groups, he did a disservice to law enforcement. Nevertheless, his version was welcomed by the press and public—as well as by certain official agencies. Understandably, they enjoyed having the complexities of organized crime reduced to a simple formula and a single enemy—LCN. Meanwhile, as everyone concentrated on crooks with Italian names, the amoral society which makes organized crime possible, and which, in turn, helps make society amoral, could continue to profit as usual.

Coppola, who had seen such men as Albert Anastasia die because they defied such men as Meyer Lansky, was released from prison shortly after his ex-wife died in Rome.

Had Valachi been right, had Trigger Mike been a high-ranking lieutenant in the La Cosa Nostra "family" of Vito Genovese, he would have returned in triumph to Miami Beach to pick up the reins of power. But Mike was branded just as Ann was branded—not as a stoolie but as a fool. She was punished for talking, but Mike had married her, allowed her to learn his secrets, and been unable to stop her tongue. He had only himself to blame.

A few personal friends might play cards with Mike and flatter him, but the real rulers of organized crime considered him finished just as, a few years earlier, they had considered Costello's usefulness at an end after his unfortunate publicity. Like Ann, Mike still had money but money was not enough. His prestige was gone and with it his power. More than that, if less important, he was hot and would remain hot for the rest of his life.

Coppola converted the loggia of his house into a place where he could raise orchids. It proved to be a safer hobby than the abortions he had helped perform on his wife.

Federal agents watched his house around the clock, taking note of everyone who came and went. Ultimately the house was sold at auction to satisfy the tax lien against it. Mike pulled a final fast one just as two years earlier Ann had predicted he would do. She had written to Jaffe:

"Knowing Mike as I do, I'll bet all the tea in China he will have a friend front for him. The friend will buy the house for a few thousand dollars above the mortgage and he [Mike] will rent the house from the front. And you may rest assured everything will be very legal and proper."

When the IRS put the house up for sale, Mike had no friend but he had his son. The son was the only bidder and he offered $24,500. The "mortgage holder" got $22,500, and the United States got $2,000. Mike, of course, continued to live with his son.

But even such a victory was small comfort. For Coppola, brewing and stewing and still on probation, was as much alone as Ann. His health was bad. In September 1966, he became ill and was taken to a Boston hospital. The hospitals of Boston had long been familiar to the syndicate. Justly famous for their skilled doctors, they were also known by the privacy they offered. The syndicate controlled Boston where corruption differed from Miami Beach only in that it lacked a suntan. Many "meets" were held by top hoods in Boston hospitals where they could combine a planning session with a bed rest.

So complete was the privacy that Trigger Mike Coppola's death there on October 1, 1966, was not reported immediately. In the interim his body was shipped to New York and buried. Federal agents didn't learn of the funeral until it was over.

In the haste with which Mike was buried, Ann Drahmann scored her final victory.

Index

Adonis, Joe (Doto), 48, 56
Alderman, Jerome S., 189
Alibi Club, 44, 45, 46
Alo, Vincent "Jimmy Blue Eyes," 55, 101
Anastasia, Albert, 55, 58, 87-88, 89, 91, 93, 94, 205
Andrews, "Screw" (Frank Andriola), 2, 21, 24, 33-34, 38, 40, 43-47, 51, 57, 59-60, 61, 62, 64, 97, 98, 104, 115, 116-117, 167, 178, 179, 180, 188, 201
Andrews, "Junior," 179
Anndra Shop, 33, 36, 64
Angersola, George, 102
Angersola, John, 59, 96, 101
Anggelis, John, 181
April Flowers, 158-159, 160, 161, 162, 190-191, 192
Arnold, Petey, 37
Arrowhead Club, 11
Augustine, Agnes, 5, 79

Bailey, George, 43
Bailey, Lawrence K., 152
Baker, Bobby, 201
Baker, Reverend Donald, 159-160
Barkhau, Reverend Harold, 106
Barkley, Alban, 140

Barnett, Barney, 78
Batista, Fulgencio, 57, 58, 87, 95
Beckley, Gil, 36-37, 46, 47, 57, 60, 61, 62, 102, 104, 105, 107, 108, 110, 111-112, 122, 134, 156, 188
Beckley, June, 105, 111, 134, 137
Bennett, Reverend George, 106, 107
Benton Frank, III, 185
Berman, Martin, 102
Bernardini, Cesare, 185
Beverly Hills Club, 10, 27, 50
Beverly Hills Country Club, 12-13, 14, 15, 17, 20, 21, 25, 29, 37, 39, 67-68, 72, 96, 105, 107, 178, 182, 188, 190, 200
Black Hand, 49-50
Blair House, 134, 136, 146, 149, 151, 176, 195
Bobben Realty Company, 24, 37
Bolita, 95, 179
Bommarito, Joe, 101
Bootlegging business, 7-8, 9, 10, 14, 20
Brady, Buck, 8, 9, 10, 12, 21, 25-26
Breckenridge, John 181, 184, 187, 188
Bridwell, Raymond, 80
Bright, Kenny, 28, 31, 106
Brink, Jimmy, 14, 18, 19-20, 21, 28, 32, 105, 156
Buccieri, Marty, 158, 159, 162-163, 192

209

INDEX

Buchalter, Louis "Lepke," 48, 54, 57, 59, 87
Campbell County Civic Association, 65, 66
Carinci, Tito, 105, 156-159, 161, 162, 164, 181, 190, 192
Catena, Jerry, 56
Chandler, A. B. "Happy," 11, 45-46, 139, 154
Chapman, Fred, 96
Chesler, Louis, 85, 99, 101, 104-105, 200
Chicago Syndicate, 102
Chloral hydrate, 8, 157, 160
Ciafardini, Pat, 45-46, 158-159, 160, 162, 163, 181, 187, 192
Clark, Andy, 31
Clark, Lefty, 102
Clark, Melvin, 44-45, 116, 158, 188
Cleveland Syndicate, 9-18 *passim*, 21, 22, 23, 27-28, 39, 42, 49, 50, 56, 57, 58, 65, 91, 95, 98, 99, 102, 106, 115, 168, 171, 182, 188, 190
Club Collins, 57
Coakley, Daniel H., 54
Cohen, Ben, 57, 76-77, 78, 93, 96, 121, 150, 175-177, 178, 193-195, 198
Cohen, Mickey, 168
Coll, "Mad Dog," 49, 51
Combs, Bert T., 12, 139, 154, 185, 187, 188
"Committee of 500," 154, 182
Cook, Henry, 38, 156, 159, 161-162, 163-164, 182
Cook, Louis, 38
Coppola, Anna (Ann) Augustine Drahmann, 10, 12, 24-25, 26, 44, 59-60, 164, 184, 191, 205, 206-207
 suicide, 1-3
 childhood, 4-6, 8
 first marriage and birth of child, 13-14
 marriage to Drahmann, 18, 19ff.
 after Drahmann's death, 33-39
 meets Coppola, 46-47, 61-62
 marriage, 67-69
 spies on Coppola, 70-71, 84-86
 beaten by Coppola, 72-73, 82-83, 109-12, 118
 abortions forced on, 74-75
 mother's death, 79
 party at Retschultze's, 107ff.
 divorces Coppola, 119-122
 meets Wanderscheid, 123
 aids IRS, 126-132, 146ff.
 beaten by hoods, 147-149
 protected by Air Force police, 151-152
 goes to Europe, 166-177
 meets Cohen in Europe, 193-194
 preparations to testify against Coppola, 195-200
Coppola, Anthony, 94
Coppola, Doris Patricia, 54, 69
Coppola, Doris Lehman, 51, 53-54, 55, 59, 69, 71, 83, 85-86, 121
Coppola, Michael (Trigger Mike), 1, 2, 3, 10, 14, 21, 47, 146-147, 149, 157, 166, 178, 184, 193, 194
 early career, 48ff.
 first marriage, 51
 Scottoriggio case and wife's death, 52-54
 moves to Miami, 56-57
 income and tax returns, 58, 103-104, 114
 courts and marries Ann, 62-64, 67-68
 sadism, 72-73, 74-76, 82-83, 88, 100, 109, 118-119
 and death of Costello, 87-92
 and Anastasia, 87, 93-94
 organizes numbers racket in Florida, 95-96
 in Las Vegas, 98-100, 124
 business in Newport, 116-117
 and IRS, 128-129, 130-133
 indicted, 152
 tax evasion trial, 197-204
 in prison, 205-206
 death, 207
Coppola, Michael David, 51, 53, 69, 206
Coppola, Ralph, 102
Cosa Nostra, La, 101, 196, 205-206
Costello, Frank, 21, 48, 67, 87, 90-92, 94, 206
Cottingham, Robert, 19, 20
Counting houses, 93
Courier-Journal, see Louisville *Courier-Journal*

INDEX

Courtney, Max, 59
Croft, John, 32, 101
Cuban National Lottery, 95
Curd, Ed, 14, 53

Davis, John L., 182, 187, 188
Dalitz (Davis), Moe, 10, 11, 17, 49, 72, 77, 101
Danforth, Harold R., 54
"Death Valley," 7-8
Deckert, James E., 27
DeMartino, Anthony, 101
DeMartino, Ben, 56, 101
DeMartino, Teddy, 101
Dennert, Arthur, 21, 27
Desert Inn, 28, 29, 67, 98-99
Devine (Blatt), Nig, 24-25, 27, 37, 44, 57, 71, 90
DeVoto, Earl, 167, 178, 180, 204
Dewey, Thomas E., 88, 196
Diamond, "Legs," 11, 49
Dragna, Jack, 168
Dragna, Tom, 102
Drahmann, Charley, 18, 19-26 *passim*, 28, 31-32, 34, 35, 63, 69, 72, 76, 111, 167, 178
Drahmann, Joan, 2, 14, 21, 33, 35, 36, 64, 68, 82, 89, 90, 92, 97-98, 108, 109, 112, 114-115, 117-120, 122, 147, 149, 150-151, 169, 170, 172, 184, 193, 194, 195, 200, 204
"Dr. D.," 75, 76, 98
Durante, Jimmy, 68
Dwyer, Bill, 48
Dyer, Judge David, 198, 202

Eastern Syndicate, 21, 22, 23, 27, 44, 47, 49-50, 77, 102, 180
Eder, Max, (Maxie Raymond), 78, 101
Eha, Charles, 40
Elks Club, gambling in, 27
Epstein, Ike, 101
Espie, David, 29-31
Esquire magazine, 92

Factor, John "Jake the Barber," 99
Farley, Rip, 22-24, 25, 40, 80
Farley, Taylor, 22-24, 80
Farmer, Evelyn, 46
FBI, 12, 46, 67, 124, 143, 148, 157, 165, 168, 170, 191

Fetzner, Bob, 148
Flamingo Club, 14, 21, 22-23, 24, 28, 31, 37, 42, 64, 99, 105, 145, 159, 201
Fleischman, Lawrence, 171
Fontainebleau Hotel, 78, 82, 104, 122
Ford, Fred M., 124
Ford, Judge H. Church, 192
Fredericks, Leroy, 165, 181, 183, 187
Fremont Hotel and Casino, 37, 91, 201
Friedlander, Jack, 57
Fruit Fly, 93, 96

Gambling business:
  in Cuba, 57, 58, 77, 105
  in East Harlem, 49-51, 93
  in Florida, 57, 59, 94-96
  in Las Vegas, 28, 87, 91, 98-99
  in Newport-Covington area, 2, 8, 9ff., 14, 19-22, 29-30, 66, 115, 154, 181, 183
  in Texas, 124
Gambling equipment, 29-30, 31, 95, 179-180. *See also* Slot machines
Garfield, Sam, 91
Garrison, Edwin, 11, 12, 50
General Development Company, 84, 99
Genovese, Vito, 56, 205, 206
George the Wop, 102
Giancana, Mooney, 100
Giancola, Carl A., 144
Giesey, Alvin, 15
Gigante, Vincent "the Chin," 91
Glass, David, 102
Glassman, Mr., 78
Glenn Hotel, 9, 10, 16, 42, 60, 105, 156, 159, 176, 190, 192, 201
Glenn Rendezvous, 17, 27-28, 40, 105, 156
Glenn Schmidt Playtorium, 40, 42, 43, 142
Gordon, George, 96, 102
Greene, Jerome, 128
Gugel, George, 17, 43, 81, 165, 181, 182, 183, 187

Handbooks, 19, 28, 57, 59, 66, 76, 97, 106, 115, 145, 183, 189, 190
Harris, Big Jim, 65, 81, 92, 186
Harris, Fat Allie, 89

211

INDEX

Harris, Matthew P., 124
Hay, Mrs. Nancy, 162
Hesch, Oscar, 42, 106, 116, 187
Hialeah race track, 70
Hill, Judge Edward G., 143, 144, 182, 183-184, 186, 187
Hirschfeld, Thomas, 161, 162, 163
Hoffa, Jimmy, 134, 140, 141, 166
Hosea, Henry, 143
House Is Not a Home, A, 196
Howard, Ulie, 28, 140
Hughes, Jimmy, 30, 31
Hummel, Bill, 167
Hy-Dee-Ho Club, 65, 186

Internal Revenue Service, 1, 50, 112, 122, 123-124, 127, 132-133, 136, 137, 168, 169-172, 178-179, 185, 189, 195, 206
International Longshoreman's Association, 58
Irey, Elmer, 130, 151

Jackson, Hattie, 79-82, 92, 181-182, 183, 184, 185-186
Jaffe, Richard E., 124-125, 127-138 *passim*, 146, 147, 149, 150, 151, 167, 168, 170, 171, 172, 175, 176, 178, 194, 198, 199, 200, 203, 204, 206
Jerus, David ("Jew Bates"), 9
Jessel, George, 90
Johnson, Keen, 16
Jolly, Judge Andrew, 46, 66, 116, 188
Jones, Cliff, 201

Karo, William H., 168
Kastel, "Dandy Phil," 91
Kefauver, Estes, 28-29, 57, 64, 67, 76, 92
Kefauver Committee, 28, 32, 37, 39, 40, 41, 140
Kennedy, Edward, 177
Kennedy, Jackie, 8
Kennedy, John F., 146, 150
Kennedy, Robert F., 2, 139, 140-141, 146, 150, 151, 153, 165, 166, 168, 170, 171, 188, 191, 192
Kenton County Protestant Association, 28
Kentucky Derby, 89-90, 97, 105, 157
Kleinman, Morris, 10, 68, 99

Kolod, Ruby, 101
Kossman, Jacob, 198, 202, 203
Kramer, Emanuel, 126

Lafata, Charles "the Wop," 8
Lansky, Jake, 48, 102
Lansky, Meyer, 10, 22, 48, 49, 57-58, 59, 77, 87, 94, 102, 177, 200, 205
Lascari, Michael, 56
Lassoff, Bob and Ben (Big Porky and Little Porky), 24-25, 61
Latin Quarter, 27, 39, 66
Layoff betting, 7, 104, 105, 188
Lederer, Louis J., 91
Lehman, David, 52, 53, 70, 85
Lepke, *see* Buchalter, Louis
Lester, Charles E., 13, 16, 17, 27, 39, 41, 43, 45, 64, 66, 80, 143, 154, 156, 161, 162, 163, 164, 178, 182, 192
Levinson, Ed, 14, 22, 27, 28, 37, 43, 57, 90, 91, 99, 201
Levinson, Louis ("Sleepout Louis"), 14, 15, 21, 22, 24, 27, 37, 40, 46, 53, 57, 59-60, 65, 89, 98-100, 101, 104, 105, 145, 154, 159, 164, 201
Levinson, Mike, 14, 57
Levinson, Mildred, 37, 38, 63, 68, 98
Levy, Justice Aaron J., 43
Lewis, Jesse K., 16, 17, 27, 28, 139-140, 153, 181
Licavoli, Peter, 8, 20, 72, 171
"Little Mexico," 7, 9, 15
Livorsi, Frank "Cheech," 78, 101
Lockhart, C. R., 29
Lombardo, Philip, 101
Long, Edward, 136
Lookout House, 13, 14, 15, 18, 19, 20, 21, 28, 29-31, 32, 33, 39, 66, 92, 140, 173, 190
Lookout Stud Farm, 20, 34, 156
Louisville *Courier-Journal*, 43, 105, 106, 139, 142, 153, 154, 182, 191
Lowe, Butts, 72
Luciano, Charles "Lucky," 48, 56, 101, 175, 176-177, 196-197
Lukens, James, 140
Lupo the Wolf, 49

INDEX

MacRae, Gordon and Sheila, 68
Mafia, 49, 57, 59, 196
Manhattan Cigarette Company, 56, 58
Manzi, Robert, 171
Marcantonio, Vito, 52-53
Margulies, Frank, 127, 128, 129-130
Martin, Fat Hymie, 95-96
Massei, Joe, 56, 69, 96
Masterson, Red "Enforcer" 10, 11, 12, 15-16, 25-26, 27, 39, 40, 61, 155
Maybury, Alfred, 42
McClellan Committee, 101, 140, 188-189, 205
McCoy, Bill, 20
McDonough, Larry, 10
McGrath, Eddie, 102
Meade, Mitchell, 191
Merchants Club 15, 17, 25, 40
Meredith, Hubert, 16
Meyers, Danny (Aaron Meyervitz), 23
Miami *Herald*, 77
Miami *News*, 97
Miami Provision Company, 56, 69
Michell, Allen B., 96
Midtown Social Club, 101, 147
Miller, Martin and Nikki, 61, 71
Miller, Sam "Gameboy," 15, 18, 20, 77
Molaska Corporation, 49
Morelli, Frank "Butsy," 53, 54
Moss, Harold, 1, 2, 3, 169, 173, 175, 195
Mother Kelly's Nightclub, 37
Mounds Club, 67
Murder, Inc., 55, 57, 87-88, 89, 94
Murphy, Judge Ray L., 16, 45, 81, 143, 144, 145, 181, 182
Musoff, Wallace, 171, 172-173
Mussman, Ralph, 15, 153, 154, 161, 163, 165, 186, 187

Narcotics, 2, 12, 48, 78, 108, 112, 115, 119, 150, 171, 196
National Labor Relations Board, 58
National Syndicate, 9, 21-22, 49, 50, 58, 93, 102
Negroes, Syndicate and, 12; in numbers racket, 38, 44-45, 50
Nevada Gaming Control Board, 100
Newport Civic Association, 39-42, 65, 115
Newport Housing Authority, 116

Newport Ministerial Association, 116, 139, 160
New York State Crime Commission, 58
Numbers racket:
  in Newport, 43-46, 178ff.
  in East Harlem, 49-51, 56, 58, 62, 88
  in Florida, 94-96
  in greater Cincinnati, 115, 117

Old Kaintuck Castle, 10
O'Nan, Roy, 96
"Operation Baby-sit," 1, 151, 168, 199
"Operation Shakedown," 195

Paisely, Thomas, 156-157, 162, 181
Patriarca, Raymond, 54-55
Payne, Bull, 44-45
Payne, Steve, 44
Peloquin, Robert, 176
Polizzi, Big Al, 72, 101
Polizzi, Charles A., Jr., 190-191
Pomeroy, Reverend Dudley, 106, 139, 160
Primrose Club, 21, 25, 26-27
Prohibition, 7, 10, 48-49
Prostitution, 2, 19, 77, 79-82, 84, 106, 115, 124, 139, 145, 154, 181, 183

Rabinowitz, David, 134
Radio, 83-84
Rao, Joey, 51, 52, 56, 58, 78, 101
Rainwater, Jack and Red, 96
Ratterman, Ann Hengelbrok, 154, 159, 161, 164
Ratterman, George W., 8, 154-165, 167, 181, 186, 188, 189, 190, 191, 192, 200
Ratterman, Father P. H., 160
Reinfeld Syndicate, 48
Remus, George, 7-8, 9, 10, 14, 25, 205
Retschultze's Restaurant, 107, 110, 111
Ritter, Frank, 59
River Downs race track, 11, 50
Rivers, Joe, 102
Riviera (Havana), 58
Riviera (Las Vegas), 98, 99
Rolf, Judge Joseph, 159, 163, 164
Roll, Norbert, 142, 144, 145, 146, 153, 165, 185, 187

INDEX

Rosato, Al, 101
Rosenthal, Frank "Lefty," 97, 109
Rothkopf, Louis, 10, 72, 168
Rothstein, Arnold, 7, 48, 57, 60, 91, 93, 94
Ryan, James 171

S & G Syndicate, 57, 76
St. Valentine's Day Massacre, 9
Salerno, Fat Tony, 2, 56, 60, 61, 63, 93, 101
Sands Hotel, 42
Scalish, John, 101
Scarglatta, Dan, 101
Schmidt, Peter, 8, 9-11, 12-13, 14, 16, 27, 39, 40, 41-43, 50, 64, 66, 67, 115, 142
Schraeder, Sam, 10, 32, 37
Schultz, Dutch, 11, 48, 50-51, 87
Scottoriggio, Joseph, 52-53, 85
Seifried, Christian, 92, 106, 140, 144, 146, 181, 182
Sherry, Madam, 77, 80
Shylock business, 57, 62, 79
Siddell, Robert, 27, 42, 66, 80, 181
Siegel, Bugsy, 10, 57, 68, 88, 93, 168
Sinatra, Frank, 68, 100, 191
Slot machines, 10, 17, 27, 67, 143, 144, 167
Snax Bar, 66, 142, 145, 146, 189
Social Action Committee (of Newport), 92, 97, 106, 144, 155, 185
Sonken, Joe "the Blimp," 37
Spinella, Mike, 177-178
Sportsman's Club, 44, 117, 178-180, 185
Staab, Frank, 191
Stacci, Joe, 101
Stacher, Joseph "Doc," 56
Stapleton, Judge Paul, 142-143
Stardust Hotel, 99
Strollo, Anthony (Tony Bender), 58
Stuart, Henry, 165, 187-188
Swinford, Judge Mac, 28

Tanico, Michael J., 91
Teamster Union, 78, 134, 140
Terrace Hilton Hotel, 157
Terranova, Ciro, 49
Thiem, Jack, 40-41, 42-43, 44, 115, 156, 181

316 Club, 80
Todd, George, 20, 33, 35
Torrice, Joseph, 101
Tourine, Charles "the Blade," 109, 148
Tropical Park race track, 59, 70
Tropicana (Las Vegas), 91
Tropicana Club (Newport), 156, 157-159, 160, 162, 163, 190
Tucker, Garson, 16, 32
Tucker, Sam, 10, 13, 14, 16, 17, 22, 26, 32, 49

Ugast, Fred, 124, 151, 152, 168, 169-170, 172, 195, 197-198, 200, 201, 202
"United Sunday," 153

Valachi, Joe, 101, 102, 205, 206
Vann, Judge Harold, 122
Vest, Judge John L., 16
Vice, Howard, 8, 10, 12

Wallace, Harold R., 189
Wallace, Richard, 130, 151, 168
Wanderscheid, Joe, 121, 123-125, 126-138 *passim*, 146, 147, 149, 151, 194, 198-200, 202, 203
Warren, Judge Fred, 64
Wehby, Emil "Jelly," 108-109, 201
Weintraub, Morris, 44, 45, 116, 167, 180, 189
Wexler, Irving "Waxey Gordon," 48, 130
Whitfield, Dave, 10, 11-12, 27
White, Chuck, 109, 148
"White Smitty," 44
Willis, Simeon, 17
Wise, William J., 16, 17, 66, 81, 106, 144, 146, 181, 184-185, 186, 187
Withrow, Thomas, 158, 162-163
Withrow, Mrs. Thomas, 163
Workman, Bugs, 91
World Series in Cincinnati, 7, 48, 186, 190
Wyatt, Wilson W., 190

York Tavern, 17
Yorkshire Club, 15, 22, 145, 190, 201

Zwick, Bob, 5, 9
Zwillman, Abner "Longie," 48, 56

www.ingramcontent.com/pod-product-compliance
Lightning Source LLC
Chambersburg PA
CBHW030149100526
44592CB00009B/195